THE TWELFTH OF FEBRUARY

MCGILL-QUEEN'S/BRIAN MULRONEY INSTITUTE OF GOVERNMENT
STUDIES IN LEADERSHIP, PUBLIC POLICY, AND GOVERNANCE

Series editor: Donald E. Abelson

Titles in this series address critical issues facing Canada at home and abroad and the efforts policymakers at all levels of government have made to address a host of complex and multifaceted policy concerns. Books in this series receive financial support from the Brian Mulroney Institute of Government at St Francis Xavier University; in keeping with the institute's mandate, these studies explore how leaders involved in key policy initiatives arrived at their decisions and what lessons can be learned. Combining rigorous academic analysis with thoughtful recommendations, this series compels readers to think more critically about how and why elected officials make certain policy choices, and how, in concert with other stakeholders, they can better navigate an increasingly complicated and crowded marketplace of ideas.

9 Multilateral Sanctions Revisited
 Lessons Learned from Margaret Doxey
 Edited by Andrea Charron and Clara Portela

10 Booze, Cigarettes, and Constitutional Dust-Ups
 Canada's Quest for Interprovincial Free Trade
 Ryan Manucha

11 NORAD
 In Perpetuity and Beyond
 Andrea Charron and James Fergusson

12 Under the Weather
 Reimagining Mobility in the Climate Crisis
 Stephanie Sodero

13 Rethinking Decentralization
 Mapping the Meaning of Subsidiarity in Federal Political Culture
 Jacob Deem

14 Natural Allies
 Environment, Energy, and the History of US-Canada Relations
 Daniel Macfarlane

15 Gender, Communications, and Reproductive Health in International Development
 Carolina Matos

16 Nostalgic Virility as a Cause of War
 How Leaders of Great Powers Cope with Status Decline
 Matthieu Grandpierron

17 The Twelfth of February
 Canadian Aid for Gender Equality during the Rise of Violent Extremism in Pakistan
 Rhonda Gossen

The Twelfth of February

Canadian Aid for Gender Equality during the Rise of Violent Extremism in Pakistan

RHONDA GOSSEN

McGill-Queen's University Press
Montreal & Kingston · London · Chicago

© McGill-Queen's University Press 2024

ISBN 978-0-2280-2252-7 (paper)
ISBN 978-0-2280-2253-4 (ePDF)
ISBN 978-0-2280-2254-1 (ePUB)

Legal deposit fourth quarter 2024
Bibliothèque nationale du Québec

Printed in Canada on acid-free paper that is 100% ancient forest free (100% post-consumer recycled), processed chlorine free

This book has been published with the help of a grant from the Federation for the Humanities and Social Sciences, through the Awards to Scholarly Publications Program, using funds provided by the Social Sciences and Humanities Research Council of Canada.

Financé par le gouvernement du Canada   Funded by the Government of Canada   Conseil des arts du Canada   Canada Council for the Arts

We acknowledge the support of the Canada Council for the Arts.

Nous remercions le Conseil des arts du Canada de son soutien.

McGill-Queen's University Press in Montreal is on land which long served as a site of meeting and exchange amongst Indigenous Peoples, including the Haudenosaunee and Anishinabeg nations. In Kingston it is situated on the territory of the Haudenosaunee and Anishinaabek. We acknowledge and thank the diverse Indigenous Peoples whose footsteps have marked these territories on which peoples of the world now gather.

Library and Archives Canada Cataloguing in Publication

Title: The twelfth of February: Canadian aid for gender equality during the rise of violent extremism in Pakistan / Rhonda Gossen.

Names: Gossen, Rhonda, author.

Series: McGill-Queen's/Brian Mulroney Institute of Government studies in leadership, public policy, and governance; 17.

Description: Series statement: McGill-Queen's/Brian Mulroney Institute of Government studies in leadership, public policy, and governance; 17 | Includes bibliographical references and index.

Identifiers: Canadiana (print) 20240387171 | Canadiana (ebook) 2024038721X | ISBN 9780228022527 (paper) | ISBN 9780228022534 (ePDF) | ISBN 9780228022541 (ePUB)

Subjects: LCSH: Canadian International Development Agency. | LCSH: Economic assistance, Canadian—Pakistan. | LCSH: Women's rights—Pakistan. | LCSH: Women—Pakistan—Social conditions. | LCSH: Equality—Pakistan. | LCSH: Civil society—Pakistan. | LCSH: Violence—Pakistan. | LCSH: Islamic fundamentalism—Pakistan.

Classification: LCC HQ1236.5.P18 G67 2024 | DDC 305.42095491—dc23

This book was typeset by Marquis Interscript in 10.5/13 Sabon. Copyediting by Grace Rosalie Seybold.

The flags of mourning were flapping
the handmaidens had rebelled
those two hundred women who came out on the streets
were surrounded on all sides
besieged by armed police.
Teargas, rifles and guns
wireless vans and jeeps
every path was blockaded
there was no protection
They had to fight themselves.

You as for two
We two crores of women
Shall testify
Against this tyranny and cruelty
hurled at our heads
in the name of the law of evidence.

Excerpt from "Twelfth of February 1983,"
poetic chronicle of the day when women were arrested in Lahore,
by Saeeda Gazdar

Contents

Figures   ix

Acknowledgments   xi

Prologue   xv

PART ONE:
TWO STEPS FORWARD, THREE STEPS BACK

1 The Year of *Qisas* and *Diyat*   3
2 Exposing Vulnerabilities   15
3 Violent Extremism and Women's Empowerment   25
4 From Women in Development to Feminist International Assistance   38
5 Field Visits under Armed Escort   50
6 Crimes in the Name of Honour   73
7 The Hudood Ordinances: A Lingering Backdrop to Legal Protections   86

PART TWO:
GENDER EQUALITY IN DANGEROUS PLACES

8 The Dark Years in Afghanistan   103
9 The Golden Years for Civil Society in Pakistan   113
10 The Forerunners: CIDA's Women's Funds   127
11 After 9/11 and "Operation Enduring Freedom"   140
12 Twilight Years: End of an Era for Canada in Pakistan   154

PART THREE:
ENTRY POINTS AND SHRINKING SPACES

13 Being a Feminist in Difficult Places   171
14 Understanding Obscurities   185
15 Security, Gender Equality, and Development   199

Epilogue   209

Appendix: Chronology   211
Notes   219
References   231
Index   245

Figures

0.1 Map of Pakistan and Afghanistan. Courtesy of Bill Nelson. xiii
3.1 World Economic Forum Global Gender Gap Report Rankings for Pakistan from 2013 to 2022. Design by Philip Browne Consulting; data from WEF Annual Global Gender Gap Reports. 34
5.1 Men and women's contribution to GDP in Pakistan, 2003–18. Design by Philip Browne Consulting; data from a 2021 UNDP report, "Development Advocate Pakistan – Womenomics: Women Powering the Economy," available at https://www.undp.org/pakistan/publications/womenomics-women-powering-economy-pakistan. 58
10.1 CIDA Pakistan Program – women's funds 1989–2010. Design by Philip Browne Consulting, based on CIDA data. 130

Acknowledgments

The idea of this book surfaced during my last diplomatic posting in Pakistan and took much longer to write than anticipated. It encompasses a wider scope than the original idea of capturing Canada's thirty-plus years of gender equality assistance in Pakistan into a story, thanks to the illuminating new research on violent extremism and its impact on gender equality efforts, notably by Simbal Khan, Jacquie True and Monash University, ICAN, and many others. I discussed the idea with many colleagues and friends in Islamabad including Rukhsana Rashid, CIDA's long-standing senior gender advisor, Neelam Hussain from Simorgh, Julie Delahanty, Shabnam Razzak, and many others. It was during the discussion with Farhat Sheikh (now a senior advisor on gender equality for Canada's development program), in the course of CIDA support for the women's unit at the National Disaster Management Authority, that the idea of documenting CIDA's long history of support to the efforts of Pakistan women's groups, the gender equality movement, and the women's movement beginning from the early 1980s came up. She encouraged me to tell the story, as did many others. In Canada, Jim Freeman helped flesh out the idea during our first conversation over Skype from Islamabad. These discussions and the initial research also resulted in the Canadian High Commission aid section commissioning a documentary film after I left, on the journey of Pakistan women, released by GAC in 2017. It was led by Rashid's research that built on and encompassed the work done while I was still at the embassy.

I am grateful to those former colleagues working in Pakistan and in Canada for the insights that helped shape this story. The Pakistan desk at GAC also has been very helpful in providing resources, and some encouragement, over the years and through changes of staff. Collectively the help from the embassy aid section and the PSU has been critical. I hope the book will be useful for their ongoing work. The historical information provided by Elizabeth McAlister and the early gender experts in CIDA such as Wendy Lawrence, Isla Paterson, Diana Rivington, and others was invaluable. Insights from Janet Dunnet, Shahwar Pataudi, Rehana Hashmi, and others who worked on Pakistan for CIDA (or on CIDA projects) in the 1980s and into the 1990s were much appreciated. Liz Smith, another former CIDA colleague, gave some early editorial framework guidance. Canada's aid history is vast and this captures but a glimpse into a small part of it.

The hours of conversations in Pakistan helped me make sense of Pakistan's unique context and understand it better. I am grateful for the many evenings at Kathy Gannon's and Mehnaz Aziz's homes, where the gatherings of interesting people never ceased. The women's dinners convened by Ambassador Robin Raphel and conversations with Maleeha Lodhi provided intellectual perspectives. The book draws on the excellent analysis of and conversations with Zahid Hussain and Imtiaz Gul, and the work of many scholars on violent extremism and counter-terrorism and on Pakistan. The guidance from MQUP editor Emily Andrews shaped the book with the directions suggested by the peer reviewers. The team at MQUP has been excellent.

Lastly this book would not have been written without the support, encouragement, and knowledge of my husband Shahbaz Ehsani. He first raised it when we were packing the last boxes before leaving for Islamabad, when he came across a dusty report called "The Other Side of Purdah – Integrating Pakistani Women into Development," dated December 1983. "This might be useful for the Pakistan assignment," he suggested as I closed one of the last boxes. I thought about it; maybe he was right. I had been encouraged to publish it twenty-seven years earlier, when there was little available on the situation of women in Pakistan, as background for Canada's aid program. Perhaps it was worth considering a second part to it – bridging the gap from 1983 to now. I didn't think about it again until some months later, standing in the humanitarian camp of internally displaced people in Sindh following the heavy monsoon rain floods, when I decided that maybe it was time to bridge that gap.

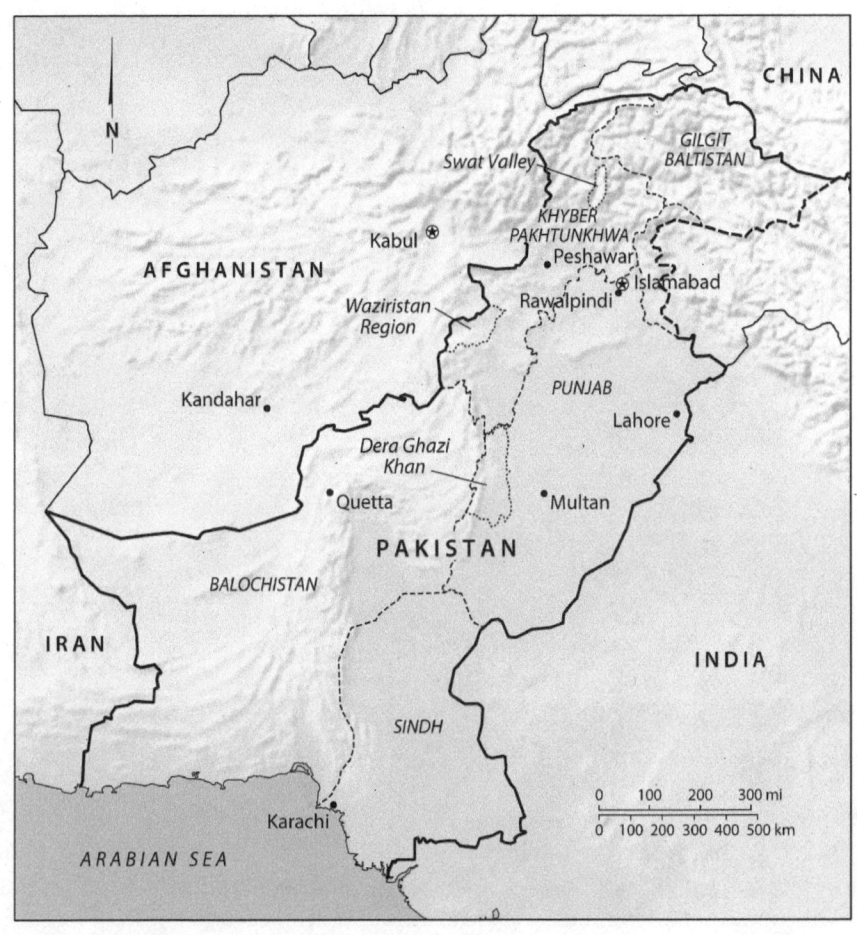

Figure 0.1 Map of Pakistan and Afghanistan.

Prologue

Watching news of the devastating floods in Pakistan in 2022 brought back memories of the Indus River floods twelve years earlier: the sights and sounds of the emergency relief camp outside Sukkor, the heat and dust from the desert of central Sindh blurring images of the historic barrage bridge in the distance. My flashbacks to the Afghan refugee camp outside Peshawar in 1984, during my first mission to Pakistan, didn't recall such overwhelming numbers of vulnerable women and children as we witnessed in Sindh the year of the Indus floods. Seeing the relief camp and surrounding areas that year was a harsh realization that socio-economic development and gender equality were still a long road ahead for many. I found myself wondering what had changed for rural women and girls in Pakistan after the decades of international development and gender equality efforts.

Having recently returned to Ottawa from a yearlong field assignment at the Provincial Reconstruction Team base in Kandahar, Afghanistan, I knew that the security situation in Pakistan was precarious. Numerous deadly attacks from violent extremists and militants, located in the border areas of Pakistan since 9/11, were causing instability and uncertainty in the country. Pakistan's close involvement in the US war in Afghanistan against the Russian invasion in the early 1980s had triggered a violent militancy and the emergence of the Pakistan Taliban. Security as the top national priority had naturally detracted from and slowed socio-economic development. How had the security situation affected gender equality efforts in the country? What had happened to the women's rights movement during the rise of violent extremism and the Pakistan Taliban?

Given its strategic role in the region, particularly as a neighbour with Afghanistan, Pakistan has been a priority country for international development assistance almost since its creation in 1947. Through the Commonwealth and the Colombo Plan for Economic Development and Cooperation, Canada, along with other countries, began to offer economic assistance to the new state of Pakistan in 1950. It was one of the first and largest Canadian aid programs for close to six decades. In 1965, Canada helped Pakistan establish its first nuclear power plant. It became a nuclear power more than thirty years later, in 1998. The famous Warsak Dam on the Kabul River is Canada's legacy infrastructure project in Pakistan. The other is a completely different area of international development – support for women's rights, gender equality, and civil society, which began in 1983 with assistance on women in development through the Aga Khan Rural Support Program. A senior-level planning mission that year kick-started Canada's pioneering support for Pakistan organizations on gender equality.

The field of international development is vast, and this story addresses one piece of it – that of progress and setbacks on gender equality and the situation of rural women that development programs tried to address during the period of the rise of violent extremism and militancy. The history of these years, connected to the decades of wars in Afghanistan and proceeding against the backdrop of turbulent regional geopolitics, is seen through a gender lens to better understand the obscured nature of forces that reversed many development gains. The Canadian experience of decades of support to and solidarity with Pakistani women's groups and civil society in their efforts to push forward the rights and equality agenda at all levels, and the evolution of the Canadian International Development Agency's (CIDA's) gender equality policies and aid projects, provides a thread through which the story is told. Tracing the pattern of gender equality through the work of groups in Pakistan, supported by Canada under five consecutive women's responsive funds beginning in 1985, sheds light on how the security situation impacted gender equality in the country, and in particular its impact on the majority of rural women. This is not intended to be a history of all gender equality programs and efforts in Pakistan – something that would take another whole book, and perhaps would be impossible to fully cover even then. Rather, this volume uses the Canadian experience of assistance for gender equality as a lens through which to view events inside

Pakistan that unfolded during the time period and how they impacted women and girls. Since most aid donors and governments follow similar types of policy and program responses on development at any given time, I didn't feel it necessary to compare the Canadian experience and program approaches with others. The scale and priority differ between various actors, but generally all are loosely coordinated to move in a similar direction, albeit at different paces and scales. Canada happened to be the leader on gender equality among the donor community in Pakistan from the early 1980s until just after 9/11. I didn't expect that a comparative assessment of other donor programs on gender equality would uncover more insights than could be gleaned from a close look at Canada's programs.

The history of extremism and militancy in Pakistan and its implications for sustainable development provide the context, in a time period when these were seen as the purview of security, not of development actors.

The rafts of books of political analysis and searching for answers to the challenges and future of Pakistan continue to be published. Development agencies produce regular forecasts and scenarios from a social and economic development perspective. Anatol Lieven responded to my question on the future of Pakistan's development over brunch one spring Sunday at the Canadian Club in Islamabad with another question, "Is there a good development scenario? What happens when a government is too preoccupied and distracted to prioritize development?" What happens is the inevitable trade-offs in which social and economic development are usually accorded secondary importance to national security. At the same time, people struggle with multidimensional poverty, continuing violent extremism and radical fundamentalism. Of the one-third of the country under the age of fourteen, more than 10 per cent are out of school, and youth unemployment is rampant. Nevertheless, social programs continue, and the strong extended-family kinship culture creates astounding resilience in society.

Many of my friends working on international relations in Pakistan have said, "There have been so many books written about Pakistan covering everything that could possibly be said" – from the well-known book of Tariq Ali in 1983 titled *Can Pakistan Survive?* to Anatol Lieven's comprehensive look at Pakistan subtitled *A Hard Country*, to *Pakistan at the Crosscurrent of History* by Lawrence Ziring, to the more recent ones such as Declan Walsh's *The Nine Lives of Pakistan*.

They all conclude that despite the odds, Pakistan survives, has not collapsed, and in some ways has even flourished despite the violent militancy and mayhem it has experienced since 9/11. In the words of Declan Walsh in 2020, "The lengthy inconclusive American intervention in Afghanistan had badly destabilized Pakistan by creating fertile ground for its *jihadi* groups." Although this book is about the fight for women's rights and equality in Pakistan and Canada's supportive role in it over a critical historical period, that cannot be separated from the war in Afghanistan and its impact on women's rights and equality in Pakistan.

Pakistan has a unique relationship with Afghanistan. They share a 2,570-kilometre (1,600-mile) border. They are significant trading partners. There are numerous cultural, ethnic, and religious connections. Over three million Afghans, mostly refugees, reside in Pakistan. As former Afghan President Hamid Karzai put it a decade back, Pakistan and Afghanistan are "conjoined twins; there's no separation." What happens on one side seems to affect the other profoundly, especially the pathways to gender equality.

WAF protests against the growing threat of Talibanization, Lahore, 19 April 2007. Photo taken by LalaRukh for WAF Lahore.

WAF protest against the Law of Evidence, Lahore, 12 February 1983. Photo taken by LalaRukh for WAF Lahore.

WAF protest, Lahore, 12 February 1983. Photo taken by LalaRukh for WAF Lahore.

WAF protest against Qisas and Diyat Ordinance under Sharia law, 10 April 1984. Photo taken by LalaRukh for WAF Lahore.

Women protestors arrested in Lahore, 12 February 1983. Photo taken by LalaRukh for WAF Lahore.

WAF protest against the 9th Amendment to the Constitution, which would have imposed Sharia law as the supreme law of the land, 12 February 1986. Photo taken by LalaRukh for WAF Lahore.

WAF protest, chador burning, January 1987. Photo taken by LalaRukh for WAF Lahore.

WAF protest against the Shariat Ordinance, Lahore, 26 June 1988. Photo taken by LalaRukh for WAF Lahore.

WAF protest about police violence against women, at the Inspector General of Police Office, Lahore, 10 August 1989. Photo taken by LalaRukh for WAF Lahore.

WAF campaign against the "Veil and Four Walls" policy of government to impose restrictions on women's movement. Poster asks: "To protect who?" Photo taken by LalaRukh for WAF Lahore.

PART ONE

Two Steps Forward, Three Steps Back

I

The Year of *Qisas* and *Diyat*

I have seen two powers rise in Pakistan, that of Mullahs and Women.
                                    Intizar Husain, Pakistani writer, 2009

Decorated with long colourful tinsel garlands around our necks, we stood on a rocky hillside just outside of a village in the Haripur district of the Northwest Frontier Province. It was the end of winter in Pakistan but still cold, with barren trees and mud-coloured ground. Smoke from wood-burning cook-fires nearby hung in the air. Our heads were not covered, but we wore *dupattas*, the scarf over the shoulders and front. Boys mingled in the crowd, some serving tiny cups of steaming hot tea. We were surrounded by men in woollen vests and shawls, with their heads wrapped in cloth turbans. No women were to be seen. As guests of the District Commissioner for a community development council ceremony, we were asked to plant seedlings in commemoration of spring, beginning the following month. It was the second day of Canada's Women in Development scoping mission to carve out a program of support for women.

That same week in Lahore, the Pakistan Women's Action Forum (WAF) was preparing for a street procession against the proposed Sharia Law of Evidence. WAF's press conference two weeks earlier marked the start of a public campaign against the Law of Evidence and the proposed Qisas and Diyat Law[1] to draw attention to the inherent discrimination against women built into the newly drafted laws. The Council of Islamic Ideology,[2] a constitutional body that advised Parliament on whether or not laws complied with the teachings of Islam, had proposed the law in April 1982. The Law of Evidence reduced the legal status of women by stating that the evidence of two women was equal to that of one man. 1984 was thus a pivotal year for both Pakistan and Canada on women's rights. The differing priorities were more than stark in contrast – Canada was offering new funding for rural women's socio-economic development. Pakistani women's rights organizations were battling a systematic rescinding of legal rights at the legislative and policy levels, which a foreign aid agency could do little if anything about.

— * —

A year earlier, the historic women's protest in 1983 on the Mall Road in Lahore, against the Law of Evidence instituted under Prime Minister Zia-ul-Haq, saw women tear-gassed, beaten, arrested, and hauled off to jail. Their photos flooded the media, and more protests followed in Karachi and other cities. A new stage for the women's rights movement in Pakistan was launched. The demonstrations took place during the most repressive years of Zia-ul-Haq's government when political activity was banned, and the press heavily censored.

The Women's Action Forum was formed in September 1981 in response to the government's anti-women policies, notably the Hudood Ordinances of 1979 (a set of fixed laws and punishment for crimes such as adultery) and what followed in later years. *Hudood* means "boundaries, limits, or restrictions" in Arabic. The Hudood Ordinances, the written Sharia law code, promulgated in the fateful year of 1979, included the Zina provision, which made sex outside marriage a criminal offence and rape a private offence. Not everyone understood the full implications of it when it was first announced. It took some cases to make it clear that "the law protects rapists, prevents women from testifying and confuses the issue of rape with adultery" (Mumtaz and Shaheed 1987, 101). A woman who had been raped had to prove her innocence or be accused of adultery and subject to penalty, including death by stoning. The Safia Bibi case in Punjab demonstrated the absurdity of the new law: Safia Bibi's father had registered a case of the rape of his daughter by a landowner and his son, and the judge had sentenced her as a rape victim, for adultery, on the basis of her own evidence (ibid., 103).

The founding of WAF in Karachi in 1981 symbolizes to many the birth of the women's rights movement. It was an evolution from earlier groups fighting for women's equality, such as the first fully fledged women's organization of Pakistan, the All Pakistan Women's Association (APWA), founded in 1949. But WAF was different; it was a response to a new urgency to address a systemic suppression of women's rights and freedoms unseen previously. "General Zia-ul-Haq's regime (1977–1988) institutionalized state-sanctioned gender discrimination through the imposition of certain ordinances of Sharia law that inherently weakened equality of women and men" (International Crisis Group 2015).

The fight for women's rights in the 1980s is etched into the history of the women's movement in Pakistan by the Women's Action Forum and what it embodied. Pakistani Women's Day is celebrated on 12 February each year in recognition of the protests by WAF and the Punjab Women Lawyers Association in 1983 against the Law of Evidence and other discriminatory laws introduced at the time. Thus, 12 February 1983 is a milestone that has not been, and never will be, forgotten. It became the title of a powerful poem by Saeeda Gazdar (Ahmad 1991), signifying the struggle of the time:

> To come out on the streets to fight, to demand
> the right for freedom,
> is against the sanctity of the feminine principle ...
> Those 200 women who came out on the streets were surrounded
> on all sides, besieged by armed police.
> Tear gas, rifles and guns, wireless vans and jeeps,
> every path was blockaded, there was
> no protection, they had to fight by themselves.
> I read the charter of freedom, and you?
> The writing in front of us is large and clear.
> Written on the wall, are you unable to read?
> ... not us, but you deserve to be murdered, for being the enemies
> of light and truth
> for being the murderers of love.

WAF put the issue of the legal challenge to the status of Pakistani women on the agenda of the global media. "Scores of western journalists sought out their members to get an insight into the discriminatory laws and their response," recalls one of the founders, Zohra Yusuf, the former head of the Human Rights Commission of Pakistan (Yusuf 2006). In Canada, the *Globe and Mail* covered the 1983 protest in an article headlined "Pakistani Women Stage Protests against Proposed Islamic Laws" on 3 March 1983. I was intrigued by the origins of WAF, which had coincided with Canada's first efforts to implement a new policy on women in development in Pakistan through programs specifically for women, and I wanted to learn more about its history. What was the state of the feminist movement in Pakistan? Was it growing in strength or on the wane? How were women's rights activists dealing with the growing violent militancy and religious extremism, I wondered?

— * —

Five years earlier, the year 1979 had witnessed a combination of events in the sub-region that bolstered the rise of Islamic movements. This confluence of events began with Ayatollah Khomeini declaring the victory of the Islamic revolution in Iran. The Soviet invasion of Afghanistan occurred the same year, and President Zia implemented his Islamization policy in Pakistan. Pakistan actually imposed Islamic law with less violence and upheaval than in Iran (Ghattas 2020). "All these events fueled a religious fervor that affected Muslims on a broad plane ... leading to a new vision being articulated for the Muslim world" (Ziring 2004, 176).

In April 1979 former Prime Minister Zulfikar Ali Bhutto was hanged under Zia's authority, causing the West's rebukes over human rights abuse during his first years in power. Zia's strategic role for the US in the region, supporting their efforts in the proxy war against the Soviets in Afghanistan, muted further criticism. The Pakistan government's policy on Afghanistan and the decision to engage with and support the Americans in the war against the Soviet Union "has wreaked havoc in Pakistan over the decades ever since," said Nasim Zehra, a well-known Pakistani journalist and writer who hosts a primetime current affairs talk show, when speaking on Pakistan and US policy at the Pakistan Institute for Development Economics as a panelist in 2020. From the start of the war in Afghanistan, the spread of extremist Islamic ideology across the Muslim world, sparked by this combination of key events in the sub-region, particularly the Islamic revolution in Iran, accelerated over the twenty years that followed.

— * —

The case of a couple condemned to *Hadd*, or the punishment of death by stoning under the Zina Ordinance (one of the ordinances under Hudood against adultery and extramarital sex), in autumn 1982 jolted women's rights organizations into coordinating their action under the aegis of WAF. Having witnessed the consequences for women under the Iranian Islamic revolution next door, which introduced severe restrictions on women, Pakistani women may have been even more concerned about such a public act. "Founders Day in Karachi" (referring to the founding of WAF) is celebrated on 16 September in recognition of the group's ongoing commitment to women's rights and promoting inclusive democracy in Pakistan.

An inspiring book by Rukhsana Ahmad entitled *We Sinful Women* translates poetry written in Urdu of the women expressing resistance to the government's Islamization campaign of the 1980s. The book's title is taken from a poem by the revered feminist poet Kishwar Naheed, "We Sinful Women" or "*Hum Gunahgaar Aurtein*," which became, in the words of civil society activist, poet, and writer Harris Khalique, "the anthem of the women's movement across South Asia … [Kishwar] wanted an equal world between women and men, and between the haves and have-nots." The book features the poems "Twelfth of February 1983," a poetic chronicle of that day; "The Hudood Ordinance" by Zehra Nigah; and "Section 144" by Kishwar Naheed. The writers and poets in the 1980s were rightfully concerned about the negative impact of eroding human rights on women, and on Pakistan overall. The joining up of WAF with the democracy movement was intentional. It signalled a more profound and unsettling sense of what the current government policies might mean for the future of society. This period in Pakistan's history is always referred to as one that marked the beginning of a turbulent and violent path that remains uncertain, and not only for women.

A nationwide media campaign called "*Chadur aur Chardiwari*" – "The Veil and Four Walls" – was mounted by the government to enforce *purdah*, the seclusion of women (Ahmad 1991), and government directives were issued to require female broadcasters to wear the chador and to ban women from sports. The government attempted to stop women from working and to segregate education to symbolize the Islamization policy. Women social activists would have nothing to do with this and fought hard against the Islamization policies affecting women. Nothing that happened in Pakistan or Iran, however, compares to the drastic images of suppressing women in the name of Islam by the Taliban in Afghanistan during their five-year rule a decade later – and, sadly, being instituted once again with their return to power in Afghanistan in 2021.

WAF's Islamabad chapter's remembrance of the 1983 protests on Pakistani Women's Day in 2020 chose the theme *In the Court of Women: Rising Violence against Women and Children*. It was an acknowledgment of the urgent need to tackle the growing violence against women and children, and a reminder that violence against women had triggered the most vigorous women's movement in Pakistan's history, becoming the central theme for women's rights groups during the 1980s (R. Khan 2009). The Islamization campaign of Zia-ul-Haq had the long-term effect of escalating violence against women (Ahmad 1991; Iqbal 2006). In the end, "women were the biggest losers under Zia" (Ghattas 2020). The issue of gender-based violence and protection of women has become a focus of WAF ever since.

The Law of Evidence came into effect in 1984 despite the women's protests. The number of women in prison skyrocketed to 6,000 by 1988, with "Zina complaints comprising most cases against women and girls" (Sarwar 2014). Years of protests, campaigns, and activism against the Hudood Ordinances have resulted in partial repeal and legal amendments that limit their implementation, but they remain in place.

"You couldn't turn your face away from what was happening at the time. The more oppression we saw, the stronger was our resolve to fight it," recalled Hina Jilani, a lawyer and activist, in the Canadian documentary film *The Journey of Pakistani Women*.[3] The late Asma Jahangir, Hina's sister, the internationally respected human rights lawyer about whom much has been written, was also involved as a member of the Punjab Lawyers Forum, an early supporting organization that formed an alliance with WAF. Shirkat Gah Women's Resource Centre, established in 1975, was instrumental in the launch of WAF in 1981. Aban Marker, a member of Shirkat Gah, hosted the initial meeting that created WAF in her home in Karachi. Aban later led a partnership with Canada's aid program in Pakistan for many years through her role in the national environmental action program and as head of IUCN Pakistan, which CIDA funded. I first met Aban in the early 1990s when we worked on Pakistan's National Conservation Strategy policy together with the Sustainable Development Policy Institute (SDPI), another key CIDA partner at the time. She was a strong and inspiring activist and intellectual.

WAF was alarmed by two major trends in the early 1980s – the growing trend to segregate women, and the various measures being adopted in the name of Islam (Mumtaz and Shaheed 1987). In their book *Women of Pakistan, Two Steps Forward, One Step Back?*, the earliest published book that documents the women's movement of the 1980s, Khawar Mumtaz and Farida Shaheed document the situation of those years. Farida Shaheed, another women's rights activist, recalled in 2017, "There was a questionnaire circulating by the government asking about whether women should participate in athletics, should drive or should work."[4] Harris Khalique recalls that it was primarily WAF – the educated women in urban areas – that came to the rescue of rural women who were the direct victims of the anti-women laws.[5] "The government's well-orchestrated move to negate women's rights and freedom, already apparent by the end of 1981, needed to be countered effectively and in the shortest time possible" (Mumtaz and Shaheed 1987, 133).

Paying closer attention to the alarm bells raised by these women activists would have provided deep insights into trends that have since become entrenched paths of division in society and have led to violent conflict. The women's movement, its struggles, and the issues they brought to the world's attention were the best barometer on the situation in the country and the impact of regional politics at play. A closer intersection of geopolitical analysis, security, and development trends might have strengthened the foreign policy analysis and response by the international community. But gender equality was far from central to foreign policy then, and no one was paying much attention to it.

— * —

The WAF campaign was in full swing against the proposed Qisas and Diyat Law as we arrived in Islamabad from Ottawa in February of 1984, one year after the infamous protests of the 12th of February 1983. The capital city is at the foot of the Himalayan mountains. The five of us quickly realized we needed not only warmer clothes for the February weather but more appropriate clothes to wear in the conservative society in which we had landed. The small boutique in the Holiday Inn had a few *shalwar kameez*, the loose-fitting pants and long tunic that make up the traditional dress of Pakistani women, which we grabbed despite the odd colours and mismatched sizes. Mine was burgundy with blue and yellow embroidery on the front. Not a perfect fit, but it worked. As I fidgeted with the shawl I had draped over my shoulder, my colleagues were already out the door. I rushed out behind them into the lobby full of small groups of international workers and Pakistanis meeting over late afternoon tea and samosas. The Holiday Inn was the most popular place for foreign diplomats and aid workers to stay, and a select location to meet with contacts, exchange information, and hammer out programs.

The month before the Pakistan mission, CIDA's president had agreed to develop a new policy on Women in Development to tackle systemic discrimination against women. A paper entitled "Managing the Process of Change," outlining what this would mean for CIDA, had been presented to CIDA's President's Committee by the new WID director, Elizabeth McAllister (the head of the WID mission to Pakistan). It was a fresh approach to renew the 1977 initial CIDA policy on WID. The Pakistan program would be the first to showcase it and to present the approach to a foreign government. Given its underpinnings on tackling systemic discrimination against women, we were cautious about how to talk to the government of Pakistan, especially given the Islamization policies and laws that President Zia was implementing, and the uncertainty and tension in the air. We were aware of the WAF protests and were anxious to meet with the group. We were also very conscious of cultural appropriateness and went out of our way during the mission not to give the impression that we were exporting a Western feminist model to Pakistan. The 1975 global Women's Conference and the UN Decade for Women that followed had unleashed questions of equality between women and men worldwide, including in Pakistan. Although sixty-one countries had ratified the Convention on the Elimination of Discrimination against Women by then, Pakistan had not yet signed.

A few days into the mission, we were driving past the president's office on Constitution Avenue to a meeting at the Planning Commission to present Canada's new WID policy and discuss with officials our plan to initiate aid projects for women. Looking out of the car window, I saw hundreds of soldiers in riot gear lined up in front of the president's office and Parliament. I asked my Pakistani colleague what was happening and why they appeared ready for action. She shrugged, saying it was simply protection around the president's office, implying it was a normal situation. Perhaps normal for people in Pakistan, by then close to five years into martial law, but it was a sign of the most repressive years of the Zia-ul-Haq regime and its readiness for street protests and resistance to the tightening of restrictions on freedom and democracy WAF and other activists were vehemently opposing. We had arrived during the height of martial law. Many Pakistanis still maintain that this was the darkest period of Pakistan's history (Hussain 2020). Yet ironically, four years later, when General Zia was killed in an unusual plane crash in the summer of 1988, the US

Secretary of State, George Shultz, described him as a "great fighter for freedom" (Ghattas 2020) due to his role in enabling the war against the Soviets in Afghanistan.

Pakistan's pivotal role in the anti-Soviet war in Afghanistan made it highly globally relevant and, for the Americans, a key ally. 1984 witnessed a surge in financial and other support from the US to the Pakistani military (Coll 2004) along with a six-year economic aid package. Zia provided logistic support from Pakistan and training facilities in the tribal areas to prepare the Afghan Mujaheddin for the battle in Afghanistan. America entrusted Pakistan's security establishment with training and conditioning the Mujaheddin to fight the war in the name of Islam – the CIA covert operation for an Afghan jihad, the largest in the history of the CIA (Mamdani 2004, 141). The US strategy of turning the Afghan civil war into an Islamic "holy war against the communists" made Pakistan the frontline state in this effort. The Saudi intelligence head recruited Osama bin Laden (Mamdani 2004), with CIA approval, to lead the Afghan jihad, consisting of recruits from other Arab countries in addition to Afghans. Bin Laden settled in Peshawar with his family in 1982 to carry out this role. The combined support of the US and Saudi Arabia for the Afghan war effort saw both countries significantly increase their (multi-faceted) support for Pakistan.

Zia's Islamization policy, the Saudi Arabia policy of support, and his own Islamic credentials helped bring the mullahs in Pakistan on side. By assisting the Americans to counter the Russians in Afghanistan, he endeared the West to him in the last Cold War conflict playing out in Afghanistan, which, more than any other location, was the high point of the Cold War (Mamdani 2004, 120). The Afghan war also led to the creation first of al-Qaeda, then of the Afghan Taliban, and, post-9/11, of the Pakistan extremist groups and eventually the Pakistan Taliban (TTP). Cold War politics was to have a profound effect on Pakistan, instigating the growth of internal militancy with its many ramifications, not least of all on women and girls.

The Afghan Mujaheddin fighters, stationed in Pakistan, were clearly against women's rights. American and Saudi support for Zia gave rise to extremist militants in Pakistan who strongly opposed women's rights, writes Kathy Gannon, a Canadian journalist and author based in Pakistan covering Afghanistan (Gannon 2005). The situation in Afghanistan was therefore already, in the mid-1980s, a strong influencing factor on women's rights in Pakistan. Political Islam and violent extremists, however, were still a marginal force in the early 1980s, undetected and unacknowledged (Ghattas 2020). We had landed in Pakistan for the CIDA WID mission unprepared for the geopolitical reality we found ourselves in.

MEETING THE WOMEN'S ACTION FORUM – KHAWATEEN MAHAZ-E-AMAL

In Lahore, we met with the Punjab Women's Lawyers Association and WAF members in the heat of a campaign against the Law of Qisas and Diyat and the Law of Evidence. Sitting in the home of a key activist that day (who did not want to be identified), the atmosphere was tense and conversations guarded; they were unsure how the security authorities would react and whether there might be more violence and imprisonments. We were aware of the fear they felt, which did not, however, deter their plans. They were certain they were being watched, as WAF meetings had been attended and monitored by the Central Intelligence Department (Mumtaz and Shaheed 1987). As a follow-up to their poster campaign across the city – "One Woman, One Testimony"; "The Proposed Law of Evidence Unacceptable," which plastered Lahore with posters – they were preparing for a procession on 12 February (now Pakistan Women's Day) with six women's organizations to denounce police brutality and the proposed Law of Qisas and Diyat. It took much courage, given that fifty women had been arrested and many were injured in the Lahore protests on February 12th the previous year. We left the meeting worried and subdued, with a sense of helplessness and realization that this was a more serious and dangerous situation than we could have imagined. We had shown up with hope and enthusiasm about the new aid policy in support of women's equal access to resources and services, and to ensure that Canada's development programs assisted women as both contributors to and beneficiaries of the development process. Our mandate was limited to socio-economic development and poverty reduction plans. The overshadowing struggle against the systemic assault on women's rights in a context of a government-directed Islamization policy and implementation of aspects of Sharia law was far too sensitive and political for a foreign aid agency at the time, especially when the government was a military one that Canada, the US, and other countries strongly supported for geopolitical reasons.

We didn't speak much about the current crackdowns on women's rights, politics, and democracy, and, like aid agencies and political analysts inside Pakistan and elsewhere, put it aside as internal political turmoil that would eventually pass. No one anticipated the laws' reverberations on gender equality, and how repealing them became almost impossible for decades. Even WAF did not initially recognize the implications of the Islamic laws or the "violation of the legal system and the sheer opportunism of using Islam for political purposes," recounted Mumtaz and Shaheed a few years later (Mumtaz and Shaheed 1987, 99). International criticism of the suppression of human rights (and women's rights) in the name of Islam was silenced at the time (Ahmad 1991). Zia-ul-Haq was even called "a champion of the free world" by US President Reagan. The uneasiness we felt that day was the recognition of systemic discrimination against women being implemented through these laws, policies, and directives. It was obvious they would adversely impact women in Pakistan, although the hope was still there that it could be a passing phase. It was beyond our mandate to do something to support those trying to change it. And WAF, to their credit, was not accepting any foreign assistance, although they were grateful for the international media attention giving visibility to their protests on the world stage.

WAF termed 1984 "the year of Qisas and Diyat." Its campaign against the proposed discriminatory laws, coordinated with various women's organizations, could not stop the *Majlis-e-Shoora* (both houses of Parliament – Senate and National Assembly) from tabling it in August 1984, nor its passage by the National Assembly in 1985. The original law proposed reduced *diyat* (blood money as compensation for murder or physical injury) for women. For proof of murder, women's evidence as witnesses was inadmissible, so if murder were committed in the presence of women, the murderers could get away unpunished. The Law of Evidence and the Qisas and Diyat Law signified the "exclusion of women's evidence over a vast field, tantamount to cutting women's worth by half" (Mumtaz and Shaheed 1987). "If Zia's regime has been a repressive one for women, it is not simply because it is a martial law regime, but because, in addition to being politically and economically reactionary, it has been characterized by socially retrogressive programs dressed in Islamic colours" (ibid., 130).

Canada, along with other Western countries and Pakistan itself, had underestimated the impact of President Zia's Islamization policy on women's rights in Pakistan. The tensions at play were not only between rights activists and government policy, nor fundamentalist Islamic political groups, but within the government itself, with the Islamization policies and their detrimental impact on women's rights versus the government's progressive sixth Five-Year National Development Plan, with its far-reaching vision for women's and girls' education and a population program in support of women's reproductive health. Dr Mahbub ul Haq, then Minister of Planning, had asked CIDA's WID director during a corridor discussion at the end of the mission to keep up the international pressure on Pakistan on women's equality issues. He was likely aware of the risks to women's rights, given that the WAF protests against the Islamization policies and laws were in full swing. Little did we know we were witnessing an historic moment, one which drastically changed Pakistan and the course of gender equality in Pakistan – and, some might argue, beyond its borders – for decades.

"The military dictator we fought then has long gone. The fight is now against the dark forces he unleashed and nurtured, who now kill innocents, claiming over 50,000 lives over the past decade [since 2001]. They've expanded their theatre of war to attack and threaten girls' schools and polio workers in Pakistan (Sarwar 2014) … The Taliban, who tried to kill Malala in 2012, intended to take forward the controversial 'Islamization' agenda that General Zia set in motion decades earlier," wrote Beena Sarwar, a Pakistani journalist focussing on human rights. Her view is held by many women's rights activists. The other key factor is that the origins of Pakistan's internal militancy are strongly rooted in historical Cold War politics. The 50,000 lives mentioned above burgeoned to 67,000 by 2017. By 2020, the Global Terrorism Index placed Pakistan seventh in the list of countries most affected by terrorism in the world (Khan 2022).

CIDA's first foray into supporting Pakistan's gender equality efforts in 1984 took place within the context of a raging women's rights campaign against discriminatory Islamic Sharia laws under a state-sanctioned Islamization policy. Moreover, it coincided with the "black wave" of Islamic fundamentalism sparked by the Iranian Revolution in 1979, the term so aptly coined to depict the phenomena of the time by author, journalist, and political analyst Kim Ghattas, and used as the title of her book in 2020 on the Middle East. The WAF protests should have been a strong warning sign to all of what was to come, but are still obscured from most of the analysis of Pakistan's drift into extremism.

2

Exposing Vulnerabilities

By 2010 Pakistan was considered a dangerous place to be a diplomat. Anti-American sentiment was high, the ongoing war in neighbouring Afghanistan was in the throes of a renewed American troop surge, and deadly suicide bombings were frequent in Peshawar and the northwest region. US drone strikes on militants were a regular occurrence in Pakistan's remote tribal areas bordering Afghanistan. A deadly bombing by the Pakistan Taliban had taken place at the Marriott Hotel in Islamabad just two years earlier, igniting layers of security restrictions and turning Pakistan into a non-family duty station for most diplomats and the United Nations. The start of the decade had witnessed more frequent attacks by militant groups and the Pakistan Taliban, which had expanded throughout the northwest of Pakistan (Khyber Pakhtunkhwa and the Federally Administered Tribal Areas) following its founding in December 2007, three years earlier.

We secured the last seats on the Pakistan International Airways flight direct from Toronto to Islamabad, packed with aid workers and supplies for the flood emergency affecting twenty million people. The devastating 2010 Indus River floods had been triggered by eighteen days of non-stop rains a few weeks before, and the monsoon was not yet over. As Shahbaz and I stepped off the plane, the rain poured, tempering somewhat the blast of 37° C heat. Benazir Bhutto International Airport was a chaotic scene of flights arriving full of urgently needed supplies and surge aid workers. We were met by the Canadian embassy staff, who helped us navigate through the pandemonium and into the armoured vehicles waiting outside.

The embassy driver stopped at the heavily guarded gates to the diplomatic enclave for under-car bomb scans, repeated again a few minutes later upon entering the Canadian compound. The building and grounds hadn't changed since the 1980s except for the higher exterior walls topped with barbed wire. The staff quarters we were allocated were the same house where I had attended a cocktail party during our mission in 1984. A lovely two-story brick home built by Canada in the late 1970s, it was now dwarfed by the rapidly expanding and heavily fortified American embassy towering beside it. We were apprehensive about living with this level of security on a daily basis, but I was nevertheless happy to be back working in Pakistan.

Despite the danger, insecurity, and visible inequities, Pakistan is a place that imprints itself on the memories of those who travel there, with its mix of ancient history and civilizations, vibrant colour, and chaos of daily life, "an important intellectual center of the Muslim world that can't be ignored, both good and bad," as the president of the Aga Khan University described it to me. From a geopolitical standpoint, also, Pakistan cannot be ignored. Former colleagues reminisce about the best social life ever in Islamabad and the warmth and openness of Pakistanis. A mix of stark contradictions – the hospitality and welcoming of foreigners amidst burning anti-American sentiment; growing sectarianism; flourishing literature, art, poetry, and journalism amidst a retraction of freedoms and the silencing of some progressive voices. A brand of religious extremism that breeds fear, erases diversity, increases divisions, and crushes efforts for equality and education for women and girls flourishes in parts of the population. Mountainous beauty, rivers, deserts, and mixed, multi-harvesting farmlands in contrast with the prevailing poverty, illiteracy, food insecurity, and lack of safe water and sanitation for millions.

That year, the 2010 floods drove a huge number of vulnerable people into emergency humanitarian camps throughout the country, especially in Sindh province, where the water eventually moved along with the Indus to meet the sea. In the words of Richard Holbrooke, the US special representative for Afghanistan and Pakistan, after his visits to the hard-hit areas of Sindh (Packer 2019), "It's hard to imagine a more overwhelming sight – the endless display of areas under water, people clinging to the dikes and raised areas, as close to their land as possible and in tents huddled along the roads, they had nothing." These sentiments were echoed during my trips to the flood areas shortly afterward. As aid workers, we were shocked at the number of people and the extent of deprivation; how did we not know that this level of poverty, malnutrition, and lack of education existed in Pakistan? The UN was perplexed that their radar had missed this level of vulnerability. It was so well hidden, as poverty tends to be, that its depth was somehow obscured from aid donors. The UNICEF representative reaffirmed at the time that Pakistan was in a constant state of what they defined as emergency because of the high level of child malnutrition, and the low indicators on health and well-being for millions of women and children. Sitting in a meeting on the flood response at the Economic Affairs Division of the Finance Ministry that September, the Joint Secretary admitted that the floods had exposed rural poverty (and the scale of the malnutrition issue) in Pakistan like never before. It was hard to reconcile this evidence from our vantage point in the capital. Had the development community become out of touch with grassroots reality, or perhaps too focused on policies and strategies and aid coordination meetings? Travel to certain parts of the country had been extremely difficult, if not impossible, for some years due to the security situation, and efforts to secure funding arrangements for programs in Pakistan were also a large part of the work.

The areas hardest hit by the floods were in Sindh province, where rural households faced the highest severe food insecurity in the country, the representative from the UN World Food Program (WFP) told us at a briefing the next day. Nearly 45 per cent of Pakistani children still suffer from chronic malnutrition, with stunting the highest in the region. WFP told us that the high prevalence of malnutrition "is at odds with Pakistan's status as a low middle-income country which risks losing the demographic dividend of a youthful population because almost half of the future workforce is stunted" (WFP 2021). Pakistan has the second-highest number of children out of school at approximately 22.8 million, and girls are particularly affected, with 32 per cent of primary school–aged girls out of school (compared to 21 per cent of boys). Some 38 per cent of the population is classified as poor, with poverty the main driver of food insecurity. The gender-disaggregated data from the humanitarian response in 2010 exposed the shocking impact on women and girls, especially in Sindh and Balochistan.

Many in the development field thought or hoped the floods would be a turning point for Pakistan on poverty and development policies, and an opportunity for the government to undertake structural economic and governance reforms. On the sidelines of a meeting of foreign aid donors on the policy reform agenda, a senior British colleague told me the floods might have unleashed a revolutionary change in Pakistan. The former World Bank director, who had returned to Pakistan as an independent consultant for the Bank, answered a question from the German representative on how donors could leverage the government to implement the reform agenda on energy sector and tax reform, as strongly advocated for by the Asian Development Bank. "Don't expect that those demands will be acted upon in exchange for increased aid; it won't work," he noted. Just a few weeks later, a dramatic policy shift by the government forwent the additional donor grant aid for flood rehabilitation in lieu of an internally designed cash transfer program. Imposed conditions on aid programs by international donors were often understandably resisted by governments, with the exception of large IMF loans needed for budgetary support, which were tolerated to the extent necessary. And Pakistan was already receiving over $4 billion per year in combined foreign assistance. Forgoing additional aid dollars was the consequence of differences in policy prescriptions against current local realities and priorities.

— * —

The five-star Serena Hotel meeting rooms were crowded with aid workers and officials attending the UN humanitarian coordination meetings. Navigating the crowds of foreign and Pakistani aid workers, embassy staff, and government officials, we moved from meeting room to meeting room, trying to gather as much information as possible on the emergency response. The hotel had become the coordination centre for the humanitarian effort, given its size and secure location. Every day, the CIDA team divided among sector coordination meetings and regrouped at the end of the day to recap the situation and report to headquarters.

Late one afternoon that hot, humid August, a group of prominent women held a meeting with heads of aid agencies to see how they could help support women and their families affected by the floods. My colleague in the High Commission suggested it was an opportunity for me to connect with these women who were active on women's empowerment issues, so I went. Diplomacy and development work depend on strong relationships, and this would possibly be one entry point into the network of gender equality leaders in Pakistan. Relationships and access to key figures and information are what make the job not only a success, but a meaningful and rich experience. The formal meeting, chaired by the popular advisor to the prime minister for the social sectors and women at the time, Shahnaz Wazirali, was an instructive introduction back into that world. Canada was known in Pakistan for its consistent and strong support for gender equality programs since 1984. The gender equality work was historically speaking CIDA's signature, or at least the most well-known, along with support to civil society organizations and the famous Warsak Dam. Riding on the coattails of that strong legacy on gender equality would help my work as a diplomat, given that the future of Canada's aid program in the country was looking not only uncertain, but dim.

Approximately thirty women from different organizations and some private activists attended; the urgency of the flood situation and its impact on women and children led to a solemn mood. The meeting was testing the waters to see if any aid money could be leveraged to match private initiatives. Pakistan gives the highest percentage per capita of any country in indigenous philanthropy. According to a Johns Hopkins study, it is double the size of government spending under the Public Sector Development Program. The sizeable philanthropy is well known and visible, so a matching approach could have leveraged that. I made some useful contacts at the meeting, including with members of the famous Women's Action Forum, that would prove critical later.

— * —

The UN World Food Programme, as one of Canada's closest humanitarian partners, had rescued our efforts to organize a visit by Canadian Minister of International Development Bev Oda, at the height of the flood response. WFP provided staff support and helicopters for the minister to witness firsthand the emergency response and food assistance that Canada was funding. I managed to secure seats on a PIA flight to the town of Sukkor in Sindh for the sizeable Canadian government delegation, along with CBC reporter Nahla Ahmed and her film crew. Together with two other officers, I visited the temporary relief camps while the minister, the CBC crew, and UN WFP officials boarded the helicopter for a flyover of the worst-affected areas. The relief camp was a shock, watching lineups of mothers with their small children being measured for body weight and treated for malnourishment in the heat and dust of the camp. Sindh province had not appeared to have so many extremely vulnerable people (the majority in the camps were women and children), at least on the surface. The government and the internationally supported humanitarian response were struggling to respond to the scope of the challenge, given the number of people in need. I found myself wondering if the approach and strategy CIDA had developed in the 1980s (1984 through 1988), so aptly captured in the CIDA WID program strategy on Pakistan entitled *Nation Builders: Women in Pakistan. A Development Strategy*, had been the right one, or if it had actually made any difference. What, if anything, had changed for women and girls, especially those in rural areas, after more than three decades of support to Pakistan's development efforts, not only by CIDA but by other donors? The early CIDA WID strategy had targeted rural women, their basic needs, and support for their role in agriculture. The reading of the situation of women in 1983 by the CIDA mission had also indicated multiple forms of discriminations, including, at the time, the Hudood Ordinances and their negative impact on the status of women. It was hard not to juxtapose that legacy of decades of aid support for Pakistan's gender equality movement and civil society against the backdrop of the rising violent militancy and religious extremism that developed over the same period. How had the rising insecurity, internal militancy, and extremist violence impacted their lives? Had the discriminatory laws been reversed? As a development practitioner, the question of whether rural women were even more vulnerable now with perhaps less access to essential services was a burning one. By 2010, the Islamists were gaining ground in Pakistan (Hussain 2010), and it appeared that some of the progress in gender equality and women's rights made over three or more decades was being rolled back. Just how far back was a question I was determined to answer.

FLOOD RESPONSE

The Friends of Democratic Pakistan (FODP), created in 2008, was a group of countries formed to strengthen relations with Pakistan and push for policy reforms while bolstering its shrinking democracy in the face of growing extremism and violent militancy. It was chaired by Germany and coordinated by a UN Special Political Representative with offices in Islamabad. Richard Holbrooke, appointed in January 2009 as US Special Representative for Afghanistan and Pakistan, saw it as a forum to help find a political solution to the war in Afghanistan, given Pakistan's critical role. The "Af-Pak" strategy of the Obama administration promoted constitutional stability in Pakistan as one of its five objectives. In October 2009, the US agreed to a $7.5 billion aid package to help pave the way for a long-term strategic partnership. The FODP was one tool to help "build an enduring relationship with Pakistan" (Packer 2019) of the kind that Holbrooke was after.[1] The US administration took a harder line with Pakistan, whom they saw that year as the real enemy in the US-led war against the Afghan Taliban.

FODP was planning a high-level conference in Dubai not long after I arrived. At one of my first meetings at the German ambassador's residence, more than forty representatives from different countries and the UN sat at the long table discussing Pakistan's future. The group of diplomats and members of international organizations hoped for a pact with the government on reforms in exchange for increased aid for flood rehabilitation and reconstruction. Unfortunately, the anticipated changes, using a collective response by donor countries, didn't leverage anything, as earlier predicted by the Bank advisor. The aid pledges of over $2 billion USD for flood rehabilitation (the UN's largest-ever disaster appeal to that date), including Canada's proposed $50 million CAD, never fully materialized.

Pakistan responded well to the flood crisis through both its military and civilian response and people's own resilience and capacity, and life returned to almost what it had been pre-flood by November 2010. People returned to their homes and rebuilt and recovered. Unfortunately, the "build back better" approach to mitigate the impact of future disasters was not enough to counter the climate-change-induced catastrophic floods twelve years later in 2022, where the damage was much worse. But in 2010, the Pakistani government politely but firmly told the international community that it wished their additional funds for flood rehabilitation to be directed to the boosted cash transfer program to affected families. The job of flood recovery and rebuilding was to be led by the government, not aid donors. The cash transfer program was an excellent one on paper but failed in the eyes of the international community to reach the scale of people in need and ensure recovery. The flood rehabilitation plans for disaster risk infrastructure were not fully implemented, and the policy choice of the government not to rebuild to flood-proof communities by accepting the offers of the international community resulted in devastating consequences down the road. In 2022 the Pakistan government appealed to the international community to launch "an immense humanitarian response" (New Humanitarian 2022) to help with the floods.

The Pakistan government shut down the UN Humanitarian subregional hubs and some of their camps in remote locations as soon as they could, too soon for the humanitarian community, but perhaps forcing people to return home helped avert chronic aid dependency. Pakistan remained much the same post-floods, and perhaps life became more difficult for many thousands of people who slipped from poverty to destitution or ultra-poverty, but on the surface, at least, things appeared to normalize.

After the flood emergency died down and the Friends of Democratic Pakistan group failed in its policy reform agenda with the Pakistani government, the hastily organized international meeting of the Pakistan Development Forum also quietly closed. The Minister of Finance spoke to the aid donor countries attending the Forum in Islamabad: "this meeting is about Pakistan, our burdens are our own, we are not seeking international support without demonstrating our own support. We will take the lead on how we wish to engage with the world. Our military, social protection agencies and citizens will help with recovery, and we will protect the poor."

Everything appeared to go back to normal, at least on the surface. The aid donor–government relationship remained a somewhat boring but routine part of the job. The evening "salon" discussions over dinner were where the more illuminating conversations took place, on the current issues and changes in society amidst the rising terrorist violence and suicide bombings, and on how the government and military were responding. The flood emergency was over, but with security getting worse, development policy and programs were impacted. Many were already lagging in implementation due to a myriad of reasons well known to aid donors and the government; the story of failed development programs is the subject of numerous accounts and analysis. But my interest was more in what was left out of the aid, political, and security analysis – the gender lens on its history and impact.

WOMEN'S ECONOMIC EMPOWERMENT

The barrage of backed-up missions from CIDA's headquarters, stalled due to the monsoon flood emergency, started to arrive to carry out project-monitoring visits. Despite the scheduling pressures, I welcomed them as an opportunity to zero in on the situation of rural women and shed some light on what had changed since the early aid programs for women's development, the 1980s' WID strategies and the WAF movement. It was a chance to see CIDA's more recent policy shift to women's economic empowerment (called WEE) in action. Just weeks earlier, CIDA's gender advisor, based in Ottawa, had posed the question to the Islamabad gender equality team during a videoconference, "What makes a WEE project? It should be grounded in human rights, and human rights need to be included in the CIDA WEE framework." The guidance framework for the WEE Program "has always maintained that without a focus on women's rights in Pakistan, progress towards women's economic empowerment will be limited" (CIDA 2010a). Since then, further research has reinforced the theory on women's economic independence as critical to equality (Lopez-Claros and Nakhjavani 2018). Senator Ayesha Raza Farooq, speaking at Canada's WEE Forum in Islamabad some years later in 2017, said, "Women's empowerment, especially their economic empowerment, is not only key to nation-building and effectual implementation of human rights but is also critical to women's self-esteem and wellbeing that has an invaluable impact on their families. What does empowerment mean to me? It is not when our incomes rise, but when we are empowered to exercise our rights." The efforts of the gender equality team in CIDA by 2010 to integrate women's rights into the WEE framework appeared to be a way of not losing sight of a rights-based approach, given the backslide on women's rights, the rise in gender-based violence, and the dramatic drop in gender equality indicators in Pakistan blatantly evident by then.

> Making progress (in Women's economic empowerment) requires a change in individuals, communities, institutions, markets, and value chains, and in the wider political and legal environment. WEE cannot be achieved unless the most marginalized women in society experience transformation in their lives. This means focusing on the intersecting inequalities experienced by women in addition to their gender, for example, on the basis of their class, caste, race, ethnicity, age or disability status, and taking action to ensure that nobody is left behind. (European Parliament Directorate-General for Internal Affairs, 2017)

As Anatol Lieven put it in 2011 in his book, *Pakistan, a Hard Country* (Lieven 2011, 4), "Pakistan is a divided, disorganized, economically backward, corrupt, violent, unjust, often savagely oppressive towards the poor and women, and home to extremely dangerous forms of extremism and terrorism – and yet it moves and is, in many ways, a surprisingly tough and resilient state and a society. It is not quite as unequal as it looks from the outside." But for the majority of poor rural women, that may not have been the reality. By 2011, not surprisingly, Pakistan was labelled the third most dangerous place in the world to be a woman.²

3

Violent Extremism and Women's Empowerment

Not long after returning to Pakistan in 2010, my friend Rushda gave me a copy of the popular book *The Reluctant Fundamentalist*, a post-9/11 novel describing the road to radicalism of a young Pakistani professional disillusioned with America and the country's vision for shaping the world. It has since been made into a movie of the same title by Mira Nair. The book is a dialogue between East and West and an early effort to describe differences in American and Pakistani culture, touching on factors that make youth – especially young men – vulnerable to extremism. Since then, international research on the prevention of violent extremism has flourished as the world is seeking to understand and grapple with its underlying drivers. In 2016, a UNDP[1] corporate strategic paper on navigating turbulence and uncertainty highlighted the systematic discrimination of women as a strategic intent of violent extremist groups:

> A particularly worrisome feature is the systematic discrimination and abuse of women as a strategic and intentional tactic of violent extremist groups. Moreover, even before violent extremism takes root, key indicators of the spread of extremist ideologies often include increased discrimination against women and girls and increased intolerance for divergent opinions, religions, and lifestyles.

As early as 2011, a study on religious fundamentalism across the globe by the Association of Women in Development (AWID 2011, 12) found evidence that religious fundamentalist actors had sought to undermine and reverse the gains made in international human rights standards for women. Nine years after that AWID study, a UNDP and UN Women report on Asia (UNDP and UN Women 2020) used expert case studies to highlight how unequal gender power structures fuelled and shaped violent extremism around the region. Breaking new ground with this research, the report showed how structures of patriarchy and harmful performances of masculinity are deeply embedded in the modus operandi of violent extremist groups. The researchers found that such groups often manipulated or built on existing gender stereotypes to incite men and women to commit violence and to find refuge and support within extremist communities. It provided key insights into the gender dynamics that underpin violent extremism in South Asia. Another study published by UN Women Pakistan (Khan 2022) found that, in Pakistan, extremist trends had deepened the exclusion of women, and militant groups have consistently targeted women's education, rights, and mobility.

The treatment of women is a barometer for instability, violence, and insecurity in society, as highlighted by the Georgetown University Institute for Women, Peace, and Security in the annual WPS Index of 2020. The Index takes into consideration three dimensions that affect the well-being of women: inclusion, security, and justice (Georgetown Institute for Women, Peace, and Security 2019). In October 2015, the UN Security Council adopted Resolution 2242, which linked the policy agendas of women, peace, and security (WPS) and preventing/countering violent extremism, calling for synergies between efforts aimed at countering violent extremism and those furthering women, peace, and security. The UNSC Report on Women, Peace, and Security (UN 2022) confirmed that misogyny is integral to the ideology and political identity of most terrorist and violent extremist groups and individuals, and is manifested in their propaganda, recruitment, and tactics. But, it concluded, the significant link between misogyny and terrorism or violent extremism is still often overlooked by policy responses.

Pakistan is rated among the worst performers by the Women, Peace, and Security Index, although it is the only country in that range not classified as fragile or conflict-affected. In 2019, Pakistan was fourth from the bottom of the Index after Yemen, Afghanistan, and Syria:

> As elsewhere in the world, two key aspects of women's security – organized violence and current intimate partner violence – are closely related across Pakistan. Women in provinces and areas

with the highest rates of organized violence also face the highest rates of current intimate partner violence, underlining the amplified risks of violence at home for women living near conflict areas. Balochistan province has the highest rates of both. (GIWPS and PRIO 2021)

Since, the 2023 index shows Pakistan replaced by other countries, with a slight move upward to ranking 158 out of 177 countries. The same indicators remain prevalent in the merged districts of Khyber-Pakhtunkhwa (KP) province that border Afghanistan, according to the study by UN Women Pakistan (UN Women 2021). "Pakistan is among those countries where 70% of women and girls experience physical or sexual violence in their lifetime by their intimate partners. As well, 93% of women experience some form of sexual violence in public places in their lifetime," said Zia Awan, the advocate heading the Lawyers for Human Rights and Legal Aid organization, in an interview in the Express Tribune newspaper in March 2017.[2] "For us, every day must be women's day," he emphasized, saying that an inefficient social justice system is the reason for various forms of violence in Pakistan.

In 2012, on a trip to the port city of Karachi, I arranged to meet Zia Awan to learn more about his work protecting and defending women from gender-based violence and so-called honour crimes. Lawyers for Human Rights and Legal Aid (LHRLA) had been a grant recipient of CIDA's Women's Development Fund in the year 2000, receiving $98,742 (over three years) for their work on mitigating trafficking of women. LHRLA's fight against honour killing had become more prominent in recent years and I was interested to hear from him. CIDA had not provided funding since 2003 when the grant ended, and I wanted to explore whether there was an opportunity to reinstate the partnership.

— * —

The office wasn't far from my hotel. Ignoring security protocols – the British and American diplomats were not even allowed to leave their consular offices in Karachi – I grabbed a hotel car and stopped outside what appeared to be an abandoned building. The entrance contained a massive anthill and dirt in the lobby near the stairs, and no lights. I managed to get to the second floor with trepidation (abduction for money was my worst fear since working in Afghanistan). Although it was dark, I could see some indication of life and office work down the long hallway. Once inside, it looked like a regular office: a busy call centre staffed by young women and men, smaller offices full of newspaper clippings and piles of documents, and a large conference room.

The Madadgaar[3] helpline call centre was operating with a sizeable staff. A few closed rooms were filled with newspaper clippings on honour crimes and other cases of GBV. At that time, the Karachi call centre was the only helpline to respond to children and women suffering from violence, abuse, and exploitation. The helpline was extended the following year to provincial centres in Peshawar and other regional capitals (International Crisis Group 2015).[4]

Zia gave a PowerPoint presentation in the conference room, showcasing LHRLA's work. I was surprised to see the lack of up-to-date technology and research skills in such a complex area, but the data were there (and the equipment has greatly improved since then). UNDP stated in 2020 that "[t]he availability and quality of sexual and gender-based violence data should be increased, including at a subnational level, not only to allow for better research and analysis but to eventually assist in the identification of areas at risk of violent extremism" (UNDP 2020). Awan's non-profit organization, working on the front lines of the worst cases of gender-based violence, was not getting the funding or capacity support it needed at that time. Although supported by the International Organization for Migration for its work on trafficking of women, this was not enough to fully tackle the challenging work of defending women from honour crimes and other forms of sexual and gender-based violence (SGBV).

The investigations were frustrating as they could do little to assist the victims. Zia talked about the laws that prohibit child marriage, sexual violence, domestic violence, *karo-kari* (honour killing), kidnapping, and harassment, which were not being enforced. "There is a lack of awareness on addressing the complaints through a proper channel, something that Madadgaar is trying to remedy." He explained that "only 10% of the violence cases are reported in Sindh and Punjab by media. The percentage of reported gender-based crimes in Balochistan and Khyber-Pakhtunkhwa is even smaller." Despite the apparent increase in media reporting, it was still not reflecting the reality. Since 2017, this trend has been similar around the world in actual reporting of gender-based violence. The poor application of laws against gender-based violence is also not unique to Pakistan.[5]

My meeting with Awan was just after one of the most sensational cases of honour crimes committed in a remote district of KP province in early 2012. It became one of the most frustrating and unresolved cases – not unlike most of them, I was learning. Five women from the Kohistan district were (reportedly) killed for dancing with men at a family wedding. The all-male tribal *jirga*, or village council of elders (in this case led by clerics), condemned the women and two men to death for "staining the honor" of their families and mixing the sexes in violation of the "law of gender segregation during the wedding party," reported many of the news articles at the time. Some said a rival family schemed to destroy a more affluent family. Another news article claimed the local administration was the hurdle, due to their inaction that empowered the clerics (Mullahs) to control community behaviour.[6]

Kohistan is an impoverished, secluded, and previously neglected district in KP province (*Swat Express Tribune* 2012). One of the poorest districts of Pakistan, it is an area where justice through the customary informal system (using local councils or jirgas) was, until recent years, legally recognized by government under a special dispensation for tribal areas. Although this governance structure changed in 2019, the customary practice may not have yet caught up. The rulings of jirgas have been considered illegal when it comes to violating legislation now in place for women's protection. As a result, jirgas can no longer order the execution of women for their definition of immorality. The Kohistan jirga used the jargon of "*na mehram*" ("male outside of family") from Islamic jurisprudence to shield itself. "These informal courts function in vast ungoverned spaces and are rearing their ugly heads in Punjab and Sindh because of the retreat of the state from its constitutional jurisdiction" (*Express Tribune* 2012). The "jirga [has conducted itself in a way] that reminds us of the days of the Taliban rule in Afghanistan [in the 1990s] and gives us a glimpse of a future Pakistan impacted by growing intolerance and bigotry," reported the editorial of the *Express Tribune* in May 2012. Yet the Pakistan Taliban and other Islamic extremist groups glorify the days of Taliban rule in Afghanistan and "look upon Taliban rule in Afghanistan as ideal government, because it enforced a particular notion of Sharia and the punishment system derived from their interpretation of it" (Sheikh 2016).

The Supreme Court eventually stepped in after pressure from women's groups and the National Commission on the Status of Women, by attempting to hold the local administration accountable and directing an investigation. Four women's rights activists flew to the district to investigate in 2012. In 2013, two more delegations visited the area for further investigation. In March 2014, the community produced a written statement saying the girls were alive (the men had fled, and the women were locked up), but they had never appeared. In 2015, three years after the incident, nobody knew whether the women were dead or alive. It was not possible to determine what had happened to them. The Supreme Court closed the case, given no conclusive evidence. It was considered a legal failure. In July 2018, the Supreme Court opened a fresh police investigation. But another murder – the killing of Afzal Kohistani (the whistleblower who exposed the honour killing) in 2019 – "deepen[ed] the tragedy that started with a video of dancing and singing and ... spiraled into a bloody tale of Shakespearean proportions, with at least nine lives claimed" (BBC World News Asia 2019). Years after this event, there have been many arrests, another murder, and conclusions that at least three of the women were killed. Not surprisingly, the Pakistan Taliban accused the media of sensationalizing the Kohistan Jirga issue.

GENDERED DEVELOPMENT DIVIDES AND VIOLENCE IN PAKISTAN'S BORDER AREAS

The stark differential in levels of development and poverty in certain provinces and regions of Pakistan is most apparent in the conflict-prone districts of KP and Balochistan. Poverty rates are the highest in the tribal districts of KP (73 per cent in the former Federally Administered Tribal Areas, or FATA districts), where militants/extremist groups have mostly been concentrated, and in Balochistan, where the rate is 71 per cent (UN Women 2021). About 73.7 per cent of the tribal districts' population continues to live in multidimensional poverty – the highest in the country.[7] In May 2018, the former FATA districts were merged with KP Province by the national government under the 25th constitutional amendment. Efforts have since been made to strengthen the state-citizen relationship, with help from various development programs to increase access to public services, such as *Sadaa-eaman*, supported and sponsored by the World Bank. This program, among many by the UN and other humanitarian and development actors, is offering cash transfers for those internally displaced by conflict/military operations against the militants, to allow these internal refugees to settle back in their homes.

Regional disparities on gender equality are also stark. A study by UN Women Pakistan in 2021 identified the restricted movement of women as a major barrier to equality in the merged tribal districts of KP (ex-FATA). Extremely low literacy levels are present in the districts of Khyber, Kurram, Orakzai, North Waziristan, and South Waziristan, at 13 per cent, compared to a national literacy rate of 47 per cent (UN Women Pakistan 2021, n53). Likewise, few women have access to any kind of media or have ever used the internet, and most women are unaware of their basic human rights, according to a UNDP project survey in the same area (Khan 2022). Compared to males, only 66 per cent of females have acquired their National Identity Cards (UN Women Pakistan 2020, n55), which are essential for accessing government services. Existing lack of skills, education, and access to services for women in these regions mean that access to economic opportunities in the post-conflict environment, including through humanitarian and development efforts, is also greatly challenged. GBV is also an inhibitor for women to participate in livelihood or economic recovery programs supported by development actors. Lack of literacy and limited physical mobility for women mean that accessing the formal justice system remains out of bounds for the majority (Khan 2022, 4). The rural urban divide in literacy, education, skill, and access to technology is well-documented, and is exacerbated by gender and other divides such as social class and ethnicity, which further marginalize already vulnerable populations and increase inequalities.

These indicators show the low level of women's equality and empowerment in the marginalized border areas of the country, where the levels of violent extremism and violence against women are also higher. Research is needed on whether there are cases in Pakistan where advancing women's empowerment may have resulted in lower levels of violence against women; however, the reverse is well-documented.

Gender-specific warning signs of violent extremism include enforced directives and social constraints on women's dress and mobility. "If you want to know what the security situation is, what the indicators of safety are, do not ask the military, do not ask the government, ask the women," said a woman representative in a study on gender and violent extremism in Indonesia (True and Eddyono 2021, 63). This research identified

> four indicators of extremism conducive to violent extremism: the shifting use of the hijab; and enforcement of dress codes,

constraints on women's mobility; social naming and "hate crimes"; and threats or acts of gender-based violence, such as early marriage, female genital mutilation, and sexual abuse. These social indicators reveal the gendered nature of violent extremism as a political identity and ideology. (Ibid., 59)

Signs of rising extremism are not only observable at the individual level, but they also manifest and can be tracked at the societal level, for instance through changes in fashion, which have been noticeable in Pakistan over the past two decades in particular (Schamber and Fransen 2022). I recalled my colleagues in Pakistan commenting on this noticeable change over the years – seeing more women wearing the long black abaya common in the Middle East in place of traditional South Asian attire. Other gender inequality indicators, such as restricting freedom of movement and banning education and employment, can likewise be early warning signals of the strengthening of violent extremism (UNDP and UN Women 2020). The WPS index data shows a straight line between GBV, oppression, and conflict. Research by Professor Jacqui True shows that increased reports of SGBV are a lead indicator of – or precursor to – terrorist violence. Her work recommends that governments closely track increased levels of SGBV (True 2020). Extreme disempowerment of women and GBV are also push factors for women to align themselves with violent extremist actors to seek power and mobility.

It is extremely challenging, if not impossible, for aid actors to reach grassroots women in these areas, even through locally based NGOs, who continue to receive threats and face security problems trying to work in the region. The Taliban continue to appeal to traditional Pashtun cultural values [and interpretations] concerning women and their honour. "This has seriously impacted CSOs working for women and child health in various parts of KP who are unable to continue and ceased operations due to direct threats and actions of the militants targeting women" (Khan 2022, n83).

Violent extremism adds another dimension to the intersecting inequalities experienced by rural women in Pakistan. Critical evidence suggests that conflict, militancy, and terrorism have impacted men and women differently in Pakistan (Khan 2022). Yet the distinct indicators of rising extremism directly affecting women's bodily autonomy and mobility are hardly discussed in terrorism studies (True and Eddyono 2021).

PAKISTAN'S GENDER GAP

Pakistan is also one of the lowest-ranked countries in the world in terms of women's empowerment. The gender gap widened slightly in 2021 compared to 2020 (by 0.7 per cent) but Pakistan still sits in the bottom tier of the World Economic Forum (WEF) gender equality index at 153 out of 156 countries (Pakistan consistently ranked second-to-last between 2013 and 2022, with only Iraq and Yemen lower). In 2006, Pakistan had ranked much better at 112th – but slipped consistently over the next fourteen years to the lowest tier, with the biggest gap showing in economic opportunities for women, and with some progress on education. The key trend is that while women benefit from education (universal primary education) and primary health care, they score extremely low on economic and political empowerment.

Pakistan is still considered to be one of the most dangerous countries for women in terms of economic resources and discrimination, as well as the risks women face from cultural, religious, and traditional practices, including so-called honour killings. Pakistan ranked fifth on non-sexual violence, including domestic abuse, according to a Thomson Reuters Foundation survey in 2018. The level of cell phone use by women is the lowest in South Asia, according to the recent WPS Index.

The drop in women's empowerment indicators is important because research studies also show that in some cases, women join militant organizations – especially the Islamist extremist groups – as an escape from the life of humiliation and destitution in their own homes. In particular, the lack of economic opportunities and prevalence of domestic violence perpetrated by husbands or in-laws push women to become radicals, as society and the legal system fail to guarantee women their rights as equal citizens (Khan 2022, 46).[8] A major insight from empirical gender and international relations studies (Hudson and Hodgson 2020) is that attitudes and norms linked to sexist ideals of dominant masculinity and subordinate femininity are strongly correlated with individual support for violent extremism and participation in political violence. Additionally, other recent reports on gender and violent extremism (Phelan 2022) recognize that it is important to address the stereotype of women as victims of violent extremism when women can also be perpetrators, supporters, influencers, and active participants in violent extremist and terrorist

Pakistan – Ranking on WEF Global Gender Gap Report

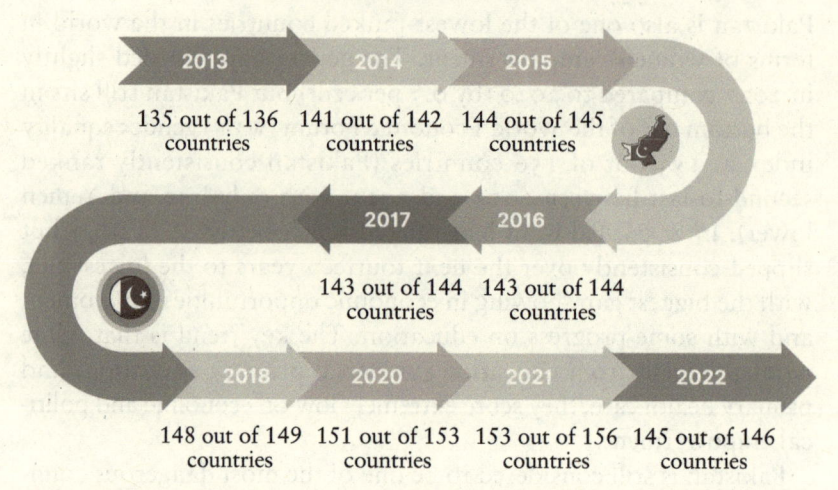

Year	Ranking
2013	135 out of 136 countries
2014	141 out of 142 countries
2015	144 out of 145 countries
2016	143 out of 144 countries
2017	143 out of 144 countries
2018	148 out of 149 countries
2020	151 out of 153 countries
2021	153 out of 156 countries
2022	145 out of 146 countries

Figure 3.1 World Economic Forum Global Gender Gap Report rankings for Pakistan from 2013 to 2022.

organizations. One important trend emerging from recent studies[9] suggests that women who experience multiple and intersecting forms of marginalization are more receptive to violent extremist messaging, and indeed may actively choose to join violent extremist groups in pursuit of economic well-being, as a means of combatting social or political inequality, or in response to perceived injustices. "There is a striking lack of evidence-based knowledge on women specific drivers of violent extremism and radicalization in Pakistan, at least that is publicly available" (Khan 2022, 16). In addition, women living in rural areas are more at risk of all forms of gender-based violence than those in towns or cities and face high levels of insecurity and harassment (UK Home Office 2020).

Extremist groups also promote gender-discriminatory harmful practices (True and Eddyono 2021) with the intent of establishing what they may consider to be a more devout Islamic state. Why and how women would support organizations that explicitly aim to reduce their basic human rights is complex, according to the findings of Johnston, Iqbal, and True in their study on Indonesia (2023). Gender inequalities and sexual and gender-based violence are therefore both pull and push factors for women to either engage in acts of violent extremism or resist them, as women can be simultaneously perpetrators and victims of violence (Fransen 2021). New research is seeking to understand how and why women resist or work to counter extremist ideologies, and the more complex question of how and why women support violent extremist groups. Both qualitative and quantitative data collected (Khan 2022) provide strong evidence that women in Pakistan have a key role as social influencers and agents of change in both supporting and spreading extremist trends in communities as well as preventing/countering violent extremism. However, research exploring women's roles in countering and preventing violent extremism is still limited (True and Eddyono 2021).

A UNDP project assessment in Pakistan's Swat district found evidence (through focus group discussions, key informant interviews, and case histories) on how violent extremist organizations exploit gender-specific grievances to attract women to their causes (Khan 2022). Testimonies of at-risk/ex-offender women in Swat described how the Taliban in the initial phase attracted their support by punishing male family members, especially in-laws, who had reportedly subjected women to domestic and gender-based violence.[10] ICAN, in its series of case studies on the role of gender and identity in shaping positive alternatives to extremism, found that

> violent extremist groups dynamically adjust their approach to gender roles according to what best suits their tactical interests. They manipulate perceptions of women's roles in society to avoid detection and strengthen their operations. Extremist recruitment propaganda plays into the economic and social restrictions women face by offering them purpose, opportunity and belonging. (Fransen 2022)

Using women's empowerment and the prospect of active roles to attract women recruits is a recent tactic of the terrorist organization Islamic State or ISIL. Young women beneficiaries from at-risk communities in Karachi described how joining violent extremist organizations provided them greater agency and mobility to participate in religious activities outside of their homes; offered them more freedom of movement, access, and agency; and increased their social capital, influence, and networks (UNDP and UN Women 2020). According to Dr Simbal Khan of Pakistan,

given the available limited research on this aspect of women's roles in extremism in Pakistan, more research is needed to understand how social exclusion and disempowerment of women impact their participation and support to violent extremism organizations and trends in the community.
(Khan 2022, 36)

WOMEN'S EMPOWERMENT AND PREVENTION OF VIOLENT EXTREMISM

If the gender dynamics of (identity and) ideology are significant factors in fuelling extremism, what role do gender equality and women's leadership play in resisting, countering, and preventing extremist ideologies and the violence they sanction, ask True and Eddyono in their study on Indonesia in 2021. Their groundbreaking research found that there is less understanding of the roles women play in countering and preventing violent extremism, while at the same time noting that there is increased international recognition of the importance of women's roles in this effort. In other words, the available research is still limited compared to the level of importance of the issue, as noted by Dr S. Khan above. True and Eddyono also noted the lack of engagement with women's groups working to counter extremism. Nevertheless, evidence on women's roles within efforts to prevent the spread of extremism in homes, in communities, and transnationally is growing. Recent studies have evaluated and compared CVE programs with and without a women's empowerment dimension and found that an increase in women's empowerment and gender equality has a positive effect on countering extremism (Couture 2014; True and Eddyono 2021). Another study on women and terrorism (Bigio and Vogelstein 2019) shows that in social settings where women are in positions of social influence, they tend to play a positive role against violent extremism and radicalization. We know from the work of feminist movements and women's organizations as well as rights-based civil society that women are challenging the rigid and violent gender norms associated with extremism and violent extremism (and fundamentalism) and are actively promoting women's rights and gender equality. If promoting gender equality is a powerful counter-narrative to extremists and violent extremist interpretations of religion that impact women's rights, then gender equality and women's leadership can play a critical role.

In the book *Equality for Women Equals Prosperity for All*, the authors found that "[e]mpirical evidence clearly demonstrates that increased economic independence is a major factor in reducing violence against women" (Lopez-Claros and Nakhjavani 2018, 88). Even more recent research has indicated the potential for dangerous backlash from women's economic empowerment that drives the need for approaches to women's economic empowerment that simultaneously address the issue of gender-based violence in certain situations. Canada's Ambassador for Women, Peace and Security made the link between women's economic empowerment and progress on reducing gender-based violence, tweeting on social media in 2020 that "Economic Independence is key to end violence against women and girls."

As far back as 1987, the Women's Action Forum concluded that "transformation of economic and social conditions leading to automatic emancipation of women is a false assumption [Mumtaz and Shaheed 1987]. It needs to be accompanied by the institutional support provided to Pakistani human rights organizations." It was recognized even then that a multi-faceted approach was needed to address systemic barriers for transformative change in gender equality.

4

From Women in Development to Feminist International Assistance

CURTAIN
Black veil cannot hide me
Bare face does not make me naked
A sun I am shining through the curtain
Darkness cannot mask me

Karime Vida, Afghan poet[1]

Although the burning issue for Pakistani women's organizations in 1984 was the government's Islamization policy and the discriminatory laws that effectively reduced women's worth, the CIDA program zeroed in on the basic needs of rural women. As an aid donor country with a strong relationship with Pakistan since 1950, Canada's strategy mirrored the vision of the government's five-year plan.

> CIDA should attempt in whatever way possible to help the government of Pakistan get projects that increase female participation implemented. This would be a first step in mobilizing the human resources necessary for increased development, as well as addressing structural deficiencies in institutional and managerial capacities in all sectors.
> (Gossen 1983)

CIDA's focus was reflective of international development thinking at the time – a shift to more equitable distribution of benefits to the population, to the sustainability of development investments, and toward increasing support for social development. In addition, there was a simultaneous demand for social justice and women's human rights.

CIDA began funding sub-projects through a local fund under the purview of the ambassador, the Mission Administered Fund (MAF), for projects up to $50,000. The small projects for women were considered "population welfare" projects in Pakistan, and the funds supported women-oriented NGO projects with a philanthropic focus such as the Family Welfare Cooperative Society, which established multi-purpose halls for women's programs; the rural development foundation doing skill training for women; many small village project committees/groups; the Small Family Welfare Group in Karachi for maternal and child health; and the All Pakistan Women's Association, among others. MAF later supported projects for income generation and early enterprise development, such as poultry-rearing by the Pakistan Girl Guides Association in Balochistan; goat breeding by women in Sehwan, Sindh; and building and equipping a skills-training centre for the Behbud Association social enterprise for women in Rawalpindi. Behbud has since grown to become a sizeable successful not-for-profit organization focussing on economic empowerment, education, and the health of women.[2] At the same time, CIDA's aid program started to integrate women into ongoing development projects in agriculture, irrigation and salinity control, energy, and other areas. The 1984 WID mission and strategy also marked a transition for CIDA in Pakistan towards social sector development, moving away from loans for large infrastructure such as power plants and transmission of hydro-electricity, the modernizing of Pakistan's railway, the supply of industrial commodities, large irrigation schemes (including the massive multilateral Left Bank Outfall Drain project, which was criticized for compounding the 2010 Indus floods), and Canadian wheat for food aid. The Aga Khan Rural Support Program (AKRSP) Program was the strongest example of Canada's WID programming in 1983 in the northern areas of Gilgit-Baltistan and Chitral. In 1985, CIDA established a WID consultancy budget to fund research studies. In September that year, another mission to Pakistan took place under the Canada-Pakistan WID consultancy project, resulting in a "women in business, small industry, and entrepreneurship" program. It was a reflection of the emphasis on income generation for women within the WID concept that evolved to enterprise development and later to a market systems approach and value chains linking to private sector development under women's economic empowerment.

CIDA'S WOMEN IN DEVELOPMENT POLICY

On a cold, dreary November day eight months after the WID mission to Pakistan, Margaret Catley Carlson, CIDA's first female president, gathered her briefing papers and walked to the executive boardroom at 200 Promenade du Portage in Hull, across the river from Ottawa, to chair the President's Committee meeting that would decide on the new policy on women in development. Maggie, as she was fondly called, started the meeting on a humorous note and turned it over to the WID director, Elizabeth McAllister, to make the presentation. "This approach is about systemic response, an institutional response and what our impact as an aid agency is having on women in the countries we work in ... It's about the effectiveness of our projects. It's not about attitudes and behaviour but accountability for adverse impacts of projects" (McAllister 1984). Not surprisingly, the new approach was unanimously approved, along with establishing a senior-level steering committee to drive its implementation across the Agency. The emphasis on setting targets and measuring impact laid the critical foundation for Canada's milestone Feminist International Assistance Policy (FIAP), launched on 9 June 2017, which took measurement and targets much further.[3] Some of the fundamentals were set by that flagship WID policy framework and its underlying theory of managing the process of change. FIAP amplified the need to measure change and impact through monitoring and enhanced gender-based analysis. It took the accountability requirement to the fullest, making results and tangible outcomes a prerequisite for funding approvals.

"The concept of a systemic response to discrimination underlines Canada's approach to employment equity in federal jurisdiction, covering race and disability as well. It underlies this new WID policy," McAllister explained in the presentation. "I have been drawing heavily on these concepts in my current term as Chair of the OECD DAC Working Group on Women in Development, especially in the development of the first DAC Guidelines on women in development" (ibid.). CIDA's president wrapped up the meeting: "I look forward to seeing a policy and implementation document that will apply to every aspect of CIDA's aid program, a challenge which I am confident we can meet by working together" (CIDA 1984b). The new policy framework also stated that "the integration of women as agents and beneficiaries of development is now further understood to be an economic imperative" (ibid.). Thus, the proposed strategic goal was confirmed: *To ensure that the full range of* CIDA *development assistance substantively assists the realization of the full potential of women as contributors to and beneficiaries of the development process.* Since the release of that 1984 WID policy, CIDA has worked systematically to promote women's full participation as both agents and beneficiaries of development, stated the finding of the gender equality evaluation in 2008. As a result, CIDA has been considered "a pioneer in promoting gender equality globally" (CAC 2008). Canada's consistent work on gender equality reached a new height once again in 2017 with the launch of FIAP, repositioning Canada as a global leader on gender equality and women's empowerment.

In a paper on *Institutionalizing Gender Issues: Effective Change Strategies* (McAllister 1997), the WID concept was traced back as early as 1970, when Ester Boserup argued that omission of gender aspects of development led to project failure. But the real turning point for WID was 1975 – International Women's Year – a year devoted to intensified action for women's advancement in the areas of equality, development, and peace, which launched the UN Decade for Women. For CIDA, it was in 1976, when the agency established a responsibility centre for WID in its policy branch. A 1979 Cabinet directive emphasized the need to integrate women in development to ensure their ability to participate as de facto agents and beneficiaries of socio-economic and political development. The agency, like other major international aid donors, was committed to ensuring that development programming included women and accommodated their needs. The major concern of the bilateral program was to take consideration of women's needs in integrated programming throughout the spectrum of CIDA's developmental activities. "WID had emerged as a best practice approach to women's development internationally in the early 1970s, although by the late 1970s, some development practitioners were already questioning the appropriateness of targeting women in isolation" (Jones 2012). The WID approach, by the 1980s, advocated for integration, rather than targeting women separately from other objectives. This approach continued to be widely applied to women's development through the 1970s and 1980s and beyond.

Shortly after CIDA's approval of the new WID policy, Forum 85 took place, a momentous gathering of NGOs from around the globe that ran parallel to the official UN World Conference for Women in Nairobi, marking the end of the UN Decade for Women. Some 15,000 women worldwide participated, many supported by CIDA, coming from what were termed at the time "Third World countries." Nasim Zehra, who was part of the 1984 WID mission, and I were amongst those attending the historic global meeting with our colleague from HQ, Wendy Lawrence, an early senior WID advisor. The day we sat together under the massive outdoor tent, activists on the stage representing grassroots organizations fuelled a fiery debate on gender equality. The voices of women from the global South were amplified, calling for empowerment of women at the grassroots.

NATION BUILDERS: WOMEN IN PAKISTAN, A DEVELOPMENT STRATEGY

In 1986, as the war in Afghanistan waged on, CIDA launched a more elaborate WID program strategy: *Nation Builders: Women in Pakistan, a Development Strategy*. It was prepared by a team of Canadian consultants paired with Pakistani consultants under CIDA headquarters team leader Janet Dunnett. It was underpinned by five detailed field studies in agriculture, education, health, small enterprises, and institution-building, each prepared by a team of Canadian and Pakistani experts. It put the 1984 WID policy (and the conceptual framework behind it) into practice with tangible actions at a country level by applying the conceptual underpinnings of equity, understanding discrimination in a practical way and moulding them into guidance and a remedy that focussed on both development's impacts on women and women's impact on development. It was a socio-economic strategy targeted to rural women, in line with the recommendations and approach of the first WID mission – to improve women's access to essential services and education, and to offer institutional support to the Women's Division of the government. Providing support to the Women's Division and other women's units within government was a high priority for sustainability and broader systematic change. The strategy encompassed women in health, education, agriculture, small enterprise development, and combined institutional development and human resource development. Training trainers and developing a cadre of professional and para-professional women, including a scholarship fund for girls, was a cross-cutting theme to strengthen women as agents of change. It included support to the government to provide services to women to "facilitate their integration into the socio-economic development of the nation" (Paton 1986). It aimed to develop a core of professional and para-professional women and remove barriers to their participation as agricultural experts, nurses, *dais* (birth attendants), teachers, and small business advisors. It also included capital investment projects, demonstration projects, and action-oriented field research, with the measurement of success being at least two good projects to be implemented in each sector over five years. It was incorporated into the broader CIDA Country Program Framework for Pakistan. As a development strategy, however, it didn't address directly the looming issue threatening women's rights and development – the Islamization policies and laws instituted by President Zia-ul-Haq that saw "the entrenchment of discriminatory attitudes towards women throughout society, but more specifically, within state institutions" (Khalique).

This early strategy was intended to tackle discrimination by addressing adverse impact and designing remedial measures to assist women in attaining skills, education, and income. It was not intended to address systemic discrimination introduced by the laws in Pakistan, nor to tackle gender relations. The shift to Gender and Development, or GAD, thinking in the 1990s sought to address what was considered an inherent weakness in the WID approach – the need for a focus on women's rights and the commensurate critical issue of practices and laws. It did mark a critical change to gender equality as a human rights issue.[4] The *Nation Builders* policy stated that "other areas such as the removal of systemic barriers to women's participation in Pakistani society, fall within the sole jurisdiction of the Government of Pakistan, as do the laws and their interpretation and may not be implemented by an outside donor" (Paton 1986, 15). The direction and parameters given to Canada as a foreign donor were clear – we understood the red lines. By sticking to traditional international development sectors of support and avoiding the laws and their implications for women's rights, the strategy avoided the burning political issues and the uncertainty of the dangerous trends of Islamization in order to obtain the endorsement of the government of Pakistan.

CANADA'S FEMINIST INTERNATIONAL ASSISTANCE POLICY

Thirty-three years later, decades of evidence demonstrated that the equality and empowerment of women and girls in the poorest and most vulnerable regions of the world increased the chances of significantly reducing poverty, reducing chronic hunger, and advancing global peace and security. "For decades, Canada has been a leader in championing gender equality in the developing world. Canada remains committed to promoting and defending the rights of women and girls globally," Global Affairs Canada posted on social media on 7 March 2017, in advance of International Women's Day that year. In Islamabad, Canadian High Commissioner Perry Caldwell quoted the new international assistance policy, saying, "If there is one thing that can achieve progress on reducing poverty and stimulating development, it is gender equality and promoting women's empowerment."

> Canada is adopting a Feminist International Assistance Policy that seeks to eradicate poverty and build a more peaceful, more inclusive and more prosperous world. Canada firmly believes that promoting gender equality and empowering women and girls is the most effective approach to achieving this goal. (Global Affairs Canada 2017)

"There is a nexus of gender-based violence and feminization of poverty," said Tahirih Abdullah, a long-standing women's rights activist, at a talk on the feminization of poverty at the Institute of Strategic Studies in Islamabad in summer of 2012. "Women need social protection measures and asset ownership – land and livestock because over 70% of rural women work in agriculture and do so mostly informally and unpaid," she told the audience that day. The shift from women in agriculture to social sectors reflected a global shift in donor thinking away from agriculture to align with gender equality. Agriculture is still at the heart of the rural economy and accounts for almost 22 per cent of Pakistan's total economy. "Women living in rural areas are the backbone of agricultural production" (Mumtaz and Shaheed 1987, 111). Agriculture is the largest employer of Pakistani women workers (Center of Gender and Policy Studies 2018), and their contribution is pivotal to food security. It is hard to miss this evidence simply driving from Islamabad to Lahore or into any of the main towns in Punjab or Sindh provinces, where women and children are working in the fields everywhere. Paintings depicting these images are displayed in some government offices in Islamabad. The former minister of Finance, Hafiz Pasha, speaking at a seminar by SDPI and the Friedrich Ebert Stiftung Foundation in 2014, attributed the reduction in poverty in Pakistan since 1980 to the agriculture sector. Women do some 79 per cent of agricultural work, but most rural women do not own the farmland they work on. Entitlement of property and transfer of land ownership to women remain legal barriers to women's economic empowerment, as does the lack of enforcement of inheritance laws.

The 1984 WID strategy had identified agriculture and running small enterprises as having the highest potential for making a difference in rural women's lives. Its focus was to support rural women in their central role in the agricultural economy and their need for education and capacity-building. It had a focus on the grassroots. But it was never fully implemented by CIDA, other donors, or the government, despite the guiding framework of Mahbub ul Haq's visionary five-year plan in 1983. The latter had as a central strategy the revitalization of the rural economy. A 2018 report on rural women by Pakistan's National Commission on the Status of Women, funded by Canada thirty-four years later, highlights that agricultural work is undergoing feminization; women's work remains largely unrecognized, unpaid, or underpaid; women work in agriculture mostly out of need and often without choice; and "law, policy and activism need to address the rights and wellbeing of women agricultural workers" (Center of Gender and Policy Studies 2018). The transition from agricultural enterprise to non-agricultural enterprise that took place after the 1980s (with an accompanying shift from income generation to enterprise development and market systems) formed the core of the women's economic empowerment approach.[5] It turned naturally again to supporting women in agriculture in the 2000s.

FROM WID TO WEE

CIDA and the Aga Khan Foundation Canada collaborated on a new "experiment" in development in 1983, the Aga Khan Rural Support Program (AKRSP). It centred on the social mobilization of communities to create participatory institutions that would "allow local populations to take the lead in managing their own development" (Aga Khan Foundation Canada 2006). Putting people at the centre of their own development led to remarkable progress on development indicators in the northern regions of Gilgit-Baltistan and Chitral where AKRSP work was focussed.[6] It also led to significant advances for women in those areas. The area was in proximity to two conflict zones, including the disputed territory of Kashmir and Soviet-occupied Afghanistan (AKFC 2006), although less affected by violent extremism at the time. CIDA and AKRSP were on the edge of new development thinking at the time, putting in place approaches that were reaching and mobilizing grassroots action in a new way.

A comprehensive look at the impact of the AKRSP program on women in Gilgit-Baltistan over a thirty-year period was done in 2012 by Dr Linda Jones, a Canadian specialist in women's economic empowerment engaged by AKFC. We met during a monitoring mission in Gilgit in mid-2012 on CIDA's support to the Aga Khan Foundation. Linda had just come from a full day in villages talking to groups of women. We discussed her study on women's economic empowerment, which showed AKF well ahead of its time in 1983 when they decided to implement a WID approach funded by CIDA and aligned with the new CIDA policy.

In its first Annual Review (1983) (Jones 2012, n36), AKRSP described its decision to implement a "separate programme targeted specifically at women and one which worked through women" since "programmes which are aimed at women but work through men have the disadvantage of leaving the women outside the decision-making process. AKRSP felt that a development programme which did not involve women was unlikely to have a pervasive impact on village development" (Jones 2012, 29n18).

From its inception, AKRSP's objective was to increase the living standards of communities "through participatory development approaches by forming and fostering broad-based grassroots organisations" (AKRSP 2009, 7). AKRSP was innovative in thinking about the strategies that would enable women to maintain control over income, keenly aware of the gender dynamics of household financial decision-making (Jones 2012, 31). The first AKRSP women's organization was formed in 1983 in Gilgit. By 1986, women in 95 villages had organized women's organizations (WOs) comprising over 5,000 households (S. Khan 2009). The cornerstone of the AKRSP approach was the pooling of assets by women's organizations for use to improve their household incomes (AKFC 2006). CIDA supported AKRSP staff to attend a seminar on Rural Development in South Asia sponsored by South Asia Partnership in Ottawa in February 1986, for support on training for social organizers in rural villages.

"AKRSP recognized that a more sustainable approach with greater outreach potential was needed and this led to the development of female village-level agricultural specialists. The first extension training for women was held in 1984, and representatives from 11 village organizations were invited to attend the residency program in Gilgit. By 1992, there were over 2,763 village-level agricultural specialists in GB and Chitral. The specialists were providing technical support to other women, demonstrating the use of new technologies such as greenhouses and drying systems, offering vaccination and other services for a fee, and acting as lead farmers from which others could learn. These specialists were often the women who became the first agricultural entrepreneurs, described in AKRSP documents as success stories."[7] The Jones review of AKRSP found noteworthy the transition from income generation to enterprise development and market development – showing the evolution from WID to WEE, with the latter implementing activities within a market development framework that involved mixed sectors. By 1994, non-agricultural enterprise initiatives had been launched; the early 2000s saw business skills training, and market development and value chains came a decade later.

By 2010, CIDA's Women's Economic Empowerment Framework echoed similarities (as well as showing key differences) with the 1980s WID strategies – coming full circle to support similar goals twenty-five years later. The WEE strategy had incorporated lessons over the years to ensure greater impact through better market development, better value chains, stronger links with the private sector, and more acute business skills, among other factors. As Canada stated in 2017, "Working with strong partners, Canada's Women's Economic Empowerment portfolio will continue to work towards improving working conditions in the informal and formal sectors and enhancing financial literacy and business development services for women micro entrepreneurs" (CHC [Facebook post] 2017). The target group was the same as the 1980s WID strategies but scaled from small projects to multi-million-dollar bilateral projects. The initial focus (and the thinking behind it) of CIDA's WID strategy on rural women's needs and their role in agriculture was aimed at the socio-economic development gap that still exists. Jones's review of WEE found that after decades of AKRSP work, "[a]griculture remains a key opportunity area for rural women" (Jones 2012). The CIDA-funded study on rural women in 2018 reconfirmed that agriculture is still the largest employer of Pakistani women workers (as noted above).

The early strategies and work on WID were focussed on much-needed fundamentals of development assistance – agriculture and basic services for rural women, who were identified as the most marginalized and vulnerable of the population (and remain so today). In addition to the small actions for WID over the 1985–91 period by CIDA, the partnership with the Aga Khan Rural Support Program (AKRSP) was critical to CIDA implementation of a WID strategy in Pakistan. Their approach of including village women's organizations within the broader community development programs helped to gain traction and expand reach to a larger segment of the target population. Other bilateral projects in health and vocational training included women, such as in the training of birth attendants. Linda Jones's study in 2012 concluded that "AKRSP's adoption of WID in the context of Gilgit-Baltistan and Chitral in the early 1980s meant that AKRSP programs could overcome socio-cultural barriers in situations where integrated programmes would most probably have failed" (Jones 2012, 28).

THE SHIFT TO WOMEN'S HUMAN RIGHTS

The UN Conference on Women in Beijing in 1995 marked a shift in global policy to promotion of women's human rights and feminist movements and networks. Removing institutionalized discrimination as obstacles to realizing women's rights took precedence over women in development programs. The enabling global policy environment was now in place to tackle discriminatory laws inhibiting women's rights. CIDA updated its 1984 WID Policy and expanded it to include the concept of gender equity in 1995. Even Canada's 1995 foreign policy statement indicated a stated commitment to reflecting Canadian values and specifically the rights of women and children and the full participation of women in overseas development assistance. The updated Policy on Women in Development and Gender Equity captured the need to change behaviour and attitudes and the critical issue of practices and laws.[8] AKRSP abolished its WID section in 1994, replacing the WID coordinator with a gender coordinator; however, AKRSP continued to focus on socio-economic development for women within the broader community development model. It was considered by some to be a more cautious approach to gender equality (Gloekler and Seeley 2007); however, it may have been expedient and practical for many reasons, including the growing sectarian and conservative religious influences in the region.

For CIDA, the gender policies that followed – the 1995 WID Policy on Women in Development and Gender Equity, the 1999 Policy on Gender Equality, and the 2010 Gender Equality Action Plan – all paved the road for FIAP in 2017. The 1999 Policy on Gender Equality, a substantive revision of the 1995 policy, was the result of a very consultative process started in 1998 under the leadership of Diana Rivington, CIDA's longest-standing Director of Gender Equality. A recognized international expert, Rivington provided significant contributions globally to policy on women's empowerment, particularly as chair of the OECD working party on Gender Equality from 1998 to 2000. One of the three main objectives of the new 1999 Policy was "realizing the full human rights of women and girls." The 2008 CIDA evaluation on the corporate gender equality policy found that

> [h]uman rights for women and girls was the policy objective with the least programming attention and fewest documented results. Such results would likely be sought only in the course of a Gender Equality (GE)–designated investment ... More consistent results were found in advancing women's wellbeing and basic needs. Still, the weakest performance in this major result area [of human rights] is found in policy change in support of gender equality. There are modest gains in human rights with an occasional success story ... [this] mirrors the low frequency and level of investment by country programs in rights issues. (CAC 2008)

The evaluation found only three success stories on mitigating violence against women in the countries under review (of which Pakistan was not one). The corporate gender equity evaluation is confusing on many fronts, especially when looked at from the perspective of the CIDA WID policy approach and its underlying framework. That WID framework put forward a methodology to analyze and measure systemic discrimination against women using "the measurement of impact and results to monitor the change in women's equality through identifying policies, regulations, directives and practices which have an adverse impact on women" (McAllister 1984). It could have been helpful for the Canadian evaluators as an early feminist evaluation and monitoring methodology. But as is often the case in large organizations, CIDA's institutional memory on WID and the foundational work of the 1970s and 1980s into the early 1990s were absorbed into new policy approaches. WID remained hidden but meaningful history in the evolution of policies towards equality.

5

Field Visits under Armed Escort

The CIDA headquarters mission arrived less than two months after the flood emergency had died down, to monitor the progress of the women's economic empowerment projects in Punjab. Our initial plans for field visits were almost skewed by the murder of the governor of Punjab, Salmaan Taseer, at the hands of his own security guard, Mumtaz Qadri, in the upscale Kohsar market in Islamabad. It happened just outside a favourite coffee shop and bookstore frequented by Pakistanis and foreign diplomats not far from the diplomatic enclave. It was 4 January 2011 and the start of a turbulent period caused by a confluence of dramatic violent events that also challenged the implementation of aid programs and development efforts in the country. The series of events that followed the assassination of the governor left all of us reeling from the effects of the growing militancy and violence.

Governor Salmaan Taseer had participated in the 1983 women's protests in Lahore against the discriminatory Islamic laws introduced against women at the time. He had been thrown in jail by President Zia in 1977, and again in the 1980s was incarcerated in Lahore Fort Jail for his protests against the laws and policies being put in place. His resistance to Zia's Islamization policy was registered from its earliest days, and he had continued trying to abate the forces of Islamic extremism, this time from a powerful position as governor of Punjab. That January, the governor had been criticizing the blasphemy law on insulting (mocking or vilifying) Islam and was publicly defending a rural Christian woman in Punjab, Asia Bibi. She was charged with blasphemy, an offence punishable by death. The governor's killer smiled as he was taken away by police, saying, "I am a slave of the

Prophet, and the punishment for one who commits blasphemy is death," as he faced the news cameras.

The murder triggered security alerts across the city and province. For Western diplomats, the immediate impact was a new set of security restrictions, making the Kohsar market and its popular restaurants, bookstores, and coffee shops off-limits, at least for the time being. Many others quietly saw this event for its more significant impact: that of representing gains for the extremists, the use of the blasphemy laws to further extremist behaviour, and a further blow to those opposing it or calling for reform. Little did we know then that this event would set the stage for a surge of support to political religious extremism, using the blasphemy laws to fan the flames, building on the strong public reaction in support of the governor's assassin.[1]

The anniversary of the guard's hanging by the state on 29 February 2016, for the murder of Governor Taseer and for terrorism, became celebrated as a three-day festival among his many thousands of supporters. A marble shrine with a green tile dome was built by his family outside Islamabad in his honour, reminiscent of the peaceful Sufi saint shrines found across Pakistan, Iran, and parts of India. He was a follower of the Barelvi sect of Islam, one closer to Sufism but now affected by shades of extremism. Tens of thousands of Pakistanis protested Qadri's execution, and thousands travelled to Islamabad to attend the funeral, while a thin crowd with few officials attended the funeral of the governor. The visible swelling of support for extremist groups was impossible to ignore. What was driving this? I wondered. At the time, no one was discussing the impact of rising extremism on women and girls in the country, at least not in aid donor development circles.

By 2016, the shrine for Qadri had become a place of pilgrimage. It was the beginning of the rise to prominence of a "radical Barelvi sectarian movement that publicly espouses violence in the name of religion" (Hussain April 2021). The supporters of Mumtaz Qadri established an Islamic extremist political party some years later, the Tehreek-e-Labbaik-Pakistan (TLP), using the defense of the blasphemy law as its main platform to raise political profile in the 2018 elections. That same year, a 700-member lawyer alliance was formed to prosecute individuals accused of blasphemy (Zehra 2023), building on this significant support and giving more voice to those with extremist inclinations.[2]

The blasphemy laws, among the others affecting women, continue to be a source of justice and human rights concerns and have severely affected many human rights activists and Christian minorities (many of them women and girls) who have been prosecuted for blasphemy, with a dramatic increase in cases between 1985 and 2011, and again between 2017 and 2020. The Asia Bibi case began in June 2009 when she was accused of blasphemy by another woman while at work in the fields. It started over drinking water from a cup that was not hers, for which the Muslim woman insulted her. Such attitudes towards minority Christians were not uncommon. A row broke out over religious beliefs, and a group of supporters demanded she convert to Islam. When she refused, she was accused of blasphemy, beaten, and eventually arrested and put in solitary confinement in Sheikhupura Jail. In November 2010, she was sentenced to death by hanging under the law that criminalized defiling the Prophet's name. Under Zia, in 1986, the blasphemy laws were updated and reaffirmed, with the death penalty specified in law. This verdict spurred the Punjab governor to speak out against her conviction after visiting her in jail in 2010. After the governor's murder, Bibi's case continued to drag on for another nine years as she languished in prison. It was reopened when the Supreme Court overturned the sentence in October 2018. Still, hundreds of protesters, led by the TLP, took to the streets and chaos spread across the country (*Guardian* November 2018). Asia Bibi was released and given asylum in Canada in 2019, resulting from intense behind-the-scenes diplomatic efforts by Canada, the UK, the US, and France. I recall officials at Global Affairs Canada in Ottawa working intensely on the case for months behind closed doors, working closely in top secret conditions with Pakistan and like-minded countries. Canada's role was pivotal in her safe release and passage.

On 2 March 2011, the Minister for Minority Affairs, Shahbaz Bhatti, was gunned down – another assassination of a powerful figure advocating religious tolerance and moderation with regards to prosecution under the blasphemy law. He had also spoken out at the time in favour of reviewing the Asia Bibi case and reforming blasphemy laws. This time, the Taliban al-Qaeda Punjab claimed responsibility. Canada's Minister of Immigration and Multiculturalism at the time, Jason Kenney, flew to Islamabad to speak at Bhatti's memorial with the following words, "As the first and only Christian minister in the Pakistani government, he understood intimately the importance of protecting religious minorities. He worked tirelessly to defend religious freedom and human rights in Pakistan and around the world, not least through his public condemnation of his country's blasphemy laws. I want to reiterate what was said in the House of Commons motion passed unanimously earlier this week. The [Canadian] House calls on the Government of Pakistan to take immediate action against those who would harm and threaten defenders of religious freedom and human rights" (Canadian Government Press Release, 4 March 2011). It signalled a more difficult period ahead for the aid program (and for the embassy) due to rising extremism, the escalation of violent acts, and growing anti-American/anti-Western sentiment in the country. But more importantly, it also marked increased difficulties for those in Pakistan at risk: for women and girls, especially those in rural areas and those from religious minorities.

A RENEWED OUTBURST OF ANTI-AMERICAN SENTIMENT

Despite the new security restrictions, including being required to obtain a "no-objection" certificate from the Ministry of Interior, we were able to plan the WEE project monitoring trip to rural Punjab. But the unpredictability of travel in Pakistan due to incidents of violent extremism manifested once again. Three weeks after the governor's murder, and just weeks before our field visit, an American CIA contractor named Raymond Davis was arrested in Lahore after killing two Pakistanis in a car chase through the crowded streets of the old city. It happened on 27 January 2011, in murky circumstances where a third person was also killed by an American car that came to rescue Davis. Widespread anti-American protests erupted across the country, calling for action against Raymond Davis as a murderer and a spy. The American embassy was furiously negotiating Davis's release on the basis of his diplomatic immunity to no avail. In the end, the Americans used the *diyat* or Blood Money Ordinance under Sharia law to secure his freedom – one of the Ordinances that has been used to perpetuate the culturally based so-called honour crimes against women in Pakistan with impunity (more on honour crimes in chapter 6). "How a single spy helped turn Pakistan against the United States," the story eventually unfolded in the media. The renewed outburst of anti-American sentiment curtailed our plans to explore the city of Lahore but did not slow the many incoming headquarters missions from Ottawa. The field visits went ahead, despite the burning of American flags and the banners everywhere with Raymond Davis's face calling for him to be hanged on the streets of Lahore. We ventured out to the old Heera Mandi area of old Lahore (the former red-light district) in the evening for dinner despite security warnings. The famous Cooco's Café was our destination point, housed in the ancient rundown *haveli* (family home) of the renowned and eccentric painter of the women of Heera Mandi, Iqbal Hussain. Cooco's sits directly adjacent to the magnificent twelfth-century Badshaahi mosque in the old walled city and is one place every foreigner in Pakistan could not miss. We were anxious to see it by night.

Lahore is an exquisite city and a place of drastic contradictions, like most of Pakistan. Its dynamic cultural scene of artists, fashion designers, writers, and activists flourishes amidst the backdrop of the old city and its seventeenth-century Mughal-era architecture, yet abject poverty is visible everywhere. The Lahore Fort, where one can wander through what is left of Shah Jahan's bedroom and the mirrored room of the harem, is an astounding building. Located near the old city's Bhati gate, the Wazir Khan Mosque is one of the most beautiful in South Asia. So, too, is the tomb of Emperor Jahangir, with its design of precious inlaid jewels. Considered the "city of literature," Lahore hosts a well-attended international literary festival every year. The Fakir Khaana Museum and its private collection of original miniature paintings telling the history of the Sikh, Mughal, and British eras was one of my favourite places to visit in Lahore. The city has many intriguing sites and hidden gems.

Sitting on the rooftop of Iqbal's restaurant that winter evening, enjoying a Punjabi meal of *aloo gosht* and *khatti dal* beside the floodlit Badshahi mosque, one could imagine a less turbulent time in Pakistan's history. Iqbal's paintings capture an image of women and children in another side of Lahore a generation earlier. Every ambassador, journalist, or writer who comes to Lahore attains an audience with the artist and usually purchases at least one painting from the overcrowded small gallery on the main floor. I was thinking ahead to the women's economic empowerment project visits the next day, anticipating images of a different side of Pakistan.

— * —

The next morning, accompanied by two pickup trucks of armed police security escorting us to the project site, we arrived at the "Pathways and Purse-Strings" project for "Enhanced market access for women producers in Pakistan," implemented by the Mennonite Economic Development Association (MEDA) from Canada, together with their Pakistani partner, Karawan. The project supported home-based work opportunities for women who could not easily leave their homes due to the customary practice of *purdah* (traditional seclusion of women) and other restrictions, such as not leaving the compound without a male family member. It linked milk collection from various homes to deliver to private-sector plants with more profitable value chains to increase women's income from the product. The projects' underlying assumption was that improving the economic condition of women would improve their decision-making power within the household and increase mobility for them. It was expected that economic empowerment through increased income would help address the social and cultural practices and behaviours that were overarching factors hindering gender equality. It began in 2007, at the cusp of the major shift in CIDA's gender strategy in Pakistan to the focus on women's economic empowerment, and built on an earlier CIDA-funded initiative of $500,000 named "Beyond the Veil."[3] This program was conceived and launched by MEDA with mostly USAID (and some CIDA) grant funding. It was "an ambitious three-year value chain development program that reached down-market to integrate poor, remote, illiterate and homebound women into more profitable value chains, leveraging their capacity for the good of the market system" (Jones 2006). It launched the women sales agent model that was continued in the CIDA-funded project.

One of MEDA's other partners was the Pakistan Social Welfare Society (PSWS) of Hyderabad, a local NGO known to CIDA from 2004–06 for its human rights and entrepreneurial training for home-based and factory workers making women's glass bangles. It had received funding under PAGE, along with the other two MEDA partners, Karawan and Sarhad Rural Support Program (SRSP), a member of the Rural Support Programmes Network (RSPN), which reaches over 54 million rural Pakistanis through community-driven rural development.

In the villages we visited, I asked women about their lives, their work, and how much they were being paid. One young woman told me that she supported her parents and four children through various sources of income; the main one was picking cotton, for which she earned roughly a dollar a day. The other sources of income were marginal. Her husband had died of the hepatitis epidemic in Punjab. She was trying to participate in the CIDA-funded WEE project to earn extra income from milk collection sales. Her youngest children clustered around her as she spoke. We talked in the courtyard of the mud house compound where the milk collecting and testing was underway (after which the women sales agents would take over and link to private buyers). Older men sat smoking hookahs on a bench, and children ran and scattered about. The rooms were rudimentary, with simple, basic furniture but no running water. Many villagers lived in dire poverty, although there were also many others who did not. For these women, carefully selected for participation in the poverty reduction project, they could not send all of their children to school; none of them appeared well-nourished. There was still little or no access to free basic health and education services despite the enormous social sector assistance by the World Bank and other donors over decades. As Samia Altaf puts it in her book on why development projects fail in Pakistan, "one of the causes of Pakistan's perennial instability is its lack of social services, and money has been poured in to improve these, but the fact remains that development programs in Pakistan have yielded extremely disappointing results" (Altaf 2011, 2). The debate over whether development has failed and why rages on. It is a combination of numerous factors, including governance issues, the inability of governments to provide services commensurate with a rapidly growing population, poor program design, and a list of others. But lessons are always being learned and new and innovative approaches developed. Access to villages such as the one we visited was limited for foreigners, especially diplomats, and visits had to be permitted by the government. The armed police were alongside and watching. We were not alone.

The Punjab milk production effort was one of three sub-projects under Pathways and Purse-Strings. The other two were seedling production in Mardan district of KP Province and embellished fabrics and bangle-making in Sindh province. The project was making strides by linking aid efforts to private-sector value chains as a way to increase income and reduce poverty for home-bound women workers. Although the sustainability of links to the private sector was at times tenuous, the CIDA evaluation in 2012 found that incomes, accumulation of assets, and capacity to save and invest in an enterprise did increase for those women involved in the project. Given the population size of Punjab, the beneficiary numbers of the project combined with similar projects funded by others should have had a major impact on poverty reduction.[4]

The next day, after a traditional Punjabi breakfast of *choly nan* and *siri paye* (flatbread and hot oily curries), we left for Lahore to see another CIDA-funded WEE project implemented by a Pakistani NGO,

Kashf, specializing in micro-finance. It took a different approach, aimed at financial literacy and business development services. It selected women who had the ability to start a micro-business when provided extra support and training. This approach was advocated in the early 1980s and even as far back as the 1970s as a way to increase women's access to income. In 1985 CIDA had funded a "women in business, small industry, and entrepreneurship" program and later the successful women's finance bank. Kashf was able to scale up its program from the initial small grant it received under the women's funds. The new project established women entrepreneur councils and provided loans for micro- and small businesses. We saw the products, mostly embroidery and clothing, which have typically been and continue to be supported for decades through women's empowerment or livelihood projects. This time the quality of the products was impressive. By 2021, Kashf's much-scaled program trained more than 26,000 women in partnership with Canada. Many other Pakistani organizations are undertaking similar programs, many much larger with stronger impact, such as the Akhuwat micro-credit program, taking an innovative approach of fraternity. All of these projects and programs combined contribute to collective impact – perhaps not visible, but things might be far worse without them. There are numerous Pakistani and donor-funded development programs like this (far too many to name) but the programs in this story are CIDA-funded and are a good indication of the type of development work at the time, given that all donor aid programs tend to follow similar programming and policy trends simultaneously, albeit with different emphasis and scale.[5]

"Any consideration of WEE should examine the terms of women's entry into the labour market, notably poor women, which requires recognizing women's contributions, respecting their dignity, and enabling them to negotiate a fair distribution of the returns to economic growth" (European Parliament Policy Dept. 2017). To succeed and advance economically, women need the skills and resources to compete in markets, as well as fair and equal access to economic institutions. To have the power and agency to benefit from economic activities, women need to have the ability to make and act on decisions and control resources and profits (Jones 2012).

What would it take to make economic empowerment of women in Pakistan a reality beyond projectized development? Two solutions were identified by the CIDA Pakistan senior advisor for women's

2003–04
Male: 82.6%
Female: 17.4%

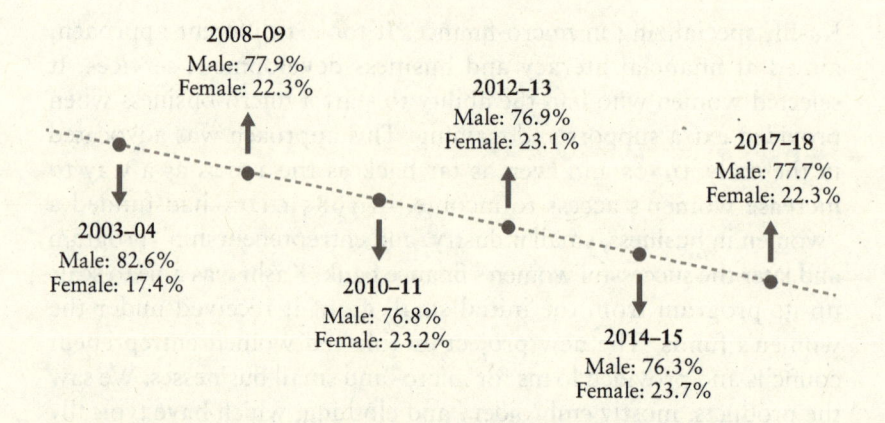

2008–09
Male: 77.9%
Female: 22.3%

2010–11
Male: 76.8%
Female: 23.2%

2012–13
Male: 76.9%
Female: 23.1%

2014–15
Male: 76.3%
Female: 23.7%

2017–18
Male: 77.7%
Female: 22.3%

Figure 5.1 Men and women's contribution to GDP in Pakistan, 2003–18. This graphic is derived from multiple years of the Labour Force Survey and Economic Survey of Pakistan, and shows the very marginal increase in women's contribution to economic production (GDP) – a function of their restricted access to the labour force.

economic empowerment in 2013 to improve the impact of CIDA-funded programs: addressing women's legal and labour rights and going to scale with programs to reach a critical mass. The combination of practical entry point projects with policy and legal interventions was the identified solution. Issues of women's mobility, access to and entitlement of property and land rights, legal equality for home-based workers, and the reform and enforcement of inheritance laws were identified as critical (R. Rashid 2013). That report made important strategic recommendations for WEE programming on legal and labour rights, endorsement of provincial policies on home-based workers, and finalization of the social protection bill for home-based workers. It also highlighted the need for stronger women-centred poverty reduction strategies, programs, and projects. The one area it did not touch on was the issue of gender-based violence and how or if it interacts with women's economic empowerment. The Kashf project, by example, had included efforts to generate public debate around GBV, gender roles, and child brides. Extra income for the family earned by women brought a sort of honour to the household as long as it was an honourable source of livelihood, recalled Canadian Linda Jones when we spoke about her work in Pakistan on WEE. "In general, men were positive. Gender roles were not quite as negative as one initially might think," she commented.

INCREASING INCOME FOR RURAL WOMEN IN SOUTHERN PUNJAB

A few months later while scheduling was underway for a field visit to the WEE project in southern Punjab, we awoke to the startling news of the killing of Osama bin Laden in Abbottabad, less than an hour away from Islamabad. The US Navy SEAL raid on bin Laden's residence in the pleasant military garrison town was launched Monday morning, 2 May 2011, from Bagram airbase in Afghanistan. Watching the BBC news account of the military operation that had taken place just hours earlier left us stunned. It took place in the town we regularly drove to for meetings on CIDA's education project there, one of the few places we were allowed to travel without security clearances. Everyone wanted to see the house where bin Laden had lived with his families, and many did until the Pakistani security cordoned it off and started arresting people, including an ambassador who tried to take photos. It was soon razed to the ground to prevent the creation of a potential visitation site.

The Osama bin Laden killing did cause more security and movement restrictions for us and again reignited anti-Americanism and the fury of a large portion of the population. Public fervour over the Raymond Davis incident had not subsided, and now relations between Pakistan and the US had sunk to a new low. The government became suspicious of Western NGOs and increased scrutiny, requiring more stringent paperwork for non-objection certificates from the Ministry of Interior. One of CIDA's partners in education, Save the Children Pakistan, was accused of being involved in the bin Laden capture because the doctor who posed as a vaccinator for bin Laden's children to obtain DNA samples had previously worked for Save the Children. Dr Shakeel Afridi languishes in jail in Pakistan, sentenced to thirty-three years in prison on treason charges. The US vowed to get him released more than once, but it was a highly sensitive issue for the Pakistan government. The head of Save the Children Pakistan was forced to immediately leave the country. The current reality was raising red flags on security that would also impact the work of Canadian-based NGOs and their Pakistani partners. Canada by then was lumped in with the US in the eyes of Islamic militants, largely due to the Canadian-led military offensive in Kandahar.

— * —

In June, the Canadian High Commissioner and I managed to obtain the necessary government security clearances to visit the WEE project in southern Punjab. We travelled during the hottest time of the year, landing in Multan just before the monsoon rains. It was mango season in southern Punjab, one consolation of the stifling weather. "Pakistan has the best mangoes in the world and hundreds of varieties," said our host when he picked us up at the airport. We drove past mangoes piled high on wooden carts at the side of the road on the way to the Multan Ramada hotel. The hotel appeared to be part of the global chain, one of the few American chains still operating in Pakistan. After a quick refresh, we headed out in armoured vehicles accompanied by the usual two pickup trucks of armed police escorting us to the rural area to meet the women engaged in the project. "Don't worry about them," the CARE project manager said, pointing at the police escort team. "We have provided extra payment for their services." By now, visiting development projects in armoured vehicles under heavily armed escort was a norm for us. On the surface, the region appeared tranquil and peaceful, but southern Punjab is known for its militant groups justifying violence, and we had recently witnessed the outpouring of support from the area for the murderer Mumtaz Qadri.

The CARE Community Infrastructure Improvement project was a five-year project to enable 4,500 destitute rural women to become economically and socially empowered through employment. The project engaged women to maintain dirt roads for agricultural use (small link roads up to 0.5 km) to improve communities' access to essential goods and services. The project included life skills training for the women and capacity-building for local and district governments on gender issues, in parallel to the women's road maintenance work and entrepreneurial activities. It was based on the lessons learned from the award-winning road maintenance project in Bangladesh by the Grameen Bank that CARE had modelled their work after. The project paid a livable wage of 6,000 rupees per month, or 250 rupees (close to $3) per day. A mobile bank would come to the area to disburse the salaries in cash payments to the women for their road maintenance work.

We drove for forty-five minutes to the area where the maintenance work was being done. The women were using hand tools for pounding and flattening the earth. They were happy to meet us and enthusiastic about the project. As we stood on the dusty road in the forty-plus-degree heat talking with the project participants, myriad women and children picking cotton in the fields around us (by hand, without gloves or hats) came into focus. I wondered how much they were earning and whether it was the same wage as the woman I met a few months ago who was earning eighty rupees per day, although they are often paid in kind. The late Najma Sadeque, a prominent journalist, human rights activist, and environmental writer who cofounded Shirkat Gah, one of the earliest feminist NGOs in Pakistan, had a month earlier said in the media that "at present, eighty percent of the work on farms is performed by women in the form of unpaid labour and they receive no formal recognition." She coined the phrase "An Acre for Every Woman" during a talk on "Food Security and Coping Mechanisms" arranged by Pakistan's National Commission on the Status of Women. When we sat down to talk a couple of months later, I asked her what had changed for rural women over three or more decades. She told me that things had gotten worse for poor rural women since Shirkat Gah came into existence thirty-seven years earlier. Her advice to CIDA was, "you must go through local community-based organizations to work in rural areas." This fundamental principle has proven to be critical to the success of any development initiative – the knowledge of local realities and the "need to understand the contextual complexities" (Altaf 2011, 3). The CARE project had formed self-help groups and group enterprises among different ethnicities and religious backgrounds – an effort to reflect tolerance, diversity, and interfaith harmony alongside the income-generating aspect. This type of community-wide education for social inclusion is now viewed as a crucial strategy to promote a culture of tolerance and peace in aid of preventing violent extremism. The project had easily integrated it as a small side activity creating social cohesion, with the potential for much greater impact than might appear on the surface. It was an early example of grassroots development activity within a project that was functioning as a counter to conflict and extremism.

Some months later, we learned that one of the CARE Canada project staff had been reprimanded by local officials for speaking out against the honour killing of women (not considered a crime in Punjab at that time) in a gender-sensitization and human rights workshop the project had organized. Such messages were not well-received by local leaders and authorities, it seemed, a not-uncommon resistance to certain gender equality efforts. Although Punjab has since taken legal action against honour killing and other forms of GBV, such changes are slow to manifest in rural villages and towns, where customary informal systems play a key role. Punjab maintains a high rate of honour killing and GBV.

The integration of a response to address gender-based violence within women's economic empowerment has been found to be an accelerator of change for gender equality in crisis-affected countries. Both the CARE and Kashf projects, as early as 2011, had integrated an awareness-building component on GBV. The more recent experience of UNDP and UN Women through projects in various countries has shown that WEE programming can have the effect of increasing and compounding experiences of GBV.[6] "Controlling for the vicious circle of GBV requires a multi-faceted and human rights approach, aiming at transforming social norms to shift unequal power relations, and engage men and boys in changing discriminatory behaviours. There is a growing recognition that a human-rights, intersectional approach provides a better understanding of the intersection of gender and other inequalities (e.g. sexuality, gender identity, ethnicity, immigration status, disability, geographical location) that form the complex and dynamic drivers that hinder or enhance WEE" (UNDP 2022b).

Marking the International Day of Rural Women in October 2017, the Canadian High Commission in Islamabad posted a message on women's economic empowerment, making the link to economic growth:

> Today ... Let's acknowledge the critical role of rural women in poverty reduction. Canada is proud to support projects in Pakistan that aim to economically empower poor rural women, their families, and their communities through improving commercial dairy practices and the business acumen of women. Canada's Community Infrastructure Improvement Project contributed to increasing incomes, improving business skills, self-reliance, and empowering disadvantaged rural women in 100 Union Councils in nine districts of Punjab and Sindh. Canada's support to increasing women's participation in the dairy sector in Southern Punjab aims to strengthen and establish dairy cooperatives, increase income and decision-making for women livestock farmers, and promote an improved pro-poor and gender-sensitive approach to the dairy sector. Women's integration into a country's economy generates dividends on multiple fronts, ranging from raising the quality of life of the family to raising the country's GDP.[7]

The project visits had given me a glimpse into the daily lives and situation of poor rural women in Pakistan. WEE was targeting a massive socioeconomic development gap that still exists. The visits brought to the fore issues of basic human rights and justice or the lack thereof, confirming that WEE is critical to women's human rights. Such programming can also function as a counter to violent extremism by providing positive alternatives to enable people to realize a better future. The informal educational strategies that the CARE project integrated, as part of the WEE project to promote tolerance and awareness on GBV, could amplify project outcomes.

The field visits in 2011 and 2012 fell between high-profile assassinations and murders inside Pakistan linked to growing religious extremism. There was increasing backlash on the War on Terror and the growing US-led ISAF presence in Afghanistan, which was facilitated logistically by the government of Pakistan through the goods moving to Afghanistan on a daily basis from Karachi port through the Khyber Pass. As the US troop presence increased in Afghanistan from 2010, so too did the support among the population for the cause of the violent extremists and their view that Western democracy is the enemy of a Sharia state (Sheikh 2016). Violence and terrorism were taking a horrific toll in the country, particularly on women and girls. There were numerous attacks on schools for girls (over 1,000 schools were destroyed by attacks between 2007 and 2017).

Canada's broader aid program had made general references to the need to combat extremism through stimulating sustainable economic growth (the programming dedicated to this objective were the women's economic empowerment projects) and securing the future of children and youth. Canada issued statements stating that "stability in Pakistan is vital for regional stability and security" and "Pakistan's determination to deal with violent extremists, who threaten Pakistan, the region and the international community, is tremendously important" (CIDA 2009). Yet, human rights remained an obscure element of the WEE framework, which was placed in the economic growth pillar of the CIDA Country Strategy. CIDA had by then reduced its gender equality work from previous years, focussing it under the inclusive economic growth objective. The aid strategy contained little analysis of the devastating impact of terrorism inside Pakistan, including its disproportionate impact on women and girls. The focus on women's human rights had disappeared from the strategic direction for Canada's aid and remained hidden and under the radar of programs at the grassroots such as the CARE project and others. The link between women's economic empowerment and progress on reducing gender-based violence was not yet articulated in guidance on gender equality, nor was the relationship between increasing numbers of terrorist attacks and increased levels of GBV. The aid strategy did acknowledge that "economic and political stability is essential to reduce the terrorist threat in Pakistan" and that "Canada's objectives in Afghanistan will prove unattainable without concerted attention to Pakistan" (CIDA 2009).

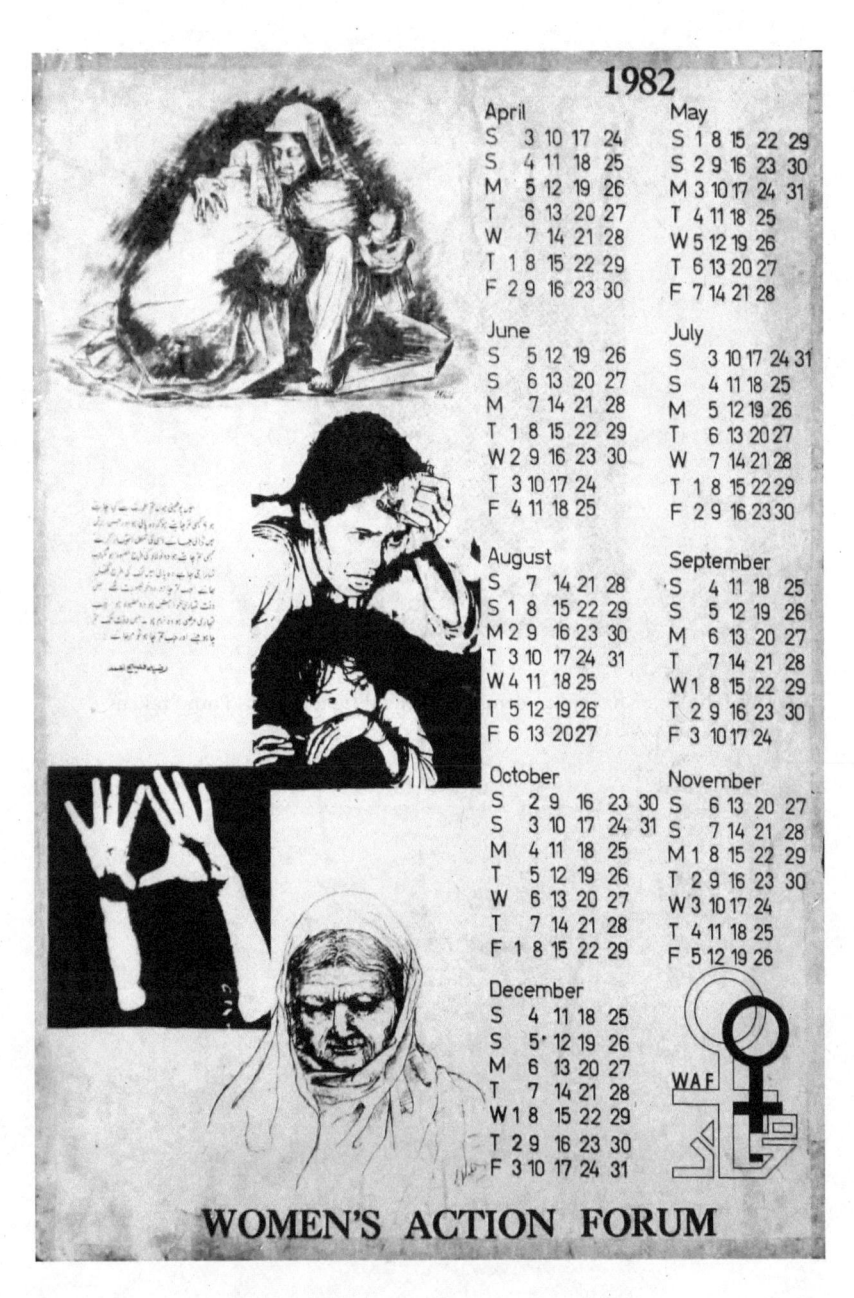

WAF calendar, 1982. Photo taken by LalaRukh for WAF Lahore.

Poster by Tehreek i Khawateen demanding equal rights, 1983. Photo taken by LalaRukh for WAF Lahore.

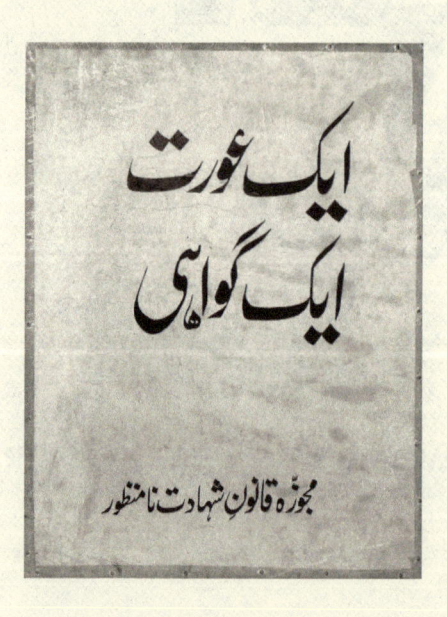

"One Woman should equal One Evidence in court" poster against the unequal Law of Evidence, 1983. Photo taken by LalaRukh for WAF Lahore.

WAF position paper, February 1984. Photo taken by LalaRukh for WAF Lahore.

CIDA WID policy, 1984. Photo taken by R. Gossen.

WAF demonstrating ten years of women's struggles, Lahore, 12 February 1993. Photo taken by LalaRukh for WAF Lahore.

Meeting with rural women in Sindh province on post-flood livelihood recovery and protection, 2012. Photo taken by R. Gossen.

Poster designed/made by Simorgh women's resource and publication centre of Lahore. "The unholy Trinity" depicts different religions, guns, and money linking to the war in Afghanistan and Islamization policies of the 1980s. Photo taken by LalaRukh for WAF Lahore.

Poster showing women's protests in the background against unequal laws, 1980s. Photo taken by LalaRukh for WAF Lahore.

1990s poster of NCSW for repeal of the Hudood Laws. Photo taken by R. Gossen.

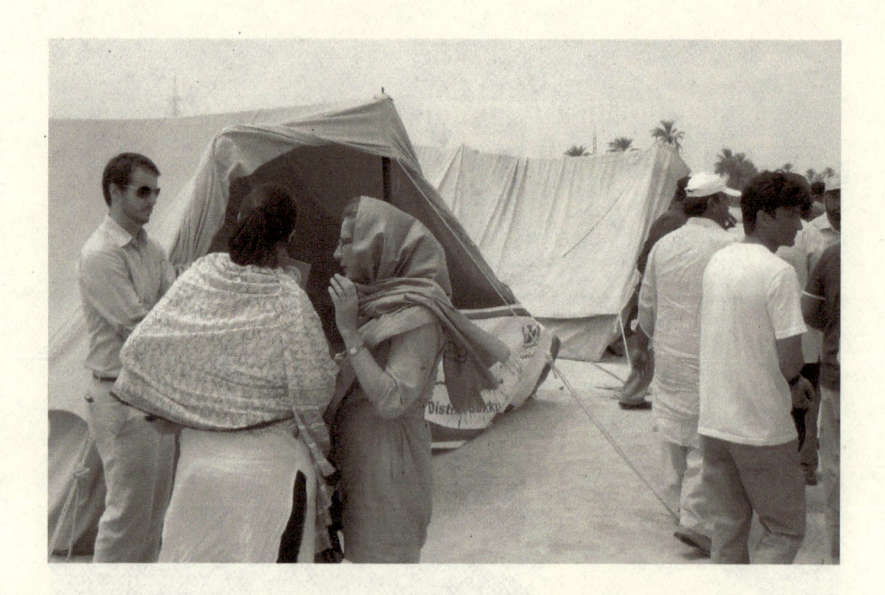

Hyderabad, Sindh, humanitarian relief camp for people displaced by the 2010 Indus River floods. Photo taken by R. Gossen.

6

Crimes in the Name of Honour

By 2012 there were almost daily news stories in the English papers about honour crimes and other cases of gender-based violence committed against women. The headlines shouted, "Couple shot dead shortly after court marriage"; the uncle opened fire on them in Sargodha. "Two women killed for alleged affairs; man arrested for killing daughter with axe in Faisalabad; to preserve honor, uncle kills niece after she returned to the village on *panchayat* orders in Khanewal district of southern Punjab. Woman claims her daughter was 'fated' to die in an acid attack after her parents threw acid on her for suspecting her of having illicit relations with a boy just north of Muzaffarabad in Azad Jammu and Kashmir. A woman's family killed a couple for marrying without the family's consent in Bahawalpur city, Punjab. Her father, brothers and uncles slit her throat and cut the nose and lips of the man in addition to breaking his legs and arms. *Panchayat* orders 'revenge (gang) rape' of a widow in southern Punjab to settle score of a rape allegedly committed by her brother." The daily barrage of articles was overwhelming and triggered the question in my mind and in many others: what was causing this form of gender-based violence, and why was it taking place? It made me wonder if this level of violence against women had existed for decades since Canada had been supporting gender equality in Pakistan and was now only reported more widely. Or was there an increase in these kinds of crimes against women? And I asked myself, was it somehow linked to the growing violent extremism and dangerous security situation in the country? Research on the links between violent extremism and gender-based violence was not yet extensive, at least not with respect to Pakistan. I set aside the *Herald Tribune* that day with a determination to understand more.

That year the Pakistan Human Rights Commission reported that family members murdered at least 943 women for allegedly defaming their family's "honour." The actual number of cases is estimated to be much higher, as fewer than ten per cent of the violent cases are reported by media, according to Zia Awan.[1] Pakistan has the highest estimated number of honour crimes against women and some of the highest violence indicators against women (Devers 2010). An estimated 5,000 women are killed each year as a result of domestic violence, with thousands of others maimed or disabled (Lopez-Claros and Nakhjavani 2018).[2]

Sexual behaviour and family honour cases, protecting *izzat* or honour and avenging insults to it by violence, were usually settled by customary law through local councils (jirgas or panchayats) or through extended family clans, often by the death of the woman concerned at the hands of her own family. In September 2020, the Supreme Court said that the word *ghairat* (a combination of being sensitive to family honour, morality, and chastity) must not be used to describe killings in the name of honour (Daur 2020). "The murderers have tried to legitimize their actions and elevate their social status by hiding behind the code of honour – or upholding the honor of the family using the cover of righteousness." The verdict authored by Supreme Court Justice Qazi Faez Isa (in 2020) also said: "Pakistan has one of the highest, if not the highest per capita honour killings in the world and predominantly the victims are women." This form of gender-based violence is mostly a crime against young people, as the average age of victims worldwide is twenty-three years old, and in Pakistan mostly affects rural women. Honour killings also accelerated significantly worldwide in the twenty-year period between 1989 and 2009 (Lopez-Claros and Nakhjavani 2018). This same twenty-year period in Pakistan witnessed the rise of an internal militancy, the growth of violent religious extremism, and a dramatic increase in violence. The correlation with the increase in jihadist extremism and Islamic fundamentalism globally during this period is striking. The 2021 study by True and Eddyono in Indonesia showed how taking a gender lens on countering violent extremism highlights that "what is at stake is countering everyday violence, that is, the community tensions and confrontation, domestic, gender-based harassment, and violence that suggest the propensity for broader political violence" (True and Eddyono 2021).

A report commissioned by CIDA in 2009 by a Pakistan consultant, did a situational analysis of women's human rights and drew links between increasing poverty, weakening security and human development indicators in Pakistan, and seemingly rising rates of rape, honour killing, and abductions. As early as 2009, the CIDA-commissioned report referenced a documented "link between violence against women and armed conflict, as rights are compromised, and conflict can make people more vulnerable to abuse" (R. Khan 2009). The report had identified an early indicator of what was to become much worse, an increase in violence against women.

"Hostile sexist attitudes toward women and support for violence against women are the factors most strongly associated with support for violent extremism ... quantitative and qualitative analysis reveals misogyny to be integral to the ideology, political identity and political economy of current violent extremist groups" (Johnston and True 2019). A UNDP and UN Women research report provided evidence of the correlation between the rise of gender-based violence (GBV) perpetrated by men and increased incidents of violent extremism, demonstrating the linkages between increasing incidences of terrorist attacks and high levels of GBV (UNDP and UN Women 2020). There is "growing evidence that in many countries hyper-masculinity – a social context which places emphasis on male aggression, violence and power over women – also helps drive violent extremism" (Khan 2022, 18).

Research by Professor Jacqui True demonstrated the links between violence against women, misogyny, and violent extremism, which is a significant finding in the field of terrorism studies. Her work indicates a correlation between sexual and gender-based violence (SGBV) and terrorism, such that the former can serve as a predictive indicator for the latter. True examined whether increased reports of SGBV are a leading indicator of – or precursor to – terrorist violence by cross-analyzing SGBV reports and terrorist incidents from the Global Terrorism Database in three countries: Myanmar, the Philippines, and Sri Lanka (UNDP and UN Women 2020).[3] She used statistical regression to provide a comprehensive analysis that demonstrates linkages between increasing incidences of terrorist attacks and increased levels of SGBV in those countries. Even though the specific causality of this association is not yet fully understood, it is clear that the relationship exists, and therefore the report recommends that governments should closely track and monitor reports of SGBV in efforts to prevent violence that can lead to violent extremism. Other gender inequality indicators, such as restricting freedom of movement and banning education and employment, can likewise strengthen early warning systems, the case study concludes. In the same report, "Conflicting Identifies, the Nexus between Masculinities, Femininities and Violent Extremism in Asia," Farhana Rahman explores the relationship between violent extremism and domestic violence against women in Bangladesh, where the latter is often considered to be an unconnected private matter. This study concludes that violent extremist groups manipulate and instrumentalize existing gender power structures and cultural narratives within communities to validate their actions. Often, the actions of violent extremist groups are depicted as alien to societal norms. However, this research demonstrates that violent extremist groups draw on pre-existing gender norms and cultural narratives to legitimize their cause, to recruit members, and even to justify attacks. Further, violence within families and communities, such as intimate partner or domestic violence and sexual harassment or assault, cultivates an environment where violence is normalized, making it easier to justify extremist violence. Thus, violent extremism and violence against women should not be viewed as isolated phenomena but rather as part of a continuum. To disrupt the draw of violent extremist groups, it is essential to understand how they position themselves within community cultural and gender norms, the study concludes (UNDP and UN Women 2020).[4]

Most so-called honour killings are encompassed by the 1990s Qisas (retribution/punishment) and Diyat (compensation or blood money) Ordinances for crimes of assault, which permit the victim's family to retain control over a crime, including the right to determine whether to report the crime, prosecute the offender, or demand *diyat*.[5] The All Pakistan Women's Association (APWA), in consultation with eighteen women's organizations, compiled a report as far back as 1981 recommending changes to the draft law, publicizing widely the inherent discrimination against women it contained. Nevertheless, the Qisas and Diyat Ordinances passed in 1985 and were enacted by the Pakistan Supreme Court under Sharia law, and became part of the penal code in 1997 in the short period between two democratically elected governments.[6] They allow the heir(s) of a crime victim to forgive or settle with the perpetrator individually, and make the state's right to prosecute secondary (Warraich 2005), thus providing a barrier to justice for victims. "This law was seen to legitimize (even encourage) murder, particularly 'honour killings' of women" (International Crisis Group 2015). It remains one of the most severely discriminating laws that affects mostly rural women, who lack education or have low literacy skills combined with other indicators of inequality and vulnerability.

Since most of these crimes are committed by a close relative or within the family, if and when the case reaches a court of law, the victim's family or relatives may "pardon" the murderer under the *diyat* provision or be pressured to accept financial compensation. The murderer thus goes free. Once such a pardon has been secured, the state has no further writ on the matter. Killing women to save the "honour" of the family has had a high level of support in parts of society despite its widespread condemnation by activists. The extended family is also an informal institution of justice in Pakistan, according to a study published by CAMP in 2015, which may partially explain this continued level of support, given that traditional methods of justice including the clan and neighbourhood have been a strong component of social control in rural and tribal areas of Pakistan (Shinwari 2015). The 2016 anti-honour-killing law changed this. Nevertheless, if the judge determines it is not an honour crime, then the Qisas and Diyat Ordinances can still apply. Promoting forgiveness over justice on a regular basis at the expense of women could be one of the worst examples of a misogynistic system severely discriminatory to women and girls, especially those in rural areas. It is a way of trying to "exonerate itself from being a crime under the cover of righteousness. It also hides motivations of vengeance beneath codes of behaviour that seek impunity on the grounds of religious authority or cultural exceptionalism" (Lopez-Claros and Nakhjavani 2018, 70).

President Zia's finance minister, Ghulam Ishaq Khan, acting as interim president for three months in 1997 (in between democratically elected governments), promulgated the Qisas and Diyat Ordinance. "In the three-month interim between the dismissal of Bhutto's first government and installation of Nawaz Sharif's Muslim League government, President Ishaq Khan, acting as a new government, made the ordinance part of the Pakistan Penal Code in 1997" (Human Rights Watch 1999, 25).

VISIT TO THE MUKHTAR MAI WOMEN'S SHELTER IN SOUTHERN PUNJAB

Multan is one of the world's oldest living cities. Called the City of Saints, its skyline is graced by famous Sufi shrines. The Tomb of Shah Rukn-e-Alam, built in 1324, is visible from any part of the city with its magnificent shining dome. Just seven hours' drive from Islamabad, in 2012 it was still not deemed safe to travel by road by the embassy security team, so we arranged to fly and landed at the small Multan airport. We were headed to a village called Meerwala to meet Mukhtar Mai, a grassroots women's rights activist whose projects had been funded by CIDA for many years.

The region, suffering from extreme poverty and extremist views, is considered repressive, especially for women and girls. The UAE controls pockets of land in the area and many sheiks from there reportedly travel to this area for sport hunting and falcon flying. It is an area where militants have flourished and "jihadists" have training camps. It is not uncommon to see road signs warning: "No foreigners allowed beyond this point." The Pakistan Taliban and other extremist groups justify their militant jihad based on the "sorry state of Pakistani society and concerns over social and economic inequality and the need for socio economic justice among many other motivations" (Sheikh 2016). These areas have been a prime target for uptake of extremist ideology (Fair 2013). Equally, they are a target area for development programs tackling poverty and lack of economic opportunities, including international donor-funded projects such as the CIDA-funded CARE project we visited the previous year.

As far back as 1997, the Asian Development Bank found that the highest concentration of rural poor in Punjab province was in Dera Ghazi Khan district. In 2009, the *New York Times* "warned that the dusty impoverished fringes of Pakistan could be the next areas facing an insurgency in Pakistan, and militants have gained considerably in the district of Dera Ghazi Khan." Not surprisingly, then, the correlation between rates of gender-based violence and incidents of extremism appears to play out here, with many well-known cases of so-called honour crimes having taken place in the region of Southern Punjab.[7] The district was the location of a sensational case in July 2016, the murder of twenty-six-year-old Qandeel Baloch by her brother, for her image as a social media star. Baloch's brother, Waseem, proudly and openly confessed on video to her murder based on "honour," saying her behaviour was "intolerable" and that "her actions had brought dishonor to his family" (Maher 2018). The case grabbed Pakistani and international media attention. In 2019, Pakistan's first government "Violence Against Women Centre" opened in Multan, under the Punjab Women Protection Authority Act of 2017. UNDP Pakistan, under their prevention of violent extremism portfolio, supported the Gender Desk in Multan in October 2020, strengthening an outlet for women to report grievances and receive assistance.

The religious fervour in the district is a particularly violent strain, according to local police authorities. Some Punjab-based militant organizations "had their roots in the anti-Soviet jihad in Afghanistan, had maintained contact with the mujahideen-turned-Taliban, and helped out the Afghan Taliban in their fight against the Afghan Northern Alliance" (Gul 2009). The violent extremist group Lashkar-e-Taiba (LET) is known to have recruited mainly from Punjab and a high concentration of its fighters have come from Multan (Fair 2013).

In 2002, Mukhtar Mai was gang-raped at age twenty-eight on the orders of a panchayat in retribution for her brother's alleged crime in Muzaffargarh district of Southern Punjab. It is one of the earliest internationally known and prosecuted cases of so-called honour crimes. Mai's brother's crime, for which she paid the price, was speaking out against his attackers. Police investigations eventually found that "three men from a rival tribe had molested the boy (Mai's brother) and that the accusation against him of having an affair with an older woman had been a cover-up" (Masood 2011). It was a blatant case of how women were used as scapegoats with impunity for male crimes. Canada was one of the many foreign embassies that provided support and funding to Mukhtar Mai early on through localized funds and the CIDA women's program funds. Mai holds an honorary doctorate from Canada's Laurentian University. She has become a symbol for advocates for women's health and security in her region, attracting national and international attention. She used the Pakistani government's compensation money and donations from around the world to build two local schools for girls.

In 2004 the late Asma Jahangir (Pakistan's renowned international human rights lawyer) wrote an article about the Mukhtar Mai case, exposing the practice against women by local informal governance bodies. She unmasked an informal justice system in place that allowed women to be judicially gang-raped. Ten years later, while still living in Pakistan, I read a media report about the ruling of a jirga who had asked the family of a twelve-year-old girl to give her in *swara* to settle a dispute. The custom of using girls as compensation for the crimes their male relatives have committed is called *swara* in the Pashtun belt, *wari* in Sindh, and *vani* in Punjab. In this case, the girl's brother raped the daughter of a man in the village who took it to the jirga, but the police intervened and arrested ten members of the jirga. It was just after the landmark women's protection bills had been passed in December 2011, making this practice illegal, and the new legislation was still fresh in people's minds.

— * —

The village of Meerwala is about a two-hour drive from Multan. It was the day after Pakistan Women's Day, 13 February 2012. We were interested to see the school and the women's shelter CIDA had funded and learn about Mai's ongoing work to support women in her community. She was an example of a local grassroots activist supported by Canada (through Pakistani NGOs), working for women's rights and gender equality in the village where she herself had faced a serious violation as a victim of a so-called honour crime. In her struggles, her husband, a local police officer who married her after she was violated, has stood firmly beside her, sharing her unflinching efforts to stand up for women in her community. More than one book has been written about her by French and American journalists. She greeted us with her usual quiet, unassuming composure, and, although not easy to engage in conversation, she showed us around the compound of the girls' school, the women's shelter, and the office. An array of photos of Canada's first female ambassador to Pakistan, Margaret Hubert, graced Mai's simple office walls. I was surprised to see so many, but perhaps they were placed there that day for our benefit. Hubert had visited more than once in 2005 and had approved Canada's initial assistance of $49,000 for Mai's work through the embassy's Canada Fund for Local Initiatives. The CFLI funds helped the school expand by paying for the construction of three classrooms, an office, and a bathroom, various much-needed supplies, and the cost of the teacher salaries. It also set up income-generating opportunities by providing livestock for thirty women from Mai's village of Meerwala. Mai's organization also established a small dairy farm with profits going to support the school.

In 2007, Canada's Program for the Advancement of Gender Equality (PAGE) – the fund established to support women's groups – provided

$99,999 for two years for capacity-building of staff and teachers, advocacy for women's rights, and fundraising for the organization. Another official Canadian visit took place that year (2007) by then-High Commissioner David Collins. The fund also provided for procuring books and uniforms for girls and furniture for classrooms, and helped pay vehicle running costs (to pick up and drop off students and teachers).

The crisis shelter for women was a relatively new development and a much-needed one. It wasn't fully utilized when I visited, but demand for such protection measures has since increased significantly. We approved additional funding for the shelter, including a twenty-four-hour helpline to provide counselling to victims, and medical and psychosocial help through a female doctor and supplies for women and children staying there. I hoped that it would be used and easily accessible to women in the area. The Canadian small projects were some of the first to support shelters in the district. Mai took us around to see these new elements and visit the school. We had a short ceremony in the courtyard where I made a few remarks about Canada's long-standing commitment to women's rights and girls' education and handed her a gift from the embassy. After a short press conference with a handful of local reporters, we ended the visit with a nice lunch with her small group and her husband in their home.

CIDA had also supported, through the women's funds, the South Punjab NGOs Forum (SPNF), a network of grassroots civil society organizations or CSOs, and the All-Pakistan Women's Association to advocate and build capacity on violence against women and to promote collective action to protect women's rights. Through the PAGE women's fund, resources were provided for training, rallies, and campaigns, organized together with a large human rights NGO – SPO – that CIDA had helped create in the 1990s. CIDA provided APWA funds for para-legal training in their multipurpose centres for women that provided health, education, and legal services. More than 600 women were trained who served as community workers (or "agents of change"), bringing a rights-based approach to development in local communities. Another organization based in South Punjab, Sangtani, was funded (between 2006 and 2008) to create awareness about violence against women and to provide women who were directly affected by violence with access to legal aid and services. They trained and used local resource persons and community members, identified and counselled women, conducted follow-up visits, and provided referrals for legal aid and/or shelter assistance. Legal aid was provided through their legal aid centre. In the process, they developed linkages with legal authorities at district government and collaborated with local elected officials, lawyers, and police authorities. In addition to legal awareness sessions, they undertook theatre performances and printed materials to reach members of the community (CIDA 2010). In Sindh, PAGE supported significant work on honour killing through a network of thirty-seven community-based organizations from rural Sindh – all of whom had already received capacity development support as grassroots organizations through CIDA funding for SPO[8] between 2003 and 2005. The network called Development Planning Management Graduates Coordination Society (DPMGCS) held a series of dialogues both in small groups and in larger public forums for sensitization about *karo kari* (the regional term for honour killing) and to design an awareness and advocacy campaign against it. They involved men and women from the communities, religious leaders, journalists, local councils, and district government authorities, including jirgas. The network also established a process of providing legal aid to the survivors of *karo kari* and advocated for legislation to check the practice (CIDA 2010, 63). This kind of development work is now advocated by experts in the field of gender and violent extremism as key contributions to preventing violent extremism, but has been an inherent part of development programming for more than two decades. Many of these programs did not receive multi-year sustained funding and without government taking them over, would run out of steam. They did at least lay the groundwork to build on.

Mai's case took many twists and turns over a decade. Despite being internationally recognized and "a symbol of voiceless and oppressed women in Pakistan" (Masood 2011), she eventually lost her case in the Supreme Court. Five of the six accused were acquitted. The Women's Action Forum (WAF) was behind the legal case, and the lawyer, Aitzaz Ahsan, took it on pro bono for WAF. WAF filed a review petition in May 2011 and obtained hundreds of signatories to an appeal to the Chief Justice of the Supreme Court, but the case remains closed. Human Rights Watch expressed dismay at the decision, saying it was a setback to the broader struggle to end violence against women in Pakistan.

Mai remains active and free in her village and a strong advocate for grassroots women. She is one example of how women's rights activists often capture a rural woman's story and add support for the case to generally further advocacy on the issue. But she has become a voice, a change-maker within the context of her local social reality. French journalists convinced Mai to tell her story in a memoir entitled *In the Name of Honour*, with a foreword by Nicholas Kristof, the *New York Times* journalist who visited her several times. In 2017, on International Women's Day, the Canadian embassy invited Mukhtar Mai and Hina Jilani as panelists to Canada's WEE Forum. It was a special forum held in Islamabad to recognize achievements in women's economic empowerment, that had been revitalized by Julie Delahanty, who led the work, during our time at the embassy. "Let's dedicate this international women's day to all those children, not just girls who suffer child marriages," said Hina Jilani at the discussion. There was no reference to honour killing in the discussion; perhaps it was still too sensitive an issue. Mai has a quiet public persona but has effectively advocated for change in practical ways, foremost remaining in her village and working for women's rights. The Canadian High Commission in Islamabad released a public statement on women's rights that day:

> Happy #IWD2017. All groups benefit from promoting women's rights. A society which upholds women's rights will also respect the rights of religious minorities; the rights of children – especially those victims of exploitation and trafficking and the rights of LGBT people.

Violence against women and girls and intolerance toward LGBTQI groups in the community have been identified in recent research as gender-specific signs of the spread of extremism conducive to violence. Support for early marriage of girls or "child brides" is also a factor that can indicate increasing extremism. It is a less controversial issue to address than the so-called "honour killing" of women and girls. Canada's diplomatic advocacy had come back to advocating for women's rights.

LEGAL PROGRESS ON HONOUR CRIMES

Fourteen years after Mai's attack, and after thousands more murders of girls and women by family members, it was the case of Qandeel Baloch that finally pushed the government to pass the legislation against honour crimes in 2016.

The provincial government of Punjab passed the Punjab Protection of Women against Violence Act in 2016 to provide greater legal protections for victims of domestic abuse. Yet, in July 2018, a village council in Multan district ordered and carried out the rape of a teenage girl in "revenge" for a crime allegedly committed by her brother. The 2016 law, which brought the penalties for so-called "honour" crimes in line with murder, proved ineffective (UK Home Office 2020) in this case, as did the 2011 women's protection bills. The deference to a customary patriarchal system continues. The challenge posed by the implementation and enforcement of laws is evident. "Factors which hamper the implementation of laws against violence are deeply rooted in social and gender inequity" (Lopez-Claros and Nakhjavani 2018, 62). The principle of justice therefore points immediately to another principle – the equality of men and women. The case study on Bangladesh in the 2020 report by UNDP and UN Women mentioned above argues that "in some rural communities in Bangladesh, the young men perceive violent extremism as a way to reclaim their traditional roles. Those young men feel ridiculed and undermined by the urban social norms and the perceived Western influences that allow women more power and autonomy. Through interview-based case studies, Rahman demonstrates how incidents of domestic violence rise when men feel their identities or roles in the community are challenged by women's economic and social empowerment" (UNDP and UN Women 2020). "The connection between extremism and misogyny has been overlooked in academic studies and the law" (Renzetti 2019).

With the passing of the Honour Crimes Law in October 2016, honour killing was finally made illegal in Pakistan. While the victim's family can forgive a murderer, the state may still prosecute the perpetrator and render life imprisonment for an honour killer. This is the result of a long struggle by the Pakistani women's movement, and by civil society organizations and activists who had been raising their voices for decades condemning the practice. The first law on honour killing in Pakistan was drafted by strong female activist voices – Shehla Zia, Tahira Abdullah, and Samar Minallah in the 1990s. Others who raised their voices early against honour killing were Nighat Saeed and Samina Khan, along with women's rights organizations, including WAF, Aurat Foundation, and Shirkat Gah (the latter two were key partners and recipients of CIDA funding throughout the 1990s). Samar Minallah, a Pashtun woman from KP, made the first documentary on honour killing.

The honour killing bill was tabled in February 2014 by Senator Sughra Imam and then passed by the Senate in March 2015, but failed to get further traction. In February 2016, documentary filmmaker Sharmeen Obaid Chinoy won an Oscar for her documentary on honour killing in Pakistan, aptly called *A Girl in the River: The Price of Forgiveness*. She dedicated the award to all the heroes working on the ground in Pakistan and to all the women in the country working for change. The Pakistani women behind the Oscar were also instrumental in getting the criminalization bill passed in the National Assembly in December 2011 because they were willing to speak up. UN Women Pakistan sent out a broad message on social media on the film's Oscar: "Let us share this great news for Pakistan and the great advocacy work of the women's organizations and survivors! There are indeed things to celebrate, and this is very much thanks to your great support and our joint lobbying." The international publicity did help obtain presidential support and commitment to take action on honour killing inside Pakistan when then-President Nawaz Sharif vowed to take action on the proposed legislation against it, which had been languishing in the system since 2014. The West's high level of interest also spurred President Nawaz Sharif to push ahead the law in March 2016, but again it failed to get enough traction to be passed. It was the case of the murder of Qandeel in July that year that helped push things further. Media articles repeatedly said: "Her death brings fresh urgency to the Honour Killing Legislation."

Maryam Nawaz, the daughter of President Nawaz Sharif, promised to move the law forward. In October 2016, three months after Qandeel Baloch's murder, the legislation against honour killing was passed unanimously in both houses of Parliament. "Now, a killer will face a minimum sentence of 25 years in jail or life imprisonment," Senator Farhatullah Babar stated on 8 October 2016 in an interview with CNN. "No murderer will be able to walk away free even if his parents or family members forgive him for killing his sister, wife, or mother in the name of 'honour.'" Qandeel's brother was finally convicted of her murder three years later, on 27 September 2019, and sentenced to life in prison in the Multan central jail.

7

The Hudood Ordinances

A Lingering Backdrop to Legal Protections

O you who have believed, be persistently standing firm in justice, witnesses for Allah, even if it be against yourselves or parents and relatives. Whether one is rich or poor, Allah is more worthy of both. So, follow not [personal] inclination, lest you not be just. And if you distort [your testimony] or refuse [to give it], then indeed Allah is ever, with what you do, acquainted.
> Verse 135, Surih An Nisa ("The Women"), of the Quran, posted on a wall facing Harvard University Faculty of Law main entrance

I met Senator Donya Aziz one afternoon in November 2011 to talk about her work on the Prevention of Anti-Women Practices Act, which had been approved by the National Assembly earlier that month. This bill was an important milestone for Pakistan on women's rights and equality, as it prohibited the outdated practices and traditions that exploited and discriminated against women. It was particularly significant that year as Pakistan was again labelled the third most dangerous place in the world to be a woman. Dr Aziz, as a member of the National Assembly (and a lawyer), had primarily authored and tabled the historic bill. I asked her how she had managed to get unanimous approval through the National Assembly for it as a Criminal Law Amendment, and in particular, how she had managed the religious right. She attributed its passage to the support of other female parliamentarians and Senator Raza Rabbani, the architect of the eighteenth amendment on the devolution of some federal power to the provinces, who helped guide those lobbying, including civil society, through its passage. With the help and support of others, Aziz had been pushing the bill for over three years. Senator Nilofer Bakhtiar presented both bills, and the Pakistan Senate unanimously passed them, providing for deterrent punishment for anti-women practices and acid crimes. "The work ahead is now putting in place measures for its implementation," she told me. Measures such as putting in place female policy units in sub-national levels of government and support in district hospitals were needed, since the latter were safe place for women seeking protection. The government has since strengthened the call for the strict enforcement of the Women Protection Act (Khan 2022, 53) to prevent the abuse and sexual harassment of women in homes, offices, or public places.

The 2011 Prevention of Anti-Women Practices Act bars forced marriages, marriages to the Quran (a practice sometimes used to keep a woman's inheritance in the family), giving away women (usually young girls) in *wani*, or depriving them of inheritance.[1] It mandates a punishment of up to ten years' imprisonment and a penalty equivalent to $50,000 to anyone who forces a woman into marriage. It also states that those who are involved in conducting weddings in exchange for settling disputes will be sentenced to five years in prison, the practice of marrying a girl to the Quran will elicit imprisonment of up to seven years and a fine of $5,500, and preventing a woman from inheriting property will result in five years in prison. The Criminal Law (Second Amendment) Act also made attacks with a substance such as acid punishable from fourteen years to life imprisonment and a minimum million-rupee (nearly $10,000) fine. Since passage of the Act, the reporting of attacks and the registration of such cases have increased, and sentences have become harsher, according to the Asia Report of the International Crisis Group in 2015 (International Crisis Group 2015, 9).

The debate on the bill, which advocates greater social protection for women, had been deferred several times, according to media reports (*Express Tribune* 2011a), after male legislators (including Shah Mahmood Qureshi, twice foreign minister and Member of the National Assembly representing Pakistan Muslim League – Nawaz [PML-N], and members of the PML-Q and the PPP) had raised an objection and some others had refused to vote. But the women's protection bills were passed in December 2011 – a strong sign of progress on measures to ensure women's rights and gender equality. The next year, the 2012 National Commission on the Status of Women (NCSW) Act transformed that Commission into a powerful and autonomous body.

Changing long-standing customary practices into crimes was a major transformation for equality in society. Women in Pakistan were forging ahead, continuing to challenge outdated practices. One women's rights NGO described the bill: "The biggest success ... of this legislation" was the acceptance that "crimes committed against women under the guise of 'customary practices' are in actuality crimes" (Lari 2011). It provided assurances of greater protection for women that were now legally enshrined, which would limit "the violation of human rights by informal justice institutions that have contributed to the rise of cases of violence against women in Pakistan" (Shinwari 2015, 142). I sent a report to headquarters in Ottawa on the importance of the historic step, even though women's rights and protection were not strongly on the radar (2011) of CIDA at the time.

The role of civil society in helping the passage in the Senate was critical. On the day of the passage, civil society members organized a peaceful rally outside the Parliament. Women's rights activists had worked with pro-women parliamentarians and supporters through the process, as they had done in the passage of the Protection of Women against Harassment at the Workplace Act, 2010.[2] The formation of the Women's Parliamentary Caucus in 2009 with UN Development Program (UNDP) support helped in researching and drafting bills, and women (and pro-women) parliamentarians were able to support the passage of these pro-women laws. "The caucus is a watershed. This is the first of its kind in Pakistan's political history," said Caucus Secretary Syed Shamoon Hashmi, who called it "a mechanism that has enabled quantitative and qualitative input for women in the proceedings of the House" (International Crisis Group 2015, 8). It showed the strength of efforts on women's political empowerment.

Other legislation has since been added in addition to the Protection against Harassment of Women at the Workplace Act (PAHWA) 2010: the Criminal Law (Amendment) (Offences in the Name or on Pretext of Honour) Act, 2016; the Criminal Law (Amendment) (Offences Relating to Rape) Act, 2016; the Women Distress and Detention Fund (Amendment) Act, 2018; the National Commission on the Status of Women (Amendment) Act, 2018; the Election Act, 2017; and the Domestic Workers Act, 2018 (UN Women 2022, 24).

Recent research and trends point to the need to support local women's organizations with meaningful financial resources, alongside women's rights advocates, who are best positioned to lead the fight against legal barriers to gender equality. Local civil society groups are well-placed to identify which laws have the most negative effects in their communities, as evidenced by the WAF early warning signs in the 1980s. Canada's early women's funds (as well as some funding from other aid actors) were able to provide resources and backing for the Pakistani women's movement, especially during the 1989 to 2009 period, in its gains on the legal front. Institutional and longer-term support for civil society organizations engaged in women's legal rights made the difference. Work on awareness-raising of violence against women and capacity-building and training of women activists, supported by Canadian aid, contributed to broadening the base for women's human rights work since the 1990s. The CIDA Women's Funds provided support for work on the implementation of laws and policies and services for women at provincial and district levels, which gave assurance of protection through the efforts of women's groups to consolidate benefits from the laws, especially on violence against women. Decades of hard work by civil society activists working hand in hand with parliamentarians were behind the progress. The WDPr lessons assessment of 2004 (CIDA 2004b) found that "as a result of increased awareness on gender issues people's demand for services increased beyond mere orientations/seminars and workshops." Today the strong demand for protection against GBV and services such as police, courts, shelters, psycho-social support and counselling, legal aid, and the implementation of legislation from the government may well be an indicator of the success of this early work.

TURNING LAWS INTO REALITY

The gap between the law and on-the-ground realities remains significant. Women's organizations called for an implementation commission to help enforce these new laws. The Human Rights Commission of Pakistan report of 2018 noted, "The fact that so many violent and unlawful practices persist and continue to escalate illustrates yet again the massive challenges to implementing the law and changing deeply entrenched societal attitudes" (HRCP 2018).

In a 2015 report on opinion surveys on systems of justice in Pakistan, it was clear that a significant portion of the population (in addition to the Taliban and other extremist groups) have lost faith in the state justice institutions, where cases can be seen to linger for decades with no resolution. Likewise, there is not complete trust in the informal justice systems either, although one study found they are often preferred for civil cases (not for criminal ones) due to swifter, albeit harsher or less just, decisions (Shinwari 2015). Pakistani analysts have consistently cited the slow legal system and its problems. The justice system "often works in favor of the haves and punishes the have-nots ... [Coupled with] official apathy, incompetence and corrupt police ... rural areas in particular bear the brunt of lawlessness and neglect" (Gul 2009). Interviews with members of the Pakistan Taliban indicate that they see the enforcement of Sharia law as necessary to address an increasing crime rate in Pakistan. In an interview with the wife of the imam of the Lal Masjid (Red Mosque) in Islamabad, Umme Hassan, Mona Sheikh reported that Hassan compared the function of religion with that of police in enforcing law and order. Hassan said in the interview, "it adds discipline to society so that order can be maintained." The Taliban also see justice as related to the enforcement of their concept of Sharia law and to punishment for offences derived from their interpretation of it (Sheikh 2016).

The law has not been appropriately applied in the case of violence against women, particularly at the district and provincial level. Many women's rights organizations have noted that judges at that level require gender sensitization to help ensure justice systems respond to the needs of women and girls.[3] CIDA had funded human rights and judicial education pedagogy training of judges from Pakistan in Canada from 2003 but had stopped it in 2012. Instead of ending it, perhaps if training on gender-based violence and women's legal protection had been added, it would have helped address an urgent gap and retained its cost-effective approach as a longstanding strategic initiative.

Increased efforts to strengthen the justice system and courts and to establish gender-based courts are since underway, notably in KP province, where the rates of GBV remain high in areas affected by extremist violence. "In 2013, the Peshawar High Court (in KP province) formed an exclusively female bench – the nation's first. We have separate courts for acid attacks; we should have similar arrangements for rape and honour killing cases and set up mobile courts to increase the justice system's proximity to women and its responsiveness to their needs," a civil judge said (International Crisis Group 2015, n121). Another historic moment in KP province witnessed the Domestic Violence against Women (Prevention and Protection) Act passed by the provincial assembly in January 2021. The legislation aims to strengthen mechanisms that provide gender-responsive justice on issues related to domestic violence. The provincial Minister for Social Welfare, Special Education and Women Empowerment, Hisham Khan, said in his public remarks, "I am confident that this law will also pave the way for more cohesive and meaningful collaboration between the security, justice and social sector service providers and will ensure that the best interests of survivors of violence are at the center of all interventions."

In 2019, Chief Justice Asif Khosa announced that Pakistan would set up more than 1,000 courts dedicated to tackling violence against women – one in each district (Woodyatt and Saifi 2019). Within a continuing culture of impunity for perpetrators, this was an important step to countering the narrative of violent extremists on the lack of social justice and on the need to enforce Sharia in order to ensure punishment for offences. New programs – including by Group Development Pakistan (GDP) and the Women in Law initiative led by Valerie Khan, Executive Director of GDP (and founder of the Acid Survivor Foundation in Pakistan, which was a strong civil society force lobbying for the second women's protection bill in 2011 criminalizing acid attacks on women) – have since been implemented, including a project entitled Increasing Women's Representation in Law, funded by Australian Aid and the UK High Commission. Another example is the training of judges and of women lawyers in KP province on the legal and judicial system and the rule of law, now being done by UNDP in collaboration with USAID and the provincial Bar Council. It is positive to see many more gender justice initiatives being funded by aid donors. Yet CIDA-funded programs for gender justice, reaching as far back as the 1990s, were incubators and small supportive steps towards a strong system, even decades later.

CIDA's evaluation of the women's funds in 2006 had recommended that gender justice be a major focus of those funds. It recommended linking community- and national-level advocacy with legislation and the judiciary/law enforcement system. With CIDA choosing to focus more on economic empowerment at the time, the women's organizations eventually went to other donors to support women's justice efforts. UK Aid, by example, supported a major gender justice program in the first half of the 2000s (perhaps building on the momentum of the organizations CIDA had supported). In 2009, despite the need and considerable work on the concept development, CIDA HQ rejected a bilateral project proposal for judicial education on gender equality developed by Simorgh (in consultation with CIDA staff at the High Commission) to address problems facing female victims of violence in the formal justice system, despite those victims' urgent need for support. Given the change in program direction by 2009, the proposed project did not move forward.

Another tribute to CIDA's early work was the partnership with Aurat Foundation in the early 2000s (under the second responsive fund for women's organizations), for the establishment of a number of information network centres for women to support women's political participation at the sub-national level. It was followed by two major bilateral projects on women's political empowerment that helped lay the foundation for decentralized work in the provinces. The Effective Representation of Women Councillors Program was instrumental in making women visible in the 2001 local government elections and supported resource centres for those elected in seventy districts. The second project (for $2.4 million), launched in 2005–06, mainstreamed women in political structures and decision-making at the lowest tier of governance, *union* and *tehsil* councils.[4] These bilateral programs built on the numerous sub-projects on women's political participation that were funded under the WDPr in the mid-to-late 1990s with the Aurat Foundation as well as Sarsabz, AGHS Legal Aid Cell, AWARD, and others. Global Affairs Canada put in place a new project for women's political empowerment, Fempower, in 2019 for $3.4 million, implemented by Shirkat Gah. It provides assistance to women legislators, provides leadership training to women councillors and community women at the district level, and offers training at the grassroots on personal status laws and GBV, among other activities. Canadian aid funded the capacity development of women's rights leaders and activists over more than two decades, who emerged through the local governance process. Increasing the participation and role of women in political processes is also now seen as an important element in preventing extremism.

THE STRENGTH OF THE INFORMAL JUSTICE SYSTEM

The "two steps forward, one step back" title of Mumtaz and Shaheed's book on the women's movement of the 1980s was still a reality in 2012 when "the Supreme Court issued orders to the provincial chief secretaries and inspectors general of police to ensure that girls and women were not exchanged to settle disputes through jirgas." The ruling arose as a result of a petition by the chair of the NCSW, Anis Haroon, against the jirga system. The NCSW found that "87 jirgas were held in Sindh alone in 2011, and 26 girls and women were exchanged to settle disputes" (Khan 2012). Pakistani feminists and activists (many of whom were supported by CIDA) have challenged this practice and the informal justice system of jirgas for decades, which helped lead to the instatement of laws against it. The NCSW in 2012 assisted the Supreme Court to declare the jirga (informal customary council/court) system illegal, and particularly the "tradition" of exchanging and giving away girls (usually between the ages of six and twelve years) in the settling of disputes, which had already been declared illegal by the Women's Protection Act of 2011.

"State law and Shariah law are both formal written codes. Customary laws (which can be described as community, familial, or 'folk' laws) are informal and unwritten but immensely strong because they reflect the cultures of the people" (Lieven 2011, 87). This common assessment of what is deemed culture or "the cultures of the people" may not, as has been determined since, always be culture, but sometimes actual crimes. Anatol Lieven goes on to say in his well-known book on Pakistan that "these codes, and not the state law or the Shariah, govern rules of inheritance, the regulation of marriage and sexual relations, and the punishment of a range of 'crimes' of the resolution of a range of local disputes" (ibid., 88). Women's rights activists have been asking for decades how such customary laws which no longer promote the welfare of women and are obsolete are still implemented by bodies of local (male) elders under informal systems of justice: jirgas and panchayats. Some analysts have concluded that the state has given way to traditional informal justice and governance structures, enabling male leaders (and in some areas the Taliban, when they were present in some remote or tribal communities) to dispense justice instead of the state (ibid.).

The informal justice system has been proven to perpetuate gender inequality and is an example of systemic discrimination, as was revealed by Asma Jahangir in 2004 on the Mukhtar Mai case. "The local Jirga system in Pakistan undermines women's rights by continuing to perpetuate their voicelessness and their vulnerability to physical, social and sexual exploitation, especially in the tribal areas," said one Pakistani activist I spoke with about the issue.

Traditional codes of conduct through jirgas and panchayats, which rule on honour crimes, have had (in some places) a stronger commanding hold on the behaviour of Pakistani society members than the state's formal laws (Shah-Davis 2011). Because the rule of tradition has reigned, it has compounded the failure of state governance. Through these jirgas or tribal councils, the governance of communities has thus allowed the non-state parallel system of regulation to flourish in Pakistan. Change is now happening, but the cultural attitudes that persist in segregating and excluding women on a local and familial level are harder to target than laws and thus harder to change. "Rewriting laws is easy; rewiring mindsets is much more challenging" (Islam and Claros-Lopez 2021).

The issue of justice and the competing judicial codes is particularly significant for gender equality. The state legal system is based on British law. Sharia law is the other formal written code. Against this sits the customary informal (including tribal) law, unwritten but immensely strong because it is "used to resolve disputes and conflicts in a manner perceived to be legitimate by local communities."[5] These parallel informal justice systems often violate human rights, especially in relation to women, girls, and religious and minority rights (Shinwari 2015). They aim at compromise, attempting to achieve community consensus and unity (but without including women), dispensing justice as compensation (using livestock, land, money, and often innocent women and girls as a means of settlement), rather than as punishment of perpetrators. In Afghanistan, this informal justice system has proven to be the most dangerous for women and the major obstacle to progress on gender equality throughout the country, especially in rural and remote areas where customary practices toward women and girls often conflict with centuries-old, interpreted understandings of Islamic law (H. Khan 2015).

Jirgas exhibit systemic discrimination as they intentionally exclude women from their councils and decision-making. This defeats their purpose as a way to maintain community consensus through consultation, given the lack of representation of half the community, and of religious and ethnic minorities, in their decision-making structure. They are seen by feminists as a way of maintaining patriarchal and tribal authority. The evolving research on links between violent extremism and violence against women leads one to see how these jirgas and panchayats perpetuate and sanction gender-based violence, and can cultivate an environment where violence is normalized, making it easier to justify extremist violence by those who may use this cultural and gender norm within the community to that end. Recent aid research has recommended that greater efforts are needed to ensure that policies address harmful constructions of masculinity and femininity promoted by violent extremist groups. Programs must work with local communities to respond to the unequal gender power dynamics that shape and fuel extremist violence, including through empowering women and girls to be agents of peace (UNDP and UN Women 2020).

The informal councils that rule on civil justice cases are known to combine customary and Islamic law and collect little evidence (Shinwari 2015, 5). The study by USIP on Islamic Law, Customary Law, and Afghan Informal Justice found that the informal structures there draw on both customary and Islamic legal sources. It further found that "the Islamic law that prevails at informal level amounts to a kind of 'folk sharia' that does not draw on centuries of interpreted law by Islamic scholars. These customary practices conflict with centuries old, interpreted understanding of Islamic Sharia law" (H. Khan 2015, 7). Customary law was found to take little or no account of the rights of women. The complicated mixing of customary law and Sharia law at local levels makes these informal structures even more precarious for women. This interpretation has been debated by Muslim feminist scholars showing that interpretations of Islamic texts differ on all accounts. More and more research on the Quran and women's rights is appearing (El-Ali 2022).

In a discussion with Farzana Bari in March 2014, we talked about the Kohistan honour killing case, where she was part of the investigation team sent to the area by the government. She spoke about the women's concern network that started with local women counsellors who strongly condemn all forms of religious and cultural extremism, as its root is in terrorism. She asked, "Why don't we speak out more strongly against these structures for their control over people's lives and why they are allowed to function with only male members? We need to continue challenging the jirga and panchayat system that remains so powerful. Why is our civil justice system so ineffective?" The women's protection legislation in 2011 declared their rulings illegal, opening the window for the state to have some control over them. As some members of Parliament are members of these councils (Shah-Davis 2011), there is an "endorsement for preservation of traditional social codes and customs even in the highest enacting body" (Warraich 2005). Honour crimes, for example, have therefore been perpetuated by structures intent on retaining their social and political hold over local communities (UK Home Office 2020).

In parallel to the women parliamentarians working with civil society at the federal level, other community-based organizations and activists have launched their own initiatives against systemic discrimination. UN Women Pakistan tells the story of Tabassum Adnan, a women's rights activist from the Swat region of KP Province who was recognized by USAID for her bravery as the first person to set up a female-only jirga to raise women's voices against the oppressive and harmful practice of *vani*. Cases of *vani* are now being reported to the police and justice system. She defied the fatwas from religious leaders against her and overcame the attempts to silence her. In November 2018, Zohra Yusuf, former chair of the HRCP, told Deutsche Welle, "In Pakistan, it is not only individuals that commit 'honour killings'; even tribal courts sentence women to death for 'dishonouring' a family or a tribe" (International Crisis Group 2015). The HRCP 2018 report noted, "Gang rape remains a primary method of panchayats and village elders to enact 'justice' and resolve conflict in their communities." Yet this clearly perpetuates a vicious circle of injustices by not punishing the perpetrators for their deeds.

Shirkat Gah, which has run women-friendly spaces since 2011, including in the Swat district, has a different approach. Instead of working with informal justice mechanisms and making (potentially futile) attempts to reform them, it engages with state institutions such as the police to address gender-based violence, thus strengthening the link between the citizen and the state and contributing to community reconstruction and rehabilitation in conflict zones. The danger of engaging with male-only informal governance systems is that these forms of governance provide the least security for women (and ultimately for both genders) and contribute to the violation of the rights of women and minorities (CIDA 2010c).

One of CIDA's (and MEDA's) former local NGO partners in Punjab, Karwan, received funding through the last CIDA women's fund (PAGE) to mobilize local journalists to raise the issue of *wani*. Local media support was essential to Karwan's efforts to pressure institutions to curb the practice. They also collaborated with local police and lawyers, and with journalists to highlight specific cases, which resulted in girls being saved from becoming victims of the outdated practice. In the district of Mianwali, Karwan formed citizens' networks against *wani* to act as pressure groups. Although they faced resistance from local elders and religious extremist groups, who saw them as interfering in local customs and traditions, they overcame it by continuous awareness-raising sessions and an ongoing social mobilization process with community and tribal elders, media groups, police authorities, local government officials, lawyers, religious leaders, and community groups. A documentary film was produced on Karwan's work, showcasing their awareness-raising efforts. CIDA's early funding of this type of work (from 2002) was critical to the cumulative steps that eventually led to changing the laws. In this case, the project contributed to the Amendment to the Wani Ordinance of 2006, which the women's protection bill that same year was built on. The writ filed in the Supreme Court of Pakistan for this amendment was supported mainly by the material provided by Karwan. The amendment ensured that those receiving females as settlement of murders or serious crimes through the custom of *wani* and those supporting the process could be imprisoned, thus strengthening provisions for victims and their families, and increased punitive measures (ibid).

THE HUDOOD ORDINANCES: A LINGERING BACKDROP

Some have argued that the Hudood Ordinances have been the biggest hurdle to women's rights and tackling violence against women in Pakistan. In 2009, the CIDA-commissioned report on women's human rights in Pakistan stated that for twenty-seven years, it was not possible to touch the Hudood Ordinances. No government could completely repeal them because they are seen as symbolic of Islamic law and justified by Islamist political parties on religious grounds. The Hudood Ordinances have been linked with a rise in gender violence in Pakistan (Critelli 2012, 1). Recall that it was General Zia who "revitalized the Council of Islamic Ideology to review existing laws and make recommendations for bringing them in line with Islam" (Mumtaz and Shaheed 1987, 17). This was a way of "strengthening state power through an increase in the disciplinary aspects of Shariah law" (Lieven 2011).

As far back as 2003–04, after the NCSW was established in 2000 under the military government of General Musharraf, a debate raged on the repeal of the Hudood Ordinances. A monitoring report of CIDA's Gender and Development Program in March 2004 found that Pakistani society was split on the issue. The divide between political parties and civil society was widening, and the report noted it was leading to increasing polarization within the civil society movement, particularly in cities such as Peshawar. President Musharraf had made attempts to curb the rising power of the radical and militant religious groups in the country and opened up the debate regarding the Hudood Ordinances. This led to their partial repeal through the introduction of the first Women's Protection Act in 2006 (Ahmad 2009).

The first CIDA-commissioned report on the status of women in Pakistan in 1983 contained a section on the context of Islamic law that attempted to make sense of the Islamization policy of the government. The Islamization underway in the 1980s by Zia was seen as a passing phase by many, including the West. The report's conclusion was a view commonly held in the West and by a majority of Pakistani society, and even of WAF at the time: "There is no cause to believe that under Zia, women's status will suffer any more setbacks" (Gossen 1983). Western countries did not think that the implementation of Zia's Islamization policy would last, much less change the legal code. The CIDA-commissioned Report went on to ask, "Is Islamization entrenching age-old customs and traditions in response to the desire of those who are not prepared to accept change; or is Islamization trying to make a fair interpretation of the [Islamic] laws in response to the needs of the present age?" This question was answered by WAF a few years later and their response was subsequently backed up by many analysts, legal experts, and academics – the Islamization policy was not resulting in a fair interpretation of Islamic law in the case of women, and was in fact putting in place dangerous regressions on women's rights.

The Hudood Ordinances were contested by some renowned religious scholars, such as Tufail Hashmi in his critique published by the Aurat Foundation under its legal literacy program in 2004. His book, *Hudood Ordinances in the Light of Quran and Sunnah*, launched in 2005, made a case on the misinterpretation of the Hudood Ordinances at the time of Zia-ul-Haq and identified the weakness of the Hudood Ordinances in light of the Quran.[6] "There should be no confusion that the ordinances were man-made laws, and the religious scholars should research and deeply study those," he said at the discussion organized by the Legislative Watch Group of the Aurat Foundation in 2005.[7] Dr Hashmi, who was also legal advisor to the Federal Sharia Court, said that "[t]he ordinances were discriminatory and had some lacunas which resulted in women languishing in jails for Hudood-related offences." His talk was reported widely in the media: "Hudood Ordinances are against Quran and Sunnah and have several clauses that are against Islam, which creates humanitarian, social and religious problems" (*Business Recorder*, 4 January 2005). "When one ruffles through Hudood Ordinances, it takes no time to ascertain that there are a number of misinterpretations of Islamic injunctions which need to be done away with, he added" (*Dawn News*, 4 January 2005). In their book on *Equality for Women*, the authors quote Anita Weiss

(2014) on the interpretation of the Quran: "there is no consensus as far as the interpretation of religious laws are concerned as they pertain to women in Pakistan. Instead, different voices have called for conflicting actions all based on Islam" (Claros-Lopez and Nakhjavani 2018, 155).

The year the Taliban took power in Afghanistan, CIDA sponsored a landmark international conference on "Islamic Laws and Women in the Modern World." It was 1996 and one of the first initiatives funded under the newly approved Women's Development Fund in partnership with the Pakistan-based Global Issues Awareness for National Trust. The conference chose six themes under Muslim personal laws, including women's evidence and the implementation of Hudood. Nine countries including Pakistan participated. It was an impressive start to the Women's Development Fund. The chairman of the Senate of Pakistan, Wasim Sajjad, opened the conference thusly: "Our present task is to find a common ground between the two opposing trends [modern theories of society with rigid classical Islamic norms] ... when a culture is in transition and the gap between culture and social structure is widening, ethical and religious values and the legal system which reflect those values are among the first objects of criticism and sometimes even rebellion" (Forum 1996). The prime minister concluded the conference saying that "implementation of the Hudood Ordinances are seldom considered in their historical perspective of the modern age or the need for *Ijtihad* – the process of frequently reviewing the details of the law in the light of changed circumstances and accumulated experience" (ibid.).

Women's rights activist and lawyer Rashida Patel, Advocate of the High Court and Supreme Court of Pakistan and vice-president of APWA, concluded at the same conference, "The process of Islamization of laws has not brought forth the intrinsic purity of Islam. On the contrary, it is based on and upholds centuries-old misinterpretations. The norms of Islamic justice and equity have been lost in these laws. These laws and their mal-implementation have annihilated the norms of the Quran. Concerted bold steps need to be taken to bring back a sense of justice and equity in Pakistan." A study by Rashida Patel on Islamic law as it pertains to women's rights as early as 1979 found that the Superior Courts of Pakistan had in a few cases reinterpreted Islamic Law, differing from earlier misinterpretation, and that "changes by judicial decisions are still few and far between and the women of Pakistan continue to suffer from age-old customs and tradition, and are borne down under misinterpreted Islamic Law" (Patel 1979, 22, found in Gossen 1983, 24).[8]

The conference (and the book published on its proceedings) appears to be the last public advocacy for women's legal rights that CIDA supported before the policy shifts to women's economic empowerment – although the WDPr did later fund, in 2004, an initiative by an organization called Rahm to develop a cadre of resource persons from two government universities to present a balanced perspective of gender issues in Islam. It also raised awareness through workshops with civil society and educational institutions in all the provincial capitals. The 2006 evaluation saw this sub-project as a strategic initiative, "given the conservative backlash being experienced by the women's movement in many Muslim countries in reaction to the western/American approach to the 'war on terrorism'" (Moffat and Ehsan 2006, 11–15).

Even the amended Hudood Ordinances retained "the roots of religious extremism" and discrimination by "criminalizing zina (adultery) and allowing testimony only by Muslim males in Hadd cases" (International Crisis Group 2015, 4n24). The *Hadd*[9] (Islamic punishment or retribution), or stoning to death in *zina* cases (the punishment decreed by the Quran), has never been used by the state. Strengthening laws criminalizing rape and sexual violence are "key successes in the struggle to eliminate discrimination against women," according to the UN Expert Panel on discrimination against women in law and in the practice of the UN Human Rights Council in 2018. Despite the passage of the women's protection bills in 2011, and steady progress made by women's rights activists to erode the Hudood Ordinances, they may continue to undermine women's rights until they are repealed in their entirety, according to some analysts. Premarital sex remains a crime in Pakistan under the Hudood Ordinances for both men and women and carries a five-year prison sentence. A groundbreaking ruling by the Lahore high court on 4 January 2021 outlawed virginity tests for female rape victims, saying there was no legal basis for them. The ruling was to apply only in the state of Punjab. The female judge, Ayesha Malik, said it "offends the personal dignity of the female victim … it is a humiliating practice, which is used to cast suspicion on the victim as opposed to focusing on the accused and the incident of sexual violence" (*Guardian* 2021). Justice Ayesha Malik was appointed to the Supreme Court in 2022, "a watershed moment in the history of Pakistan," said many Pakistanis on social media, and a strong signal for gender justice going forward.

PART TWO

Gender Equality in Dangerous Places

8

The Dark Years in Afghanistan

The wars in Afghanistan, beginning with the American-backed war against the Soviets in the early 1980s, had a profound impact on Pakistan. Afghanistan was in chaos by 1992, with the Mujaheddin (often called holy warriors) about to defeat the weak communist government, and elements of what was to become the Taliban coalescing. I was based in Ottawa at the time, handling some Pakistan files and the few Afghanistan projects CIDA had with UN agencies, but was unable to travel officially to Afghanistan due to security restrictions since things were getting dangerous. Canada's aid program to Pakistan was still one of CIDA's top three, but Canadian aid was almost nonexistent in Afghanistan. Despite the American sense of accomplishment at the departure of the Soviet Union from Afghanistan, the situation was far from ideal there, with the Mujaheddin fighting among themselves and the consolidation of the Taliban beginning to play out a narrative that was not what the West wanted but to which everyone had, at least publicly, turned a blind eye.

After the Soviet withdrawal from Afghanistan in February 1989, "the US lost interest in Afghanistan" (Gannon, AP News, 15 February 2020). American aid to Afghanistan was cut, and aid to Pakistan significantly reduced, despite the influx of more than two million Afghan refugees – later increasing to three million, making Pakistan host to one of the largest refugee populations in the world. The US also put sanctions on Pakistan over its nuclear weapons program. CIDA analysis of the Pakistan aid program strategy a year later concluded that "[t]he dramatic scale-back of US assistance to Pakistan had ramifications and led to the strengthening of Pakistan's relations with Saudi Arabia" (CIDA 1991). Pakistan had been receiving support from Saudi Arabia throughout the period of Zia's rule, particularly for the Afghan Mujaheddin groups and a network of madrassas along the border with Afghanistan, but Pakistan felt betrayed by the US and further solidified its relations with Saudi Arabia under Nawaz Sharif as prime minister. (Saudi Arabia also supported the Afghan refugee camps near Peshawar.) The unsettled situation in Afghanistan after the departure of the Soviets and the fall of the communist government, coupled with the reduction of American presence and support in both Afghanistan and Pakistan, created a vacuum that cast a shadow of uncertainty on the region.

For Canada, the early-1990s period of return to civilian rule and democracy in Pakistan saw a surge of Canadian aid for civil society organizations and a shift of funding from women-in-development–type projects to women's rights. As American aid declined, Canada increased aid, which was directed more to Pakistani NGOs and civil society than to government – a nuance perhaps to demonstrate concern over the nuclear program. Under a new goal of fostering sustainable development, CIDA's support for social development, gender equity, and environmental programs through Pakistani NGOs was aimed at standing up a critical pillar of democracy: civil society and pluralism.

CIDA funding for women's rights began earnestly in the early 1990s under the second women's support fund. It marked a change in aid strategy from women in development, which had focused on women's basic needs and capacity development, to a gender and development (GAD) focus on women's rights.[1] The 1990s was the decade of support for democratization and social development by international development agencies. Indicative of the time, the World Bank launched its major (and often criticized) ten-year Social Action Program, implemented from 1993 to 2003. CIDA supported its design on gender and on increasing positions for women working in basic health services. In 1999 CIDA signed a project for $6.7 million with the government on communications within the social action program to improve the quality of work in all sectors covered by the program.

As Canada stepped up funding for civil society and innovative and progressive projects in Pakistan, we mostly ignored Afghanistan from a policy perspective, aligning with the Americans in the post-Soviet withdrawal, leaving the flailing communist government to struggle against the Mujaheddin and a rising powerful Taliban. I recall UN officials coming to meet me as the Afghan desk officer in Ottawa to plead for drug control and other programs that Canada had little funding for. I didn't know what to say – there was no funding available. No Western aid donor was providing any significant aid to Afghanistan, and CIDA didn't pay much attention to the UN request. The result of the entire international community turning its back on Afghanistan, and American inattention to the armed Islamic fighters they left behind in the border areas of Pakistan, is now well-known – Afghanistan spiralled further into poverty and isolation, coupled with the rise of an army of armed militants. The country became, along with the border areas inside Pakistan, a haven for the Taliban, al-Qaeda, and Osama bin Laden after 9/11. Bin Laden had assisted Afghanistan in the 1990s, "pouring money into the parched economy, for roads and power plants and set up a network of camps and fortifications to house hundreds of terrorists in training as well as a private militia" (Miller, Stone, and Mitchell 2002).

The communist government in Afghanistan fell by 1993 after several years of bitter fighting by the US-backed Mujaheddin, which included the Haqqani network from Pakistan.[2] It was two years after the collapse of the Soviet Union and the end of the Cold War. The Mujaheddin continued fighting with each other over the next two years, wreaking havoc on Afghan society and creating more vulnerability by killing tens of thousands of civilians. Some of these Mujaheddin went on to join the Taliban, who rose to power by 1996, were pushed out by the Americans in 2001, and took control of Afghanistan again in 2021.

THE FORMATION OF THE AFGHAN TALIBAN AND DEMOCRACY IN PAKISTAN

In September 1994, after arriving and checking in at the familiar secure Holiday Inn in Islamabad, my colleague and I decided to visit the famous weekly Afghan market in Islamabad to browse Afghan carpets, antiquities, and jewelry placed alongside the numerous items left behind by Russian soldiers. It was not unusual to find rare Afghan antiquities for a low price. People in Islamabad recall that busy weekly Afghan market and its treasures with nostalgia. It was a destination during every aid mission to Pakistan: a display of remnants of a failed Russian war beside beautiful pieces of tasteful Afghan culture, sadly being sold at a rock bottom price.

Returning to the hotel, we stopped for lunch at the Chinese restaurant to prepare for our first set of meetings. We were there to plan CIDA support to Pakistan's new National Conservation Strategy, initiated by Aban Kabraji, head of IUCN Pakistan (and a key founder of WAF). Sitting two tables away from us was Boutros Boutros-Ghali, then-Secretary General of the UN, in an intense private meeting with Pakistani officials. He was staying in the hotel to attend the meeting of the Organization of Islamic Countries (OIC), at which Pakistan gave its support for the Middle East peace process. Were they discussing the Middle East or the rise of the Taliban, consolidating next door in Kandahar? I wondered. My colleague was intent on watching the historic meeting, pondering what was being discussed. I was impatient to get on with the demanding work we had at hand, designing a large-scale environmental policy program for CIDA funding. But it was an historic moment, so we lingered over our tea watching the meeting with the UN Secretary General.

The OIC conference was opened by Benazir Bhutto, prime minister of the Islamic Republic of Pakistan at the time. The conference communiqué of 7–9 September 1994 stated:

> She welcomed the participating delegations. In her truly inspiring inaugural address, the Prime Minister presented the vision of a politically enlightened, economically vibrant, and socially advanced Muslim Ummah, in harmony with itself, playing a vital role in the maintenance of international peace and progress as the world moves into the new millennium.

At the same time across the border, "a group of men led by Mullah Omar lynched a warlord and his henchmen for killing a boy after raping him. That incident heralded the formation of a Taliban militia, which captured the Afghan capital, Kabul, two years later and established its repressive regime, especially for women and girls" (Hussain 2010). They instituted a Virtue and Vice Minister in charge of the religious police, banned girls' education, forbade women from working, banned music and television, and forced women to wear complete burqas in public, covering them head to toe. The Ministry was later banned by President Karzai but reinstated in 2021 by the Taliban de facto regime, as the Ministry for Prohibiting Vice and Enforcing Virtue. For women in Afghanistan, 1994 was a milestone year marking the beginning of what was to be a very dark period as the Taliban visibly emerged.

In Pakistan, it was a time of growth for the gender equality movement; but religious conservative elements were also consolidating while the return to civilian rule and democracy was being heralded. Those working at odds with the objectives of the gender equality movement included Farhat Hashmi, the woman whom some have called a product of the Zia era. She began the Al Huda[3] Institute of schools for women in her home in Pakistan in 1994 and continues to lecture on her approach to conservative Islam.[4] Farhat Hashmi, who regularly lectures by video in Mississauga, advocates hijab and the importance of women veiling as a duty to Allah, and encourages purdah, the segregation of women from men and strangers. In addition, the cultural directions supported in Al Huda discourage listening to music, dancing at weddings, celebrating birthdays, watching films or entertainment on television, reading fiction, and spending time with male friends, as behaviours that are considered inappropriate and not in line with Islam (Ahmad 2009). Ahmad's analysis of the Al Huda schools also shows that "they promote an Islamic identity for women that can be seen as exclusionary and isolationist, separating women from others of different cultural and religious backgrounds" (ibid.).

> Hashmi was setting new social and moral standards for Pakistani society, going even further than what had been achieved by Zia and edging closer to full Saudi-style Wahhabi Islam, with a complete rejection of all accretions or even traditional culture in general, in a country where music, poetry, dance and literature were part of the DNA, where even trucks [were] decorated with an explosion of artful color ... there was never any open call for violence, but the women were increasingly isolated from society, encased in a set of rigid rules that made them intolerant of other ways – an unhealthy fanaticism, a kind of latent radicalism. (Ghattas 2020, 261)

The juxtaposition of Canada's support for Pakistani groups promoting women's rights and equality with the growth of ultraconservative trends exemplified in the Al Huda schools for educated women in Pakistan (which later opened in Canada) is worth more than a few minutes of reflection. Canada later unwittingly strengthened the organization's reach across borders to North America by accepting Hashmi's immigration in 2005, even as it worked at cross purposes to the efforts and values of the feminist movement in Pakistan and promoted anti-Western views. There was seemingly little acknowledgment or understanding of this trend in society within the embassy or coming from CIDA's Pakistani advisors or partners and what it could mean for aid and gender equality efforts.

In her book *Transforming Faith, the Story of Al-Huda and Islamic Revivalism among Urban Pakistani Women*, Sadaf Ahmad reflects, "philosophies such as the one permeating Al Huda ... leave no space for multiple truths." In contrast to the growing movement of Al Huda schools from the mid-1990s to now, encouraging ultra-conservative Islamic approaches towards women's behaviour, Canada was rapidly increasing funding support to Pakistani organizations that were promoting a different approach to women's rights and development.

SCALING UP FUNDING FOR WOMEN'S RIGHTS IN PAKISTAN

In 1996, the year the Taliban took power in Kabul, and only months after the historic Beijing Women's Conference in September 1995 on Equality, Development and Peace, CIDA launched the pioneering Women's Development Project Fund for Pakistan (WDPr 1996–2002). The WDPr started implementation during the period of Taliban rule in Afghanistan, and on the cusp of what was to become known as the "Talibanization" of society in Pakistan. It was a dark period for women in Afghanistan, but in Pakistan, it was still a period of growth of the gender equality movement and increased support for women's equality, despite the deepening of the backlash extremist forces were unleashing against women's rights.

The $4 million fund was the most significant funding for women's rights and women's organizations of any of CIDA's global programs. It was the fourth consecutive women's fund in Pakistan and the main mechanism for channelling Canadian aid directly to Pakistani women's organizations during 1996–2001. In 2000, the UK's aid agency, the former DFID, modelled the fund – a recognition (among aid donors) of CIDA's forward-leaning and ground-breaking approach. The fund put the focus squarely on women's rights and equality, with the intent to grow and strengthen women's organizations working at the policy and grassroots levels and support the feminist movement. This approach became a priority of Canada's Feminist International Assistance Policy (FIAP) over two decades later and of the global compact on women, peace, and security in 2021. A call to action in 2020 to commemorate the twenty-fifth anniversary of the Beijing platform for financing women's rights and strengthening feminist movements echoed CIDA's early approach of supporting the vibrant feminist community in Pakistan.

Meanwhile, next door in Afghanistan, the UN appealed for $133 million in humanitarian aid, especially for the plight of a large number of widows in Kabul (as a result of war), but received a fraction of the appeal. When Madelaine Albright visited an Afghan refugee camp in Peshawar in November 1997, she "denounced the Taliban's policies toward women as 'despicable.'" Former ambassador Robin Raphel, later a senior US State Department advisor on Afghanistan, recalls in *Ghost Wars*, "The US was open to talking with the Taliban regime initially, but the outrage at the severe curtailing of women's rights and the Sharia law public punishments quickly changed that" (Coll 2004). Hilary Clinton also took up the mantle of women's rights, and, speaking at the UN at the time, said, "even now, the Taliban in Afghanistan are blocking girls from attending schools" (ibid.). Upon their return to power in 2021, the Afghan Taliban immediately blocked girls from attending high school, justifying it based on "references to national custom and tradition" (Rubin 2022).

The Afghan Taliban had implemented an extreme interpretation of Sharia law "that appalled many Afghans and the Muslim world" (A. Rashid 2001, 2). Their actions, now well known, included closing girls' schools, limiting women's freedom of movement, and banning girls' education and women from the workplace, including those working for international organizations. Women were not to be seen or heard – essentially erased from public life. The Taliban chose women as the symbol of implementing their interpretation of Islamic law. In the words of Ahmed Rashid, the Taliban had "inspired" a new extremist form of fundamentalism across Pakistan (ibid.), symbolized most vividly by the treatment of women and seen to be reversing gains in equality between men and women and rights which women in the West had fought for so hard. By 1999, a unanimous resolution of the UN Security Council censured the Taliban for its treatment of Afghan women on grounds of undertaking discriminatory practices towards women. Ironically, in 2022 the UN Security Council again issued statements to the Taliban condemning their restrictions on women (on 29 August, 27 December, and also on 27 April 2023).

> The Taliban have increasingly restricted the exercise of basic human rights, including freedom of peaceful assembly, freedom of opinion and expression, quelling dissent and restricting civic

space ... [these restrictions] aim at the rights and freedoms of Afghan women and girls, limiting their involvement in social, political and economic life, including the ban on secondary schooling for girls and the decision to impose face coverings on women. (Ramiz Alakbarov, Deputy Special Representative of the UNSG in Afghanistan, 23 June 2022, speaking to the UNSC)

SHIFTS TO THE CONCEPT OF GENDER EQUITY

By 1994, Canadian government policy on gender equality underwent a shift. At the corporate level, CIDA established a WID and Gender Equity Division in HQ that year, and in 1995 updated the 1984 WID policy to include the concept of gender equity. It was described as a policy shift, although what this means is hard to determine. It appeared to be a new emphasis on women's rights as opposed to basic needs, but the description was not much different from the past policy statement: identifying equality of women as a priority and the full participation of women as equal partners in sustainable development of their societies. The publication of the 1995 corporate policy on women in development and gender equity coincided with the fourth global conference on women in Beijing in 1995, which elevated women's rights in government policy agendas everywhere. It changed forever the view that feminism was a Western-only concept. The WID approach was buried with the new emphasis on women's rights and equality, with barely a decade of attempts at its implementation. Soon the term was no longer used and quickly became outdated. The 1999 Policy on Gender Equality – a much more substantive revision of the 1995 policy – made clear the policy shift to the human rights of women and girls (as discussed in chapter 4).

Mirroring CIDA's new corporate policy development on gender equity, the Pakistan Program published a new strategy document, *From Plan to Action ... CIDA's Women in Development Program in Pakistan*, which was a revision of the 1986 WID strategy, *Nation Builders*. First revised in 1991, it was modified again in 1995 to articulate the change to a "gender equity approach with an emphasis on improving the position [rights] as well as the condition of women" (Moffat and Ehsan 2006). This time the revised strategy acknowledged the negative impact of discriminatory Sharia laws on justice for women and on the "misuse of Islamic teachings ... and various interpretations of Islam as a means of maintaining control and oppressing women"

(CIDA 1995). It referred specifically to the Law of Evidence (1984) and the Hudood Ordinances (1979) as "Pakistani laws (that) openly discriminate against women" (CIDA 1995, 31) in its section on Human Rights called "Protect and Promote the Human Rights of Women." This was the first time a CIDA strategy on gender equality had mentioned the negative impact of the Hudood Ordinances since the 1983 study, which had left the question open. It was a significant change from the previous strategies, which had either excluded or bypassed the discriminatory laws as either too insignificant to warrant much attention or analysis, or too sensitive and politicized an issue for development programs. It was the first aid strategy to identify some of the indicators such as the Hudood Ordinances' impact on women's rights. But there was no substantial analysis of implications of the societal trends on gender equality programming, nor any direct response strategy. The broader CIDA program frameworks and plans had not yet picked up any of this type of gender analysis. The first mention of the discriminatory and controversial laws in the wider Program strategies was five years later, in the 2001 Country Program Framework, completed just before 9/11. Ten years after the first CIDA WID strategy, and twelve years after WAF sounded the alarm on the implications of regressive policies and laws on the status of women, there was finally acknowledgment in development sector strategies, by CIDA and other aid donors, of the negative impact of the laws that were openly discriminating against women and inhibiting meaningful progress on gender equality. Although the analysis was thin, and it did not directly mention other signs or risks of backlash against gender equality efforts (as political Islam and violent extremists were still not well understood as a force for reversing women's rights in the 1990s), it was nevertheless there.

— * —

The Women's Development Project Fund was followed by another large responsive fund approved by CIDA a year after 9/11, the Program for the Advancement of Gender Equality (PAGE). Because of the WDPF's success in directing support to civil society activists, many of them feminist organizations, the PAGE Fund put an even greater emphasis on women's human rights, violence reduction, political participation, and economic empowerment and less on women's basic needs in health and education. Its budget of $7 million and the increase to $9 million in 2005 (following the 2003 post-9/11 relevancy review of CIDA's Pakistan Program strategy) reflected not only the central role of gender equality in the CIDA Pakistan Country Program Framework of 2001–02, but also the priority on directing funding to women's rights. PAGE had more success than its predecessor in reaching women in conservative communities facing higher gender disparities (such as in parts of KP province and ex-FATA regions), and developed initial strategies that were showing signs of success by 2007, with plans to broaden this work.

Although not intended to counter extremist tendencies manifesting in society, the work of groups supported by Canada under the women's funds over the period of the growth of violent extremism reveal key insights into approaches that are now considered pre-emptive or have the ability to help counter extremist narratives. A review of the five women's funds over the twenty years between 1989 and 2009 contain significant findings (chapter 10 takes a closer look) on the role of women's groups and organizations in countering extremist narratives, in taking leadership roles locally on pushing back on extremism ideology and potentially helping to prevent radicalization.

In the political and security sectors, the attention to women's rights and development strategies and programs for gender equality was still superficial at best. Had there been more attention paid to the analysis on women's rights and gender equality challenges in 1995 and better coherence among policy analysts from the aid, political, and security departments, the world might have seen the early warning signs of the future spread of violent extremism. The rise of the Taliban in Afghanistan and the spillover of violent extremist groups into Pakistan were having a deep effect on the Pakistani state and society. The implications for women and the state of gender equality were under the radar, yet to be fully manifest and understood. It was not yet a time of prevention, pre-empting, or mitigation of these developments. In Afghanistan, even the UN ignored the treatment of women and the ban on girls' education (Gannon 2005) at the time. The UN Special Envoy tasked with brokering a peace deal between the Mujaheddin and the Taliban said at a news conference, "don't talk to me about women. I don't mention women. That is a cultural issue. I am trying to negotiate peace" (Gannon 2005).

9

The Golden Years for Civil Society in Pakistan

While the situation darkened for women in Afghanistan during the 1990s, it was an active period of growth of civil society and rights-based organizations in Pakistan. It became the golden years of aid support to civil society, social development, and the promotion of democracy, and the years on which CIDA's legacy in Pakistan as a forward-looking and progressive aid donor was built. And although the 1990s have been called the democratic period in Pakistan (because of the move away from the military dictatorship of the 1980s), the situation of radical Islamists across the border, spiralling Afghanistan into its darkest period, was reverberating in Pakistan.

I had heard much about Canada's legacy of helping to build civil society in Pakistan not long after starting my assignment in 2010 from many corners, including all the heads of NGOs and think tanks who paid official visits to the embassy hoping for continued funding. In our conversations they recalled the years of the special relationship and partnership with Canada and how CIDA funding had created strong networks across civil society through the South Asia Partnership in Pakistan (SAP-PK), Strengthening Participatory Organizations (SPO), Aurat Foundation, Sustainable Development Policy Institute (SDPI), Sungi, and the Aga Khan Rural Support Program (Moffat and Ehsan 2006), to name a few. It was at one of the not-to-be-missed networking dinners hosted by the UN Women representative that I was reminded of this unique history of Canadian aid. The house and patio were full of an interesting mix of intellectuals, artists, activists, and officials, including a group of CIDA's key Pakistani development experts and advisors. Before the buffet dinner and BBQ was served and dancing started, they talked excitedly about those years of collaboration and partnership: "This is a story that needs to be told and Canada should get credit for it." Under the colourful outdoor tent in the garden, lit by hundreds of small lights, we discussed the growth of civil society in the 1990s; the stimulating atmosphere of art, music, and intellectual discussion and great food fuelled our discussion and my interest to investigate this Canadian aid legacy that appeared to be slipping into obscurity.

The story was that Canada had supported the growth of a vibrant civil society working for democracy, human rights and social development, and the uplifting of the rural poor at a crucial time in Pakistan. The 1990s had begun badly for Pakistan in its relationship with the Americans, who had applied sanctions for the nuclear weapons program and cut aid. CIDA, in contrast, increased aid funding during this period. In 2001, the CIDA program strategy identified in its lessons learned that "the capacity of civil society in Pakistan to contribute to democratic development and the delivery of social services is a well established and relatively reliable avenue for channelling donor support" (CIDA 2001). "CIDA funding has had considerable success in supporting the creation and development of civil society organizations ... this should be built on," said the Goss Gilroy evaluation report of the aid program in 2006.

For years CIDA supported the expansion of progressive and innovative approaches to human development and poverty reduction and building awareness among rural communities and oppressed parts of the population of their rights (political, humanitarian, justice, socio-economic). The civil society movement worked hand in hand with the move to foster democracy, the women's movement, and organizations striving for equality for women. CIDA supported the establishment of the NGO called the South Asia Partnership Pakistan, working to uplift marginalized populations, and funded the creation of new leading-edge think tanks such as SDPI. Building the capacity of activist groups, policy institutes, and women's organizations was a major objective including funding human rights training in Canada for many of their staff. These groups had a rural development focus and extensive grassroots outreach, which CIDA support helped them sustain. Support was also given to university partnerships that lasted decades, such as the McMaster University School of Nursing relationship with the Aga Khan University for the establishment of its school of nursing and the development of women health professionals (1994–2001), and later the McGill University relationship with the Lahore University of Management Sciences for capacity development of NGOs working at community and district levels.

In 1987, CIDA created and sustained, for over a decade, what became a leading rights-based NGO in Pakistan, Strengthening Participatory Organizations or SPO. It was registered as an independent non-profit in 1993 and remains an active rights-based organization working in social development and gender transformation.[1] First called the Small Projects Office of CIDA, it was created out of excess local funds from the sale of Canadian commodities to the government. In 1993, it was transformed into an independent NGO with the guidance of Tariq Banuri, Ferida Sher, and Javed Jabbar working with Ralph McKim, the Canadian Program manager. In a conversation in Canada Ralph recalled, "With CIDA and several influential Pakistani development practitioners, we began the transition of SPO from a funding agency to a capacity-building entity, from Small Projects Office to Supporting Participatory Organizations (SPO) from a bilateral agreement with government to a Pakistani non-governmental organization. From there SPO went on to greater things." It was then renamed to Strengthening Participatory Organizations.

One of my last events in Islamabad as Head of Cooperation was attending the twentieth anniversary of SPO at the Marriott Hotel in 2013. It was nostalgic for many that day, including me, as it recalled brighter days of SPO's rise in its fight for human rights, gender equality, and the uplifting of the poor. The Marriott Hotel ballroom (having recovered from the 2008 bombing) was as usual decorated with bouquets of gladiolas and gilded, gold-trim-upholstered chairs and banners for the event. The panel on the platform was an array of SPO's past leadership, including some of the feminists who had formed WAF and fought in the early days for women's rights against the Islamization policy of Zia. Celebrating the past progress on social development was somewhat muted that day by the pressures being faced by civil society from the government, together with reduced funding from donors, as frequent suicide bombings and terrorist attacks were still taking place around the country. The security issues faced by such organizations and their staff were the unspoken but present thoughts on everyone's mind.

CAPACITY-BUILDING OF GRASSROOTS WOMEN'S ORGANIZATIONS

The work of Strengthening Participatory Organizations with grassroots women's organizations was a unique early endeavour, likely due to the feminist leaders such as Ferida Sher on its board. In 1991 SPO began to support "rural community-based organizations and adopt a more supportive role concentrated on capacity building" (Canadian High Commission Pakistan 2000). As early as 1996–97, it established a Women's Emancipation Program, which promoted the formation of community-based women's groups. Between 1993 and 2003 alone, SPO helped establish and fund 305 localized grassroots women's organizations. In 1999 it strengthened its national centre and regional office in Multan to build capacity at the grassroots in communities so that "residents work cooperatively to take charge of their own problems and solve them" (Naqeeb 2006). The book SPO, *A Brief History*, compiled in Pakistan, contains lessons from the 1990s on this early work of supporting grassroots women's organizations.

SPO's emphasis on establishing and building capacity and funding local women's organizations throughout 1994–97 coincided with the rise to power of the Taliban in Afghanistan and their oppressive policy towards women. While women in Afghanistan were being visibly stripped of basic rights, in Pakistan, SPO mobilized and funded grassroots women's organizations under their capacity-building program, called the 'Development Planning and Management Program' or DPM. At least twenty-seven grassroots women's organizations were formed, and many more received *choti* or micro-funding (approximately $1,000) out of SPO's Social Sector Fund to provide them institutional core support. In 1996–97 three special multi-year programs on village education for women were undertaken in rural Balochistan, KP, and Sindh provinces. In 1998–99 five women's "clusters" developed, and fifty-five female groups were formed, of which seventeen women's organizations completed the full DPM capacity-building program and graduated to become Female Development Organizations, which were then eligible for the SPO social sector fund grants. SPO's role since 1994 in organizational capacity-strengthening of women's organizations is precisely what the 2017 Feminist International Assistance Policy called for more than twenty years later. The work of these pioneers in the field laid the groundwork for the broader policy response decades later. Many Canadian NGOs and women's organizations were voicing the need for this type of work since the 2017 FIAP policy launched. The period marked a notable shift away from basic needs to capacity-building for grassroots women's organizations.

By 2002–03, women's groups mobilized under the village education programs were transformed into women's organizations with expanded scope and activities through SPO's training and workshops for community-based organizations or CBOs. The attacks of 9/11 hampered SPO's efforts to mobilize female groups and caused a setback in SPO's women's emancipation program in the Northwest Frontier province (now KP). Women were "discouraged from continuing their association with an internationally funded NGO by hostile elements within their communities" (Naqeeb 2006). The extremists were becoming bolder and the threat to the state from rising militancy more severe. The hardest-to-reach women living in the border areas of Pakistan with Afghanistan, whose rights either have never been realized or are under assault due to security and conflict concerns, are still the most difficult to reach for NGOs. After 9/11, despite a great deal of effort by the women's fund staff, very few projects manifested in these remote areas. By 2004, PAGE staff elicited only one project in Balochistan, the province where violence against women – mainly honour killings and domestic violence – has increased steadily. The project did, however, take what the staff called a cluster approach, providing strategic support by grooming a group of local NGOs with gender-focused capacity-building (Moffat and Ehsan 2006, 9-1).[2] 2020 saw record cases of violence against women recorded in that province (Quettavoice, October 2020). "Impunity is the underlying factor behind violence against women," said Advocate Ishaq Khan Nasar (Quettavoice, June 2020). CIDA's 2008 strategy had a special program to support socio-economic development in Balochistan in support of Canadian interests in Afghanistan. A separate proposal for Balochistan was developed for strategic consideration under Canada's engagement strategy for Pakistan in 2009–10, but it never materialized.

THE AGA KHAN RURAL SUPPORT PROGRAM WOMEN'S ORGANIZATIONS

AKRSP, with CIDA funding (as the first donor to support AKRSP), mobilized women's groups and built their capacity in the northern Gilgit-Baltistan region starting in 1983. It was the most significant development project in Pakistan that targeted rural women, and the first that facilitated the formation and funding of village-based women's groups. The cornerstone of AKRSP's approach was to encourage women to form women's organizations to pool assets and use them to improve household income. They went on to support gender programs for over thirty years, supported by multiple donors (USAID, DFID, the World Bank), although Canada remained a strategic partner. AKRSP forged a long partnership with CIDA (S. Khan 2009) that continues today.

AKRSP has documented its experiences working with women's organizations from Gilgit and Baltistan in various commissioned reports. The creation of women's organizations (WOs) provided a collective way of supporting self-reliance. The formation and development of the WOs has also been critical in improving the mobility and confidence of women, enabling them to participate in local development processes. AKRSP supported the establishment of women-only markets and women's multi-purpose centres and shops. "Given the socio-cultural context and segregation in most AKRSP communities along with the very different circumstances for women than men, the women-only activities were often a useful approach up until the present day in Gilgit-Baltistan" (Jones 2012).

The original intent of the WOs was to integrate women into the development process, "to generate equity capital for common projects; and accept responsibility for collective effort."[3] "Generating equity capital" refers to the formation of savings groups that would contribute to village projects (e.g., skills-building programs for youth, equipment for economic activities) but also provide a pool of money against which village women could borrow for their own needs. This latter function was and continues to be a strong motivator for women to join a WO (ibid.). Women were encouraged to form organizations to improve household income. Generation of their own capital through "savings gave women a new kind of empowerment ... Savings also enabled easy access to credit and built the capacity of women's organizations to manage village organization banking" (S. Khan 2009). The creation of Village and Women's Organizations and the federation of these into Local Support Organizations has been extensively covered in AKRSP reports to CIDA (Jones 2012, n3).

AKRSP went on to support small-scale income-generating projects for women and vocational training. AKRSP "has been one of the pioneers in developing a unique service delivery approach to women's development, by focusing on building collective strength and capacity of women" (Gloekler 2003). "One of the most powerful outcomes of AKRSP's community development approach has been the education of girls. The combination of increased household incomes and the empowerment of women through women's organizations paved the way for more girls to go to school, contributing to the high literacy rate among women in the region" (Aga Khan Foundation Canada 2006). Some of these women then supported their daughters to attend university outside of the region. WOs have filled many roles over the years in the AKRSP Program – savings services, a conduit for AKRSP programs and grants, selection of trainees and agricultural specialists, and a place for women to collectively discuss and solve problems (Jones 2012).

It was these localized women's community-based organizations that made the difference. In contrast is the situation of women in the newly merged tribal districts near the Afghan border, which have suffered from conflict and not received the commensurate level of development support during the same period, where the indicators tell the story. Women's literacy rates are abysmally low at 13 per cent, their movement constricted, and they usually remain confined to the home. The area has been plagued by terrorism and has been a home to violent militants for years (UN Women Pakistan 2020). The Rural Support Programs Network mentioned above was built on the success of AKRSP and its approach to supporting people as protagonists of their own development. The program set up in KP province, the Sarhad Rural Support Program, initially funded by USAID and the provincial government, has brought the lessons of the AKRSP program to the area, as seen by their participation as the Canadian partner in women's economic empowerment projects.

> AKRSP had always taken certain gender issues into account (e.g., segregation, mobility) long before the approach became fashionable in development, and to some extent this is the reason that women-focused programs worked so well to catalyze change in the more remote and conservative communities of Gilgit-Baltistan. (Jones 2012, 28)

In the 1990s, AKRSP initiated small infrastructure projects in water supply schemes, adult literacy, and an accelerated professional development program for women for degrees in natural resource management. But AKRSP, too, became "vulnerable to pressure from the outside regarding women's activities, particularly from religious leaders ... resulting in the women's program coming to a halt in Baltistan and Chitral in the late 1990s" (Gloekler and Seeley 2003). Gender and women's programs faced resistance from religious and conservative forces and, in response, tended to "follow a policy of compliance" (ibid.), taking a practical approach to women's development utilizing its strength in service delivery and capacity-building. This may have been a reaction to the increasing involvement of women in local politics and their gaining seats on the district councils, resulting from AKRSP focus on individual capacity-building and women's empowerment. It is also indicative of what some religious leaders and extremists such as the Taliban fear: the empowerment of women.

In a meeting with the vice chair of the Aga Khan Development Network at the Aga Khan University in Karachi in 2011, Sohail Khan told me that their health services program was using the AKRSP women's community collective savings groups in Chitral for maternal and child health initiatives reaching the ultra-poor, which Canada had funded as part of the G7 Commitment the previous year. As we admired the beautifully built university, he praised the thirty-plus years of partnership with CIDA and how it had helped over a million lives and built sustainable development in Pakistan.

A year later, flying in the Aga Khan helicopter, I hoped to witness the legacy of the CIDA-AKF partnership on women's development. Manoeuvring between some of the highest mountains in the world, the pilot landed atop a mountainous plateau in Baltistan. We disembarked and walked down to the village to meet the community. The historic Sost tunnel, built with CIDA funds and constructed by one of the first village organizations under AKRSP, was nearby. The original stone that marked its foundation had the year 1983 and AKRSP, CIDA visibly carved into it. The tunnel was still in use as community infrastructure for water control. As we visited communities in remote villages, it appeared that progress had been made, but the other legacy was the many faded and rusty CIDA signs with the Canadian flag along many roads in the area.

We gathered for a small ceremony in a tiny village. The community leader spoke, and the women came forward to place traditional colourful hats on our heads. I was asked to sign a ragged guestbook – dating back to the early 1990s when I had last worked on the Pakistan program. In it were the names and original ink signatures of one of the CIDA program managers who had visited in 1991. Not so many had signed since and I think I was the third one after the mid-1990s.

Clearly Canada was the main visitor, but the community had carefully preserved the book despite the lack of visitors notable since security concerns began to detract from diplomatic travel.

AKRSP, like CIDA itself, was going through a transition after doing the same work in the same areas for so many decades but finding that sustaining it at scale was costly under reduced aid budgets. With funding getting harder to obtain, especially from Canada, could AKRSP continue? These were also questions the organization was asking itself at the time. I felt that I was witnessing the end of an era that had delivered innovative, leading-edge development results in communities, but was struggling with the perplexing issue of how to scale up meaningful jobs and entrepreneurship to meet demand, especially among youth. "There was a heavy reliance on AKRSP as a provider of services that could only be sustained as long as the specific program was funded" (Jones 2012). This was the same conundrum CIDA was facing in its bilateral WEE projects – how long could what were considered high-cost projects be continued? The CIDA partnership with AKRSP for this work has since been able to evolve and expand successfully with continued aid funding.

Sectarian violence had also manifested in northern Pakistan, brewing since the 1990s. By 2012 Shias accounted for 70 per cent of the victims of sectarian attacks of car bombs and suicide bombs during religious processions. Just a few weeks after our visit, a bus in Gilgit-Baltistan was stopped by militants and Shia men were pulled out and shot (August 2012). It was the third time that year Shia men had been targeted in such a way in Pakistan (Ghattas 2020). AKF had done a case study on sectarian problems and the potential for tensions. Linda Jones's report from her fieldwork in 2012 mentioned that "in most places, the effect of conservative belief systems is lessening its impact on day-to-day life and women's economic empowerment" (Jones 2012, 43). As violence ebbed and rose, it was a confusing situation to understand, and it was dealt with as one-off incidents. AKRSP was also working in the Kalash Valley region of KP province, an area affected by sporadic violent extremism. No one wanted to consider what the longer-term implications were, despite the trends. CIDA and AKF did not acknowledge the shrinking space for development projects and the change in the context from the 1980s and 1990s. The government restricted travel to the north around 2012 (which some years later opened again). I wondered at the time how the current corporate CIDA Gender Equality Action Plan of 2010–13 would guide development officers in dealing with security issues stemming from violent extremism and sectarianism affecting gender equality programs.

Looking at the AKRSP example provides a lens into aid approaches working at the grassroots with women that helped community-building, stimulated small-scale local economic development to fight poverty, and supported inclusion and social cohesion as much as was possible given sectarian tensions. The AKRSP model has helped establish other rural support programs, many of them as part of the (N)RSPN network. The model is an example of integrated programming at community level designed to make communities resilient to shocks and external influences (such as violent extremism). There are many other successful development models in Pakistan, many without any external financing, but AKRSP was chosen here as an example of Canada's early commitment to supporting gender equality at the grassroots with a community-based focus, and of a longstanding partnership with AKRSP in Pakistan. These programs have for decades helped fight poverty and hopelessness and build individual and community resilience in underserved parts of the country – the kind of efforts recognized as having a role in preventing radicalization and the spread of violent extremism. Community-centred programs and pro-social actions have shown to build social cohesion by increasing social learning, interactions, and dialogue, which, although not often the stated goal, have had positive effects such as reducing social isolation. Sustained, effective, and scaled development, when done right – not imposing external models, but enabling and supporting stirrings from the grassroots – can be a positive counter to extremism.

CIDA EARLY SUPPORT ON GENDER JUSTICE

CIDA also began work on gender justice programming in the 1990s. The WDPr provided numerous sub-project grants to organizations such as the Pakistan Women Lawyers Association, War against Rape, training for police and jail officials, and para-legal awareness training by the All Pakistan Women's Association. It provided funding to small local organizations such as the Goth Sudhar Sangat Aghamani in Dadu, Sindh province, for its work on honour killings, child marriage, and establishing a resource centre with legal and human rights information; and for Tahaffuz to form grassroots institutions and build capacity for advocacy in twenty-four districts in southern Punjab and interior Sindh. It also included an initiative to support the Simorgh women's resource and publication centre,[4] a small, strategic nonprofit feminist organization based in Punjab. CIDA supported Simorgh's project, Regional Judicial Education on Equality Issues (1997–2007), as part of the Asia Pacific Forum for Judicial Education on Equality. Simorgh's socio-legal journal *Bayan* was operationalized within this project, and the original *Bayan* had regional outreach enabled by a regionally representative advisory board that included Justice (ret.) Dube from Canada as a member. The journal was suspended in 2006 due to lack of funding but revived after 2019 as part of Canada's women's political empowerment project, Fempower. For logistical reasons, according to Simorgh, the advisory board has limited regional representation but still includes Justice Dube.

A CALL TO ADVOCACY AND DIALOGUE ON GENDER EQUALITY

By the mid-to-late 1990s, consistent with CIDA's direction to fund civil society, especially human rights organizations, and its recognized leading role in gender equality internationally and in Pakistan, funding was scaled up to support a proactive, independent gender advocacy group to influence the development agenda of aid donor institutions and the government and collaborate with civil society through its subgroups. Called the Interagency Gender and Development Group (INGAD), it was funded and led by Canada, and evolved out of CIDA's formation in 1985 of an Information Network on Women in Development to share information and coordinate programs being undertaken by a few aid donors and UNDP. It aimed to build broader interest among donors on gender issues. Over the years, it evolved to become the Interagency Gender and Development Group, reflecting the shift from WID to GAD, to improve donor coordination in policy and program development and engage the government of Pakistan on gender and development issues. In 1998–99, under the women's development project fund, a contribution of $18,000 was provided to the INGAD secretariat for strategic policy work and research.

By 2000, it had expanded to reach twenty-nine members, encompassing all the major bilateral and UN agencies. With a broad research agenda, it undertook gender analysis within Poverty Reduction Strategic Plans (the PRSPs were in vogue in development at the time), completed a UN statement on gender in Pakistan, facilitated the Beijing Plus 5 process, and prepared a national action plan on women for Pakistan.

It also had as an objective by 2000 to "lobby for the repeal of all laws discriminatory to women" (INGAD 2000) and provide support for the repeal of the Hudood Ordinances. In addition, it collaborated on gender projects through its various committees and subgroups.

INGAD was an exciting platform to move women's human rights forward, just as religious fundamentalism was growing and becoming a more dangerous force opposing gender equality objectives. By 2003, INGAD met monthly. Its key counterpart was the Ministry of Women's Development, Social Welfare and Special Education. CIDA also funded INGAD through the PAGE Fund in 2003, 2004, and 2008–09 for its work on gender mainstreaming in government. The mainstreaming work did not include departments of government dealing with national security policy or issues. Naturally security agencies were not an arm of the government that aid agencies worked with, although security sector reform touched on the aid mandate in the 2000s; but this was not an area of CIDA work, especially in Pakistan.

After the change in program direction to women's economic empowerment mainly through bilateral programs, and with the programming and advocacy role on women's rights removed (partly due to the end of the Women's Funds), INGAD lost its compass. INGAD began to falter without strong leadership from Canada. Other larger donors had moved in and funded gender equality, gender justice (UNDP funded by DFID), and human rights and were not participating in INGAD any longer. After USAID launched its large Gender Fund in 2009 implemented by Aurat Foundation and DFID launched its gender program, INGAD lost its purpose and *raison d'être* against these larger players and forums. In 2008, CIDA still chaired INGAD, which was funded through the PAGE Fund and meeting monthly at the CIDA Program Support Unit office. "By June 2008, CIDA was still recognized as the most significant donor in gender programming due partly to its chairing of INGAD I was told in a briefing after arriving."[5] This was perhaps CIDA's own internal perception or wish, but it didn't align with the reality of a changed context for Canada. The 2009 Country Strategy had identified INGAD as a key forum for policy dialogue on gender issues in Pakistan. By 2010, INGAD was a shadow of its former self, a floundering platform given Canada's backtracking on women's rights and halting of support for Pakistani women's organizations. By 2011, INGAD barely met. The life flow of INGAD somehow mirrored Canada's three-steps-back trajectory on support for women's rights in Pakistan and its waning leadership role in Pakistan and the international community.

My introduction to INGAD was at a meeting of over fifty aid workers crowded into the Canadian Club main room on a hot muggy August morning in 2010. CIDA was co-chairing the hastily called meeting on the scale-up of the flood emergency response with the UN Office of Coordination of Humanitarian Assistance on behalf of the Interagency Gender and Development Group. It was a large and chaotic meeting focused on the gender impacts of the floods and how to urgently get more emergency supplies to displaced women and children. The INGAD meeting was hijacked to address urgent humanitarian coordination that day as the flood emergency brought a frenetic pace to aid workers in the capital, desperate for the latest information and entry points on where help was needed most. I tried my best to co-chair, but it quickly broke into side discussions of small groups of people exchanging the latest developments in their sector. After this meeting, however, I didn't hear much about INGAD until 2013, when the World Bank Representative convened it as a platform to engage on gender equality advocacy with the government through the development of a ten-point plan on Gender Equality, consulted on and endorsed by a much smaller although functioning INGAD. By 2019, INGAD was revived after UN Women took it on, a testimony to the platform as a durable entity for gender equality. CIDA's legacy on supporting policy advocacy and facilitation of consultations and dialogue between civil society and government, initiated decades earlier, is now seen as an essential element of peace-building and political processes in prevention of and solutions to conflict in the Women, Peace, and Security agenda.

— * —

Canadian support to civil society and grassroots organizations across Pakistan in the 1990s and into the first part of the next decade helped build capacity on rights, social development, and equality, strengthening the foundation on which work continues today by other donors and aid actors. While it did not stem the spread of extremism, it strengthened groups stepping up action that was an alternative and counter to extremist agendas. The funding support for Pakistani gender equality and other civil society assisted their efforts in strengthening a democratic society and advocating for rights and equality. These major Pakistani NGOs, including SPO, SAP-PK, SUNGI, AKRSP, the Rural Support Programs Network,[6] and all the organizations funded through the five Women's Funds, combined their work with other networks of organizations and individuals to ensure that the extremist interpretations of laws were modified, and that some measure of gender equality was sustained while also strengthening communities. With its links to and support from the international level, CIDA support helped make space for civil society voices. All civil society networks have recounted how helpful international solidarity can be in working against intolerance.

After CIDA cut funding to civil society, UK aid established a sizeable program with all of CIDA's former strategic partners. The Aawaz Voice and Accountability Program brought together some important civil society organizations in Pakistan: Aurat Foundation, South Asia Partnership-Pakistan, Strengthening Participatory Organization, and Sungi Development Foundation – all key CIDA partner organizations from the 1990s. Together, they formed an integrated network – managed by a private company called Development Alternatives International – to strengthen Pakistani citizens' capacity to voice their priorities collectively, bring about reform, and hold the government accountable. Aawaz, meaning "voice" in Urdu,[7] improved women's effective public and political participation, and tackled violence against women and girls and religion-based conflict. Aawaz reportedly operated in 4,500 villages and settlements in 45 districts across Punjab and Khyber Pakhtunkhwa, reaching more than 10 million citizens, of which 8 million benefited directly from improved services, reduced violence, and increased political participation, according to its public reports. The project was almost a replica of CIDA's 1990s funding for NGOs, a testimony to Canada's legacy. It built on the capacity those organizations had established and benefited from their strengths, skills, and experience in which CIDA had invested for more than two decades. The program was instrumental in achieving groundbreaking legislative changes in Punjab: the Child Marriage Restraint Act 2014 and the Punjab Protection of Women Against Violence Act 2016, in collaboration with civil society, legislators, and political parties. It contributed to the passing of three landmark pieces of legislation: the Anti-Honour Killing Law, the Anti-Rape Law, and the Hindu Marriage Law. Its success led to an Aawaz II to empower and protect youth, women and children. The US- and UK-funded human rights and gender equality programs pressed ahead with efforts to support those doing this work, helping to address issues leading to legitimate grievances and countering in a peaceful way the growing violent extremism and its narrative.

10

The Forerunners

CIDA's Women's Funds

> The key mechanism for [CIDA] gender equality support has been a series of increasingly larger responsive funds, starting in 1989.
>
> CIDA 2010

The momentum generated from the successful Women's Development Fund, approved in 1996, led to its successor, CIDA's Program for the Advancement of Gender Equality or PAGE Fund, designed just before 9/11. It was an exciting time for CIDA in its leadership role on gender equality in the donor community as the main aid agency supporting the women's movement in Pakistan. The five CIDA women's funds between 1989 and 2009–10 provided multi-year core support to Pakistani organizations, helped establish new ones, and consolidated networks from the grassroots. Partnerships with Pakistani organizations through these funds gave Canada access to a wide network of civil society, human rights activists, and intellectuals who had their fingers on the pulse of the nation. Gender equality was still one of three areas of focus of the aid program, with the objective to improve women's human rights, health and education, and economic empowerment. It was the first and only country program for CIDA with gender equality as a main theme. Other CIDA programs looked to the Pakistan program as a model on gender equality programming.

In 2006, CIDA headquarters decided to document the evidence and success of the PAGE and WDPr funds to make the case to increase the PAGE budget to $10 million. PAGE was to play a more prominent role in the overall aid program, continuing to strengthen the gender equality work and partnerships with civil society. An evaluation mission of gender experts went to Pakistan to look at both the Women's

Development Fund and the PAGE fund to provide justification to expand and increase it. "CIDA was the instigator of a strengthened gender equality movement. There was an army of solid, strong, and progressive people that CIDA was working with in Pakistan. They worked well together," recalled Linda Moffat, who travelled to Pakistan for the evaluation, when I interviewed her about the report. The heads of the major NGOs that CIDA funded and sustained throughout the 1990s and into the mid-2000s were pushing the human rights and gender equality agenda. "Muhammad Tahseen, the executive director of SAP-PK, brought the others into the gender equality discussion to brainstorm on what they could do to be more proactive on women's rights and needs," she continued. "The conversations were amazing. The grants to women's organizations over many years helped create and sustain a movement for equality and rights that could not be suppressed by extremists." The evaluation in 2006 of both funds confirmed that their value to CIDA was that they gave it a "respected profile as a lead donor in supporting women's rights and gender equality in Pakistan" (Moffat and Ehsan 2006).

The purpose of CIDA's two large women's funds – WDPr and PAGE – was to grow and strengthen the gender equality movement in Pakistan, and evaluative evidence shows that this was achieved by 2006.

> In support to 100 NGOs and institutions across the Country, the funds helped to build and strengthen an extensive cadre of organizations that are more committed and capable of taking action on gender equality ... accounting for a robust gender equality movement in Pakistan. (Moffat and Ehsan 2006)

Pakistani activists still talk about how Canada came forward in the late 1980s and 1990s to support Pakistan's pro-people and pro-women agenda. Advocacy for women's rights and women's development was one of the essential pillars of Canada's bilateral relationship with Pakistan. Farida Shaheed, in an interview for the Global Affairs documentary on Canadian support for gender equality, noted that Canada influenced Pakistan on gender equality and helped enable key decisions. Support from the international community was significant in strengthening their activist efforts at home. Over chai tea in his office one winter day in 2012 in Lahore, Muhammad Tahseen took me through some of the history of that dynamic time: "we were breaking new ground and reaching the grassroots with Canada's help," he said; "this should be documented."

In 1996 the Women's Development Fund prioritized human rights – violence reduction, political participation and economic empowerment, health, education, and economic advancement for women. Over six years, seventy-three sub-projects were funded, with the last completed in 2004. "It served to 'incubate' and build the institutional and networking capacity of women's NGOs raising awareness and acting as catalysts for change" (CIDA CPF 2001). PAGE was the fifth consecutive locally administered women's fund for delivery of gender programming, with the first beginning in 1989. PAGE continued until 31 March 2010 to complete projects underway, and funded eighty-seven sub-projects. There were twenty-two projects funded to address violence against women, legal rights, and other women's rights (ten WDPr and twelve PAGE projects). A 2004 operational review by Isla Paterson of the PAGE women's fund stated the prevailing consensus in CIDA at the time: "The long investment in program continuity (on GE since 1989) has been a major contributor to the discernable progress in advancing women's issues and gender equity in Pakistan in which CIDA is an acknowledged leader" (Paterson 2004). Paterson noted that "[t]he continuum strategy appears to have no planned end date. From 1989, Fund stakeholders appear not to have considered that they might someday end" (Patterson 2004, 6).

The funds had a combined total value of merely $14,450,000 (if combined with the MAF funds, the amount is approximately 10 per cent higher). While this is not a large amount of money, hundreds of projects were funded with accumulated impact and some with extensive individual impact. It demonstrates how such a small amount of grant funds can have strategic impact well beyond the size of a budget. When combined with grants provided to the women's funds/organizations through the gender components of the bilateral projects of SPO, AKRSP, SAP-PK, and the Aurat Foundation Women Councillors Programs, plus the annual Embassy Mission Administered Funds directed to small women's organizations, thousands of grassroots women's organizations received CIDA support. "The use of seed funding to leverage or influence larger programming and create space for civil society to effectively engage with Government is one of the successes of the responsive funds," wrote Rukhsana Rashid, CIDA's gender advisor from 2000 to 2010, in her reflection on thirty years of CIDA's gender equality programs (R. Rashid 2016). Isla Paterson, in

Period	Program	Amount
2002–10	Program for the Advancement of Gender Equality (PAGE)	$9,000,000
1996–2002	Women's Development Project (expanded)	$4,000,000
1994–96	Women's Development Fund	$500,000
1991–93	Women in Development Support Fund (renewed)	$500,000
1989–90/91	Womens Support Fund	$540,000

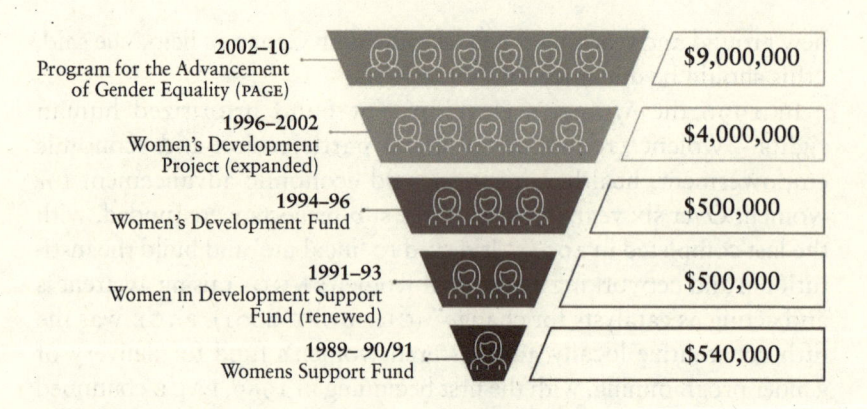

Figure 10.1 CIDA Pakistan Program – women's funds 1989–2010.

her Acknowledgments to the *Operational Review* of PAGE in 2004, recalled, "Nearly twenty years ago, as a new employee in CIDA's WID unit in Policy Branch, I was involved in the initial discussions with the Pakistan desk to begin a women in development program. It was a thrilling experience to see, in a small way the bountiful harvest of these first few seeds" (Paterson 2004). Small grants were key to resourcing feminist organizations.

During the twenty-year period of CIDA's five women's funds, much was achieved at the policy and legal level, despite the turbulence of those years and the growth of religious extremism hindering progress on women's rights.[1] The Pakistani government established a National Commission of Inquiry on the Status of Women in 1994 which undertook a report in 1997 recommending the repeal of discriminatory laws, a drastic increase of women's political participation through affirmative action, and other suggestions; also in 1994 women's police stations were set up on an experimental basis at nine locations and legal aid centres established within Dar ul-Amans (government-run homes for destitute women) (Gloekler and Seeley 2007). The government also formulated a National Action Plan in 1998 to guide gender equality policy and programs, established a permanent National Commission on the Status of Women (NCSW) in 2000 (on the recommendation of the Commission of Inquiry), and approved a National Policy for the Development and Empowerment of Women in 2002.[2] The Permanent Commission on the Status of Women to reform discriminatory legislation and safeguard and promote women's interests was a key move. It undertook consultations throughout the country and established permanent standing committees on violence, discriminatory laws, media, and employment. The government also set an endowment fund to strengthen family courts. In addition, it made efforts to tackle the issues of violence against women and honour killings. As a result, the National Assembly passed the first Protection of Women Act (a Women's Bill of Rights) in 2006, with its pushback on the Hudood Ordinances, and established a gender crime cell on violence against women for collecting data, policy development, and investigation of GBV. A code of conduct tackling sexual harassment of women in the workplace was presented to Parliament as a legal ordinance and directives were issued in government offices. The code was also adopted by several private institutions and civil society bodies. The important gender equality work underway today has been able to strengthen further the foundation of this cumulative effort. It is worth noting that much of the national policy work on gender equality ceased by 2009 as the transition of gender equality was devolved to the provinces, but later resumed once the provincial departments were operational. Provincial Commissions for the Status of Women (PCSWs) were mandated in 2010 to review provincial legislation and policies to promote empowerment, ensure gender equality, and counter discrimination under the eighteenth amendment of the Constitution. When I met with Senator Rabbani to discuss the historic amendment not long after it passed, he told me that it was a necessary step towards decentralization of responsibilities to the provinces for women's rights and development, and that it would take some time for their ministries to become operational. I wondered what might happen to the gender equality policy agenda and programs in the meantime. The provincial women's departments did struggle initially to steer policy, and there was a gap, but with added support from the UN and other aid donor countries, they began to gain momentum.

Much of the work behind the progress at the policy level during the years from 1989 to 2006 can be attributed to the contributions by the CIDA women's funds to Pakistan women's rights organizations, including: the preparation of a national action plan on women for Pakistan by the Federal Ministry of Women's Development (MOWD); the facilitation of the Beijing Plus 5 processes by an NGO coordinating committee;[3] consultations on the 2002 National Policy; technical assistance to the MOWD and Ministry of Finance to integrate gender issues into the Poverty Reduction Strategy of 2003; and strengthening capacity of newly elected women councillors at sub-national levels. The women's fund contributed to women activist movements to shape public policy, grassroots movements, and advocacy and awareness at all levels. The purpose of the last fund (PAGE), approved just after 9/11, was to enable civil society organizations and government to accelerate and influence policy and programming to advance gender equality. It was highly successful in achieving this goal. It supported gender equality advocacy, the role of the media, and gender mainstreaming in government. Journalist training in Sindh and Balochistan undertaken through PAGE enabled news features on gender-based violence, improved networking between NGOs and journalists, and resulted in more informed reporting. By 2011, there was extensive and well-researched reporting on gender equality issues, and frequent reporting on honour killing and gender-based violence evident in the daily news and media.

In 2020, the Center for Global Development in Washington posted a blog calling for "research linking investment in women's rights organizations to legal reform and beneficial outcomes for women and girls, [to] further solidify the case for investment in local women's rights organizations" (O'Donnell and Kenny 2020). The advocacy, lobbying, campaigning, awareness-raising, training, networking, and other initiatives funded through the women's funds can be directly correlated as a contribution to the institutional, policy, and legal progress made by Pakistan on gender equality and women's rights over those twenty years. Although the women's funds in Pakistan had provided this evidence a decade earlier, it had remained obscured in government files and archives.

CONSOLIDATING NETWORKS FROM THE GRASSROOTS TO POLICY

Canada's Feminist International Assistance Policy renewed the call for investing in women's organizations at the grassroots identifying it as a top priority. It mirrored the winning strategy of CIDA's gender equality approach in Pakistan from 1996 to 2009 by emphasizing that women have the potential to assist the rising of other marginalized groups in their own communities. "Reaching women in communities as 'powerful agents of change', with the ability to transform their households and communities" (remarks by Minister Bibeau in 2017) had become a top global policy priority. FIAP amplified the call for increased funding of grassroots women's organizations among activist networks around the world. CIDA's success story from the 1990s in Pakistan was now considered a model for the way forward on gender equality globally twenty-five years later.

The WDPr (1996) helped establish and create grassroots women's organizations. It demonstrated commitment to emerging organizations. "Initially CIDA struggled with who to support so in some cases women's organizations had to be created to take on the gender equality agenda," Linda Moffat recalled. SPO rose to the challenge with their capacity-building program for grassroots organizations that assessed, linked, and supported small women's organizations. This is an early example of how aid funding and collaboration with civil society enabled them to get resources to women's organizations and support efforts at the grassroots.

> PAGE galvanized awareness and support for women's rights at the community level and has empowered both men and women to advocate for space in expressing their needs, hopes and dreams. Changes at the community level have also contributed to shaping the national discourse and agenda on women's rights. (CIDA 2010)

This feedback loop from grassroots into national policy and discourse was critical in ensuring that programs were attuned to the local reality and context. As early as 2004, the documented lessons from WDPr cited "identifying ground realities and designing activities accordingly achieve greater results" (CIDA 2004b). Being present in communities was essential, and one of the failures of the women's funds was that they could not establish sub-offices or assign staff outside the capital, Islamabad, mainly due to a lack of operational resources.

FIAP also gave the aid policy a stronger mandate on violence against women. "We must put an end to violence against women, to early and forced marriages. Every girl must be treated with dignity and respect," said Canada's Minister for International Cooperation in February 2017. In Pakistan, CIDA-backed CSOs galvanized pressure on Parliament to pass legislation on violence against women. And much was achieved on the legal front between 2009 and 2016 (see chapter 7), which could trace its support to efforts of this handful of CSOs and individuals working diligently, relentlessly, and strategically with female parliamentarians over decades.

The gains on legislation and changes in laws to protect women did not occur overnight. The PAGE project undertaken by Karwan in Mianwali Punjab in the first half of 2000, which created citizens' networks against *wani* as pressure groups (discussed in chapter 7) to fight the custom of settling murders and serious crimes out of court using women as compensation, is a successful example. PAGE partners were carrying out awareness-raising and provision of services at the community level even when their lives were at risk. This work needed government backing to help protect the rights of women as articulated in the Constitution of Pakistan (1973). Between 2006 and 2008, one project funded by PAGE with Shirkat Gah (one of the leading original initiators and founders of WAF) enhanced the capacity of community-based organizations and local government on violence against women (and on reproductive health). Shirkat Gah engaged the local influencers on these sensitive issues. The PAGE recommendations to expand work on gender justice, violence against women, and sexual and gender-based violence were highly relevant to the time and context but unfortunately were not acted upon by CIDA, although, as seen later, the work was carried forward with support from other donor countries. The 2006 evaluation referred to the "somewhat scattered violence against women movement" (Moffat and Ehsan 2006) that should continue to be supported through PAGE but needed a rejuvenated strategy to move forward. The evaluation recommended advocacy and capacity-building towards a gender-responsive, women-supportive justice system – seen at the time as the key to reducing violence against women – as part of this strategy. It suggested that human rights was too broad a theme and that violence against women needed to be addressed separately with its own strategy. It recommended separate strategies for violence against women and women's political participation – neither of which were considered until well over a decade later.

The scale and reach were and remain the challenge. Pakistani human rights groups and organizations, while active in rural towns and villages, could not sufficiently reach enough of the population potentially vulnerable to extremists, who were present in regions and villages where others were not. The United States Institute for Peace found in its research that "[t]o effectively deal with the ongoing threat posed by terrorism, regardless of its ideological leaning, policymakers must be armed with better data and also local insights to inform their policy responses" (Reed and Aryaeinejad 2021). In Pakistan, increasing security restrictions on travel and on program implementation contributed to the limitation of development programs in certain parts of the country affected by militancy. A better understanding of highly localized root causes that drive people to support extremists is essential in devising responses. This has been a key lesson for development and other actors for the prevention of violent extremism. "Most sub-projects challenged and addressed highly sensitive issues and deeply entrenched attitudes and practices" (Moffat and Ehsan 2006).

PAGE supported an NGO called Khwendo Kor, which means "sister's home" in the Pashto language, working in KP since 1993, for its project entitled *Masawat*, meaning "equity." Implemented in five union councils in Peshawar, Karak, Bannu, and Lower Dir, it focused on building the capacity of local government personnel to undertake gender-sensitive plans. Public dialogues were held, trainings undertaken. Maryam Bibi, the chief executive, conveyed the challenges but also the successes of working with women in a conservative area affected by Islamic extremism, but also the dangers of a conflict zone. By the time I met her, PAGE was long wrapped up and there was no mechanism for Canada to continue supporting Khwendo Kor, but we continued to meet and discuss the situation of women in that region.

The Women's Fund did not have much success working in the areas bordering Afghanistan, the (former) Federally Administered Tribal Areas (now part of KP province), and had limited activity in the Northwest Frontier region (now KP), where religious fundamentalist groups were gaining ground. Not having enough reach through local partners to these closed, conservative, and tribal areas – where gender disparities are the most pronounced in the country resulting from restrictions on women's freedom of movement and where gender-based acts of violence such as honour killing and child marriage were considered cultural norms – was the inherent weakness of the women's development fund. Pakistani partners and non-governmental groups operating in these areas were limited (and NGO capacities were weak), projects were less forthcoming, and distances restricted staff ability to support and monitor projects (CIDA 2010). Women were mostly restricted to their homes and villages, hence projects had to engage with them within their localized environment, requiring an enduring local presence for organizations, which was not possible, due in large part to the security situation and the presence of violent extremist groups and the Afghan Taliban.

Security and restricted access to certain districts were more of an issue once the Pakistan military began offensives against militants by the mid-2000s. Parts of the border areas had become a safe haven for al-Qaeda after 9/11. The WDPr admitted its failings in reaching women in the border provinces and regions near Afghanistan. "The Afghan war hampered some sub project field activities, and some partners were threatened by 'locals' who disagreed with Pakistan's support of the American coalition in Afghanistan," said the staff report in 2004. This was a diplomatic way of raising the serious issue of local NGOs having to restrict travel and close offices and pack up and leave the regions where extremist groups were gaining influence in the population and creating an atmosphere of fear. The Afghan Taliban had begun stepping up attacks on US-led coalition forces and their allies in Afghanistan. Al-Qaeda insurgents had made South Waziristan in the border area their main base. The Pakistan army launched a military operation against them in the district in March 2004. Work of foreign-funded NGOs anywhere near the area would have been impossible. Security forces also restricted access to certain areas, especially for NGOs. Canada had sent (non-combat) troops to Kandahar in Afghanistan in 2002, and by mid-2006 had ramped up a combat military presence across the border. We won't ever know if threats were made only to those receiving Canadian funding, but the security risks were there. The 2006 recommendations for the women's funds to do more in these regions was a difficult one to implement given this context. A gender-based conflict analysis to better understand the social and political and security reality of the situation of women in those regions might have helped, but this tool was not yet available.

The recommendations for PAGE in 2006, although appropriate, underplayed the severity of and growing dangerous context for women, which began to be unleashed the following year. The role of women in promoting and facilitating extremism and radical Islam was also not on the radar. The conscious shift of focus to WEE put most of the 2006 evaluation recommendations and those of the study on women's human rights on the shelf. The WEE projects, as seen years later, were important entry points for bringing much-needed assistance to many rural and urban poor women. They also opened the way for broader women's rights initiatives through concrete measures to empower women, along with dialogue and awareness-raising. But the gender focus had shifted from women's human rights and funding women's organizations and grassroots activists to more of a private-sector angle through links to value chains and market development.

The organizations supported through the women's funds ranged from grassroots to policy. PAGE moved forward policy and helped women's rights groups based mainly in urban areas. The impact of these "forerunner" funds supporting local women's organizations and strengthening a gender equality movement and network is important in the historical context. "Supporting feminist movements is one of the most important decisions we can make to prevent violent conflict," pointed out Jacqueline O'Neill, Canada's Ambassador for Women, Peace, and Security, on behalf of Canada at the UNSC open debate on WPS in October 2022,[4] urging the international community to focus on and address the factors that force women leaders in conflict and crisis to be resilient in the first place. Increasing funding to feminist movements is a key component of feminist foreign policies.

CIDA's strategy at the time was on the right trajectory based on years of established close relationships with civil society organizations working at the grassroots, who were guiding the direction to ensure external funding was not imposing approaches that did not reflect local realities and contextual complexities, but was rather amplifying stirrings from the grassroots supportive of what Pakistani women living in communities across the country saw as their needs and priorities. In Peshawar, by example, the Pakistan village development program, funded by PAGE, supported the strengthening of grassroots institutions for women's empowerment in the years 2003 to 2006 – years when violent extremist groups were consolidating there. The funds "served as an incubator and testing ground for young human/women's rights activist NGOs to gain experience and maturity and for other NGOs to become committed to gender issues" (Moffat and Ehsan 2006). In 2004, the lessons learned from the WDPr concluded that remaining strategic in the approach was enabled by addressing practical entry points on women's basic needs; and those small injections of funds had led to policy initiatives and shifts. One example is the Lawyers for Human Rights and Legal Aid project funded in 2001–02 for its successful campaign to establish a juvenile court and assist with the drafting of the Prevention and Control of Human Trafficking Ordinance later approved by the Federal Cabinet. "CIDA funds played a catalytic role in women's equality," Rehana Hashmi told me in our interview on the history of Canada's support to civil society. "The collaboration with government was solid in some cases. Some organizations were also delivering needed services – an area where government needed civil society help."

— * —

A year after FIAP launched as official aid policy, Global Affairs Canada stated that Canada was testing innovative solutions to advance gender equality and empower women and girls in the global south through the fund for innovation and transformation. CIDA's Pakistan women's funds of the 1990s to the mid-2000s (over approximately ten years from 1996 to 2006) were doing just that. The harsh world of global geopolitics drove a wedge into Canadian funding for this process. The foundation was laid, and the fundamental change it enabled never really disappeared from the work of these organizations. Pakistan is an example where civil society has been able (in some cases) to coerce governments to change their direction where human rights violations are happening.[5]

The women's funds were more than a 'window into the grassroots' and what was happening throughout the country. Those participating in hundreds of projects carried insights, knowledge, and information and were a monitor and a barometer of the situation in their regions, including on rights abuses and on rising extremism and radicalization. They connected the local to national and sub-national levels and were a bridge between them. Their knowledge may have benefited the security sector and others searching for solutions to extremism and violent extremism. The women's funds and their network of local organizations held a key to identifying issues and solutions and were not only an early warning system, but also an identifier of risks to peace and development and to social cohesion, working from the front lines of critical response strategies and programs. The UN 2023 Counter-Terrorism Visibility Report recognized this: "Women can be very effective in detecting early signs of radicalization, but their roles should extend to community shaping, and resilience building against radicalization. Women's role in intelligence is key, particularly in communities where they have trusted relationships" (UN Office of Counter-Terrorism 2023, 61). This recognition indicates the importance of a gender equality lens and strategy for intelligence agencies as well.

The work undertaken in the 1990s and after 9/11 could be seen as a type of response and contribution to conflict prevention and prevention of violent extremism, although it wasn't called that then. We were supporting women activists at the national level, women in communities, and women leaders at the front line of the response to gender discriminatory practices in their communities – now being touted as an important defense against the rise of violent extremism. The partners CIDA was supporting have decades of experience, insight, and strategies for peace-building, for social cohesion, for uplifting communities and fighting for social change, for equality for all. What were considered small initiatives, when combined with other development programs, were in fact transformative actions networked from grassroots to policy. What was needed at the time was continued support to all groups working with communities to improve their development prospects. Small one-off projects in many cases were also a hindrance to real progress. The 2006 PAGE and WDPr evaluation provided evidence that PAGE sub-projects had started awareness-raising on women's human rights in parts of KP and FATA where extremist groups were enforcing measures restricting women's lives and education. Years of partnerships through the gender funds have increased our understanding of the importance of this type of support for a human-rights based, more inclusive society. The recognition of the lack of reach to the remote areas affected by violent extremism was notable, and perhaps could have been tackled had there been a higher risk appetite or perhaps through consultation or collaboration with security and intelligence actors. Today, with national plans for counter-terrorism in place, aid and political actors can link with those responsible to open dialogue on approaches that can help preventative responses. Pakistan's National Counter-Terrorism Authority published a national narrative against terrorism and extremism.

The Canadian experience provides insights for international development assistance on how certain approaches can be most effective in leaving a lasting impact. More research on how gendered approaches can push back on or provide an alternative narrative to extremism will increase understanding of development responses – especially when working in solidarity to support those on the front line of a response and enabled by government programs.

11

After 9/11 and "Operation Enduring Freedom"

Post-9/11 was an unsettled period of shock for the diplomatic community in Pakistan. Canada immediately evacuated all spouses and children back to Canada following the deadly attack on the Twin Towers in New York on 11 September 2001. The following month, during Thanksgiving dinner at the Canadian Club, the remaining staff learned that all expatriate employees except for those deemed "essential" were being sent back to Canada on a flight leaving in six hours. The news dampened the evening event as everyone worried about what it would mean for themselves and their families. People quickly left to pack. The Thanksgiving decorations on the tables seemed to fade and the pumpkin pie sat untouched as the realization hit home. Things were not going back to normal, and their families would not be coming back to join them in Islamabad. Foreign Affairs Canada had designated Pakistan permanently as a non-family duty station.

The deployment of American troops in Afghanistan to defeat al-Qaeda and the Taliban stirred anti-American feelings, particularly in the border areas of Pakistan. The bombing next door was a daily reminder of the crisis affecting the region. The US invasion of Afghanistan, "Operation Enduring Freedom," was initially about defeating the Taliban and al-Qaeda and capturing Osama bin Laden. It "triggered a massive political shift in the northwest territories of Pakistan," wrote Zahid Hussain in 2010, referring to the installation of conservative Islamic governments in the two provinces bordering Afghanistan, which "was to have profound ramifications" (Hussain 2010). The regions had hosted Afghan refugees since the 1980s and the shared culture among Pashtuns residing on both sides of the border meant that Afghans regularly travelled back and forth. Parts of the population had always been sympathetic to the Afghan Taliban, but the support for extremist interpretations of Sharia law now increased at the level of provincial political authorities. Rigid Islamic rule was enforced, and the Pakistani provincial administrations pledged to end coeducation. NGOs working in female education were targeted by the Mullahs (Hussain 2010). The 9/11 attacks opened the eyes of world leaders to the violent extremism that had been brewing since the 1980s but had not been recognized as a serious threat in Pakistan and other parts of the world. Those working for international development agencies found their work curbed, including many of CIDA's civil society partners working in KP province.

Exactly four months before 9/11, CIDA had sponsored a regional study mission of six gender experts to Pakistan to work with the four gender advisors based in Islamabad. The mission findings flagged the need for enhanced knowledge on Islam and violence against women. The group had astutely observed that "civil society/NGOs are more advanced than the government in responding to specific violence against women" (R. Rashid 2016). The tensions in the air in Pakistan were evident, yet understated in the report, not unlike other gender or development reports of the time. Spearheaded by CIDA HQ to encourage south-south cooperation, dialogue, and learning, the mission "allowed for in-depth discussion and sharing of experiences; for linking micro with macro strategies for maximum understanding of the bigger picture of CIDA as an Agency and gender equality as a policy in the context of the global movement" (ibid.). The learnings and recommendations from this mission were used in the design of the PAGE women's fund and form essential historical records of gender equality programming in Pakistan. They fed into program development at all levels, and not just in Pakistan.

In Afghanistan, the US-led Operation Enduring Freedom took on a female face with the objective of freeing women and children for a more hopeful future. The image played on the conscience of the Western world with women the symbol, portraying the clash in ideological perspectives of Islamic extremism and Western democracy. The regressive Taliban stance against women's rights and freedom was (and remains) abhorrent to the West.

In early 2002, the Bonn Agreement led to a transitional government in Afghanistan made up of mainly the northern alliance. The UN representative who organized the Bonn Conference of international diplomats, Lakshmi Brahimi, was approached by Pakistan to include representation of what then were considered by some as moderate elements of the Taliban in the political process that established the interim government. The US was firmly opposed to it.[1] The situation put Pakistan in a difficult position. Having supported elements of the Taliban from the beginning and having been the first country to recognize the Taliban regime, they were now a close ally of the US, who were ousting the Taliban from any political or transitional process at the time. While Pakistan shared the US interest in eliminating al-Qaeda, it did not share the US objective of eliminating the Afghan Taliban. Tensions mounted in the US-Pakistan relationship and the new Kabul government viewed Pakistan with distrust. Just after the Bonn agreement, the *Wall Street Journal*'s South Asia bureau chief was kidnapped inside Pakistan in January 2002, while researching a story on militancy in Pakistan.

> Daniel Pearl's kidnappers handed over the journalist to Al Qaeda, with Pearl reportedly killed by Khalid Sheikh Muhammad, the 9/11 mastermind. In May 2002, police found Pearl's body buried in a nursery on the outskirts of Karachi. Pearl's kidnapping was the first violent response of Al Qaeda that linked Pakistani militant groups to the American attack on the Taliban regime. (Hussain 2021)

Karachi had become a base for radicalized extremist groups. The links between militant groups in Afghanistan and Pakistan were becoming more evident. I recalled the boxes of "Osama bin Laden" candy, manufactured somewhere in Karachi, circulating around the CIDA offices at the Provincial Reconstruction Team (PRT) military base in Kandahar, with colourful pictures of him on each wrapped piece. They were practically free – easy propaganda.

TALIBAN INSURGENCY IMPACT IN PAKISTAN

By 2003, the Taliban insurgency in Afghanistan had begun to regain some strength. In Pakistan, 2003 witnessed an attack on the Christian church in the diplomatic enclave where CIDA's Head of Cooperation and other diplomats were attending Sunday service. Their children were downstairs at Sunday school and remained unharmed. An American diplomat was killed and the CIDA official suffered some injuries. The tragic event shook Canada's political and security assessment of Pakistan and ended any chance of diplomats' families returning to Pakistan. It was a major factor in triggering the relevancy review of Canada's 2001 five-year aid strategy, approved two months before the 9/11 attacks, to make sure the CIDA program was still on the right track given the security context. The review recommended that the program determine aid delivery channels less vulnerable to security disruptions and recommended an expansion of the CIDA Program Support Unit, a local private-sector entity housed outside the High Commission put in place to support aid operations. Assignment of Canadians throughout the country became a dangerous proposition. The overall program approach and portfolio of projects did not change. Adjustments to operations were made, but no changes to programming.

The analysis of the situation and how it might impact development objectives in the country was thin. The pre-9/11 CIDA Program Framework for Pakistan (approved just before September 2001) had included a reference to the "terrorism and Islamic extremism or Talibanization which leach into [parts of] Pakistan" as a result of the Afghan war and the "humanitarian tragedy" (CIDA 2001) there. However, dealing with violent extremism and conflict was not the purview of development agencies in those years. There was no guiding framework for development in the context of violent conflict, much less extremism. Thinking about how aid programs might be adjusted to take into account the reality of growing extremism and its impact on society and gender equality was nonexistent, and it was not yet identified as a risk in implementing the program framework.

The country strategy relevancy review reinforced the existing program framework and narrowed the thematic focus. It confirmed that gender equality be retained as one of the three priority pillars with a specific program goal and objective on women's rights: *Improvement in women's human rights, economic empowerment, and access to social services*. The Americans also reviewed their aid strategy for Pakistan. By 2004, the US offered a new enhanced aid package to Pakistan as partial support for the country's essential role as an ally in the war against the Afghan Taliban, and to encourage Pakistan to take military action against them and the al-Qaeda elements taking refuge in Waziristan.

Given the turbulent impact of the Afghanistan wars in Pakistan since the 1980s, perhaps 9/11 was seen as simply another moment of crisis that would not dramatically alter Pakistan. The War on Terror, however, proved to be more than a moment of crisis, lasting over twenty years and affecting Pakistan and the region profoundly. The post-9/11 period witnessed a further decline in gender equality indicators, which continued to drop steadily over the next fourteen years on the World Economic Forum Global Gender Gap Index.

SCALING UP THE WAR AGAINST THE TALIBAN IN AFGHANISTAN

2005 was the start of a new phase of the international war effort against the Taliban in Afghanistan, with a significant expansion of the International Security Assistance Force's (ISAF's) role and presence. Militant violence, and the intensity of the Taliban war against the US and its allies, also increased from 2005 in Afghanistan (and was also noticeable in Pakistan). The initial approach after defeating the Taliban, to build a new government in Afghanistan and undertake post-war reconstruction, was faltering and the war was far from over. More resources were needed to support the nation-building policy imperative. Following the formation of ISAF in Afghanistan in 2001 and the NATO assumption of command of ISAF by 2003, the subsequent expansion and the approach to winning the war evolved to embody human security dimensions including governance, reconstruction of infrastructure, and increased basic services to the population through expanding government capacity. It integrated a gender dimension in response to the harsh policies of the Taliban. Canada assumed command of ISAF in 2004 and became the largest contributor to ISAF, providing 2,000 troops. As a result, Canada took on an active role in Afghanistan and the leadership of the Kandahar Provincial Reconstruction Team (PRT). PRTs were meant to shore up the provincial governments in each province, build their capacity, and help provide services and infrastructure to the population. They were a coordinated military, security, and civilian response intended to strengthen the institutions of the state in Afghanistan. Run by the military and functioning as military bases throughout the country, the attempts by 2007–08 to enhance their civilian role resulted in an increased presence of foreign (in the case of Kandahar, Canadian) aid workers, political and prison officers, and police. For Canada, it was considered a whole-of-government or comprehensive response with the aim of implementing an integrated approach across institutions of military, police and prisons, political and human rights, development, and humanitarian concerns. The cooperation and tensions of this well-intended WoG approach were an interesting daily challenge that broke new ground in working across organizational mandates; but that has already been the subject of many other books, theses, and articles.

In mid-2006, Canada's commitment to ISAF in Afghanistan provided a large deployment to Kandahar to assist in "stabilization patrols in support of the overt peacebuilding efforts later defined in the Afghanistan compact" and to set conditions for sustainable economic growth and development, strengthening state institutions and civil society, removing remaining terrorist threats, rebuilding capacity and infrastructure, reducing poverty, and meeting basic human needs. The accompanying Canadian civilian role was to support this and help foster democracy and reconstruction and support humanitarian efforts. But as the insurgency gained ground, the combat role increased against the Taliban. In early 2006, the Canadian political counsellor from the High Commission in Pakistan, Glyn Berry, was killed by the Taliban on a mission to Kandahar, sending shockwaves through the department. Well-placed intentions to help the Afghan people were becoming a life-and-death reality. The original peace-building–type mandate had morphed into an active combat role alongside efforts to rebuild and strengthen the Afghan government. Canada requested additional NATO/ISAF assistance in the south.

In October 2007, Canada announced the creation of the Independent Panel on Canada's Future Role in Afghanistan, headed by (the late) John Manley, former deputy prime minister, to "review, analyze and make recommendations on Canada's engagement in Afghanistan beyond February 2009." The Manley Panel outlined a reconstruction and development aid strategy for Afghanistan and Kandahar as part of Canada's whole-of-government approach, with three priority signature projects for Kandahar: the construction or rehabilitation of fifty schools, the eradication of polio, and the rehabilitation and repair of the large Dahla Dam and its irrigation system. The Panel's comprehensive report and recommendations were to dramatically change the trajectory of Canada's aid to Afghanistan (and subsequently Pakistan) for the foreseeable future. Canadian aid to Afghanistan increased exponentially and Afghanistan became Canada's top international security and aid priority, with commensurate allocation of budget resources directed strategically by a high-level Afghanistan Task Force at the Privy Council Office.

GROWING EXTREMISM AND ITS IMPACT ON WOMEN IN PAKISTAN

By 2006, violent extremist groups were undertaking beheadings and public executions in the northwest and FATA regions of Pakistan, showing themselves to be more brutal than their counterparts in Afghanistan. Swat Valley, only 150 miles (241 km) from Islamabad, was witnessing severe militant violence, which reached a height between 2007 and 2009 when the Tehreek-e-Nafaz-e-Shariat-e-Mohammadi (which became part of the Pakistan Taliban in 2007) barred women from working and girls from attending schools and, on occasion, publicly flogged those who did not comply with its version of Sharia law (Khan 2022). Broadcasting on the several FM radio stations in Swat, the militant leader, Mullah Fazlullah, told women to pull their daughters out of government schools, which he called the centre of all evils, and called for women to wear the veil. He also advocated against the polio vaccine, a major aid initiative and investment of Canada in both Pakistan and Afghanistan at the time. He and his followers set up parallel administrations in Swat Valley, establishing Islamic courts that imposed Sharia law. They executed many women, especially those who criticized the Taliban for preventing girls from attending school (Hussain 2010).[2] And critical for aid programs, Mullah Fazlullah stated in a video outlining a militant charter to residents of Kurram Agency: "People dealing with NGOs should be arrested. Those having connections with NGOs should also step forward and explain themselves" (Sheikh 2016).

The Swat Valley, a beautiful part of the country, had once been a favourite day trip for diplomats. I recalled our trip there in 1984 with embassy colleagues to see the ancient Buddhist statues and stupas along the way. We stopped for a picnic out of the back of the jeep, enjoying the peaceful valley views. In 2016, the famous seventh-century Buddha of Swat statue was attacked by Taliban operatives, destroying its face. Militants continue to retain the capacity to mount targeted attacks against women health workers, and women working in community-based and civil society organizations (Khan 2022, 26n80). In a notable change of popular support by 2022, large public protests were held against the presence of the Taliban in Swat, indicating a growing lack of tolerance of the Taliban in the area. People living there were voicing concern about the Tehrik-e-Taliban Pakistan (TTP) and their alliance with the Afghan Taliban, back in power across the border.

— * —

In March 2006, CIDA sent three Canadian gender consultants to Pakistan with a mandate to "increase engagement in women's economic empowerment (WEE) and focus on how to integrate women into higher value markets" (R. Rashid 2016). The policy shift of CIDA to women's economic empowerment, away from the focus on women's rights, began with this mission. It was followed by another mission in June with a private sector development specialist. Yet that same year, the evaluation of CIDA's existing women's funds had recommended that women's human rights and access to justice remain CIDA's priority for gender equality. The WEE strategy in 2006 downplayed human rights and was also silent on the growing extremism and militancy in the country that had accelerated and spread since 9/11.

By 2006, CIDA's gender program in Pakistan had grown to encompass five multi-million-dollar bilateral projects in addition to the $9 million PAGE women's fund, with planning underway to expand this even further (Moffat and Ehsan 2006). In 2005, the CIDA gender equality portfolio was at least $20.9 million. A three-year $2 million PAGE Strategic Alliance Fund project with UNDP, for Gender Mainstreaming in the Government Planning and Development Division and Departments, was approved. The same year, three additional bilateral projects were added to the gender equality portfolio: women's employment concerns and working conditions with the UN ILO and Ministry of Labor and Ministry of Women's Development for $3 million; support to implementation of the Gender Reform action plans with the Asian Development Bank for $4.5 million; and support of women's participation in local government elections with the Aurat Foundation for $2.4 million. The local government project implemented by the Aurat Foundation followed a $2 million bilateral project from 2002 on effective representation by women councillors, also implemented by the Aurat Foundation, a strategic partner for CIDA under both large women's funds (WDPr and PAGE). In addition to this impressive funding portfolio for gender equality were the sizeable gender equality components of other bilateral aid projects, such as AKRSP with its remarkable results through women's village organizations, and SPO with its hundreds of grassroots women's organizations under the Women's Emancipation Program. "Gender equality has been one of the defining strengths of CIDA's Pakistan Program," concluded the 2006 Goss Gilroy evaluation. Canada was clearly a leader in funding gender equality in Pakistan and had a highly respected profile with likeminded countries. "The impact was significant. The aim of the Pakistan program in the immediate future is to increase the total budget allocation for gender equality programming to be in line with the other two priority areas and to focus on women's economic empowerment" (Goss Gilroy 2006). "CIDA had a comparative advantage in advocating gender as a program and policy objective among both government and civil society." The term "comparative advantage" meant that Canada held a unique position on policy discourse with government and civil society on rights and equality issues from this expansive network of partners. The significant impact was the depth of strategic relationships in Pakistani society that Canada had at the time nurtured over years of partnerships and the importance of this type of support for a human-rights-based, more inclusive society. Unfortunately, the height of this work and the vision for greater gender equality programming did not last long because Pakistan was cascading quickly into a combustible period with the rise and expansion of the Pakistani Taliban in 2007. The evaluators had captured the mood and the intent of CIDA Pakistan in 2006, but this was soon to be dampened by events in war-torn Afghanistan and the spread of militancy in Pakistan.

The month after the 2006 CIDA-sponsored WEE mission, the Lal Masjid/Red Mosque eight-day siege took place, the aftermath of which led to Osama bin Laden's declaration of "holy" war against the Pakistani state. This reflected al-Qaeda's intent to extend their war to Pakistan (Hussain 2010). It was a milestone in the history of the growth of extremism in Pakistan, unrecorded in any aid program analysis. The 2007 siege of the Red Mosque (or Lal Masjid) in the heart of Islamabad – a seminal moment in Pakistan's history as the military stormed the mosque in a deadly battle with militants that they called "Operation Silence" – ended with more than 150 people killed. The Red Mosque's leaders talked of all-out war as the government threatened to shut it down. It had become the headquarters of the growing radical Islamist resistance to President (General) Musharraf, whom they saw as an American puppet (Hussain 2010). The movement from the Red Mosque had as its main objective "to destroy the failed political system in Pakistan, which has betrayed the majority of the country's poor, and to establish a Sharia state in its place" (ibid.). Poverty and inequities in society had helped fuel support for the Lal Masjid movement, including groups of young burqa-clad girls. The young women who supported the Red Mosque (Lal Masjid) incident were students of Jamia Hafsa, who came from "impoverished families in small towns [near border areas with Afghanistan] and were purifying the streets of Islamabad for what they saw as moral corruption of westernized Pakistani elite"[3] (Haq 2016). In response to the government raid on the mosque, young women activists participated in rallies for violent jihad (Sheikh 2016). The shocking occurrences associated with the Red Mosque incident in 2007 should have served as a striking example of rising extremism and of women in participating in violent acts (Khan 2022).

The Red Mosque incident had inspired militant groups to unite in defense of Islam (Hussain 2010). The Pakistan Taliban, Tehrik-e-Taliban Pakistan (TTP), was formed on 14 December 2007 in South Waziristan to unite Pakistani militant groups under one charter that called for enforcement of Sharia law and defensive jihad against the Pakistan military (Hussain 2022). Their vision of implementing a Sharia-compliant political order through force also allied with the Afghan Taliban and al-Qaeda and its "jihadi ideology" (Mir 2022). They all shared the same motivations: to fight invading forces in Afghanistan, the Pakistan army, and government with the objective of defending Islam and establishing Sharia political order. They saw Western democracy as the enemy of their particular concept of Sharia (Sheikh).

Canada's foreign policy in the region was preoccupied with Afghanistan and its deployment of a large military force in Kandahar, and with obtaining visible and measurable results there. As more Canadian soldiers were killed in Afghanistan, Canada's relations with Pakistan, like those of the US, were increasingly viewed through the prism of the war in Afghanistan. Reports of Pakistan's ongoing support for the Afghan Taliban, whose leadership took safe haven (where al-Qaeda was also suspected of hiding) mainly in North Waziristan, were confounding international efforts in Afghanistan. One summer day in 2008, in preparation for my deployment to Kandahar, I attended a conference on Afghanistan and Pakistan of the Five Eyes intelligence[4] alliance in Ottawa where Pakistan, US, and ISAF (including Canada's) objectives were presented by CSIS as opposing forces.

"How could this situation possibly end the war against the Taliban with conflicting objectives?" I asked the presenter. He admitted that this was the overriding conundrum – a reality with which we were all struggling, and with no solution in sight.

2007 MARKS ANOTHER CHANGE IN PAKISTAN AND AFGHANISTAN

2007 marked the beginning of the seven most violent and turbulent years in Pakistan with the creation of the Pakistani Taliban and its bold expansion in the country, the assassination in Rawalpindi of Benazir Bhutto after her return to Pakistan, the eight-day siege of the Red Mosque in Islamabad (after which suicide bombings increased in reaction to the army operation against the Mosque), and the start of intense drone strikes by the US in border areas. In 2007 the US publicly called Pakistan an al-Qaeda safe haven. Unrestricted US drone strikes on the tribal areas bordering Afghanistan intensified from 2007 to 2009, targeting Taliban sanctuaries in Pakistan, and many Taliban commanders were either killed or arrested in Pakistan (A. Rashid 2011). The civilian casualties of these operations fanned the flames of anti-American sentiment. The UN humanitarian efforts increased to take care of thousands of displaced people who fled the tribal districts to seek refuge in other areas.

Pakistan had entered a dangerous period by 2007 (as had Afghanistan), one that didn't abate until 2014 (mirroring the period of Operation Enduring Freedom in Afghanistan). The militant groups gaining strength in the border regions with Afghanistan and wreaking havoc throughout the country caused a growing concern among the security agencies and the international community, and were directly impacting thousands of lives. In Afghanistan, the Afghan Taliban controlled more than half of the country's provinces. The impact on girls meant it was no longer safe for some to continue attending school in parts of the country.[5] In Pakistan, despite the increasing security problems and their ramifications for women's security, neither the program evaluation nor the Women's Fund evaluation the same year made more than a passing reference to this dramatically evolving situation, and its potential implications for the aid program, for women's human rights, or for gender equality programming, much less for the toll it was taking on the Pakistani people and society. There was a widening gap in aid and security policy analysis of the context, with the political analysis somewhere in between. The decline in gender equality indicators, evident by this time, although referenced in some documents, was not seen as a link in any way to the spread of terrorism or the deteriorating security situation.

In Afghanistan, the policy push for civilian presence in the military mission and for education throughout the country continued, although for aid actors, it was becoming almost impossible to realize such results. The Manley Panel Report had committed Canada to support the construction or rehabilitation of fifty schools in Kandahar Province. We relied heavily on our Afghan government counterparts in Kabul to monitor this, given security restrictions on visiting the sites in 2008–09 and beyond.

In Pakistan, CIDA chose a strategy that moved away from supporting the work of Pakistani organizations on women's rights and capacity-building of civil society and grassroots women's organizations (now seen as an effective approach to peace-building and preventing violent extremism and conflict) just as violent extremism was rapidly rising. What caused CIDA's muted response to human rights and its underplaying of the impact of extremism factor? Why had CIDA dropped the focus on women's rights? I wondered. What made it an either-or choice? Adding to the policy conundrum were the differing views on approaches to gender equality at play internally in CIDA, not unlike the ongoing global debate or the debate inside Pakistan itself. One of the positive recommendations of the joint Canadian-Pakistani WEE missions was to begin planning a program for home-based workers in the informal sector, still a priority in Pakistan for the millions of women facing mobility restrictions and observing purdah or living in areas affected by insecurity from violent militancy. By 2009 there was a full pipeline of WEE proposals from Canadian and Pakistani partners. The 2009 report CIDA had commissioned on women's human rights was off the table. And there was still no mention of how the growing militancy and security issues might affect women and girls disproportionately.

THE ISLAMABAD MARRIOTT HOTEL BOMBING

In September 2008, a devastating terrorist attack by the Pakistan Taliban on the Marriott Hotel (the favoured former Holiday Inn) in Islamabad killed fifty-four people, including five foreign nationals, making it the largest in Pakistan's history. This was the hotel where we had stayed on numerous aid missions to Pakistan over the years, including the first WID mission in 1984, and was the centre of meetings and workshops on international development and diplomatic events. The Marriott bomb attack resulted in even more severe security restrictions on diplomats and aid workers. Clips of the burning hotel were emotional images for the world, including diplomats and aid workers in Pakistan. A colleague emailed me the pictures of the bomb attack, recalling our many days spent in the lobby and restaurant hammering out project proposals in the 1990s. The capital was no longer immune to the violence taking place in the border regions near Afghanistan. Canada rapidly moved all staff to Canadian properties inside the diplomatic enclave and increased security guards at all locations. A sense of impending doom permeated the daily lives of many living in Pakistan.

In 2008, Ahmed Rashid, the well-known author and analyst of the Taliban, called Pakistan "the center of global Islamic terrorism." Canadian Foreign Minister Peter MacKay visited in January to persuade Pakistan to try harder to stop the free movement of insurgents between the two countries. In 2009, the Obama administration stepped up its drone attacks in Pakistan's tribal areas. It was evident that NATO forces could not win the war in Afghanistan while the Taliban had sanctuaries inside Pakistan. Pakistan was becoming a more dangerous place.

The Obama administration "Af-Pak" Strategy, announced in March 2009, linked American aid to Pakistan to its efforts to counter terrorism. In Washington, more attention was now focused on Pakistan than on the war in Afghanistan, with the hope that Pakistan might provide the solution (Hussain 2010). Canada's aid policy framework for Pakistan also emphasized the importance of Pakistan in supporting Canada's broader regional objectives (CIDA 2013) and the growing international focus on Pakistan because of its critical role in the global war against violent extremism as a strategic consideration. In November, CIDA identified border issues with Afghanistan and reinforcing Canada's efforts in Afghanistan as priorities of the aid program in Pakistan, and proposed a program to stabilize the Afghan border. CIDA officials seized this as an opportunity to stress the importance of the aid cooperation presence in Pakistan. But Pakistan's Afghan policy was at odds with US and ISAF policy in many areas. Pakistan was seen as the unpredictable wild card in the American and ISAF effort in Afghanistan.

The failure to appreciate the severity of the threat posed by the Pakistani militant groups was a failure not only of the US but also of the Pakistan government. The second fundamental flaw over the years has been the failure to admit that combating the militant threat require more than military campaigns. It required and still does, a comprehensive social and political plan. (Hussain 2010)

In March 2009, six months after the Marriott Hotel bombing in Islamabad, Canada ended twenty years of the Gender Responsive Funds with the rejection of the $18 million second PAGE II Fund. CIDA had just commissioned a major women's human rights analysis report, which was underway at the time and completed four months later. It recommended that CIDA support work at the provincial and district levels for implementation of laws, policies, and services to achieve women's human rights, and to build on existing civil society networks to move women's rights issues from the policy and institutional/legal level to on-ground service delivery. The report did provide some analysis and picture of the situation of violence against women and recommendations to tackle it. CIDA had also commissioned a report on women's human rights for Baluchistan and KP provinces, which found that Pakistani civil society organizations there "are being stretched enormously as they try to foster local level women's leadership and other development challenges, while responding to emergency needs of displaced populations affected by armed conflict" (R. Khan 2009). The report and its recommendations were not acted upon nor finalized, caught in the confusing policy shift around the war in Afghanistan.

12

Twilight Years

End of an Era for Canada in Pakistan

The year 2009 was a difficult one for Canada and NATO forces in Afghanistan. The war against the Taliban deepened and the operating environment became more dangerous for Canadians based in Kandahar. Achieving the benchmarks set by the Manley Panel for progress on reconstruction and governance goals was hampered by the ongoing war. Some say that by 2009 the war in Afghanistan was already lost (Hussain 2022). Canada began to look less favourably on the aid program to Pakistan, as many believed by then that Pakistan was playing a double game, harbouring and giving safe haven to Afghan militants, thus thwarting NATO-ISAF efforts to defeat the Taliban in Afghanistan.

CIDA's Pakistan and Afghanistan programs were administered by the same director-general, but the program strategies had not been integrated like in the US "Af-Pak" approach. The subsequent rejection by CIDA's Minister of a combined strategy for Afghanistan and Pakistan, which included border programming and a special program for Baluchistan, separated the Pakistan aid program from the Afghanistan program. In retrospect, it was likely a practical decision, given that aid within an active militarized war zone in a country such as Afghanistan was totally different from the context in Pakistan, despite both countries being affected by the Taliban militants residing in Pakistan border areas and crossing into Afghanistan.

The bombing of the UN WFP office in Islamabad in October 2009 killed five and injured many others, forcing the UN to temporarily close all its offices and eventually move to a Level 4 emergency where no spouses or children were allowed to accompany UN employees in Pakistan. The CIDA program continued project implementation despite the increased security concerns and restrictions. It was difficult to visit almost any project site: a non-objection certificate had to be obtained from the Ministry of Interior and official requests to travel to most parts of the country were frequently turned down. Embassy security clearance also had to be obtained from the internal security unit. Our Pakistani partners and collaborators were also impacted, as many had left or were preparing to leave the country. For some it was because of increased risk and at times threats to their safety. In April 2009, militants from Swat Valley seized control of Buner district, just seventy miles from Islamabad, and "ransacked the offices of international aid and development agencies working in the district and took away their vehicles, briefly taking some employees hostage" (Hussain 2010). They set up Sharia courts in the newly controlled districts. A TV broadcast of a Taliban flogging of a seventeen-year-old girl in a Swat village for coming out of her house unaccompanied by a blood relative helped sway public opinion against the Taliban. President Musharraf launched a military offensive in Swat against the Pakistan Taliban. It led to a humanitarian crisis there as people fled the fighting. Canada stepped up humanitarian aid to support those displaced by the conflict. Radical Islamist ideology appeared to cut across all segments of society with varying degrees of success, coupled with a "conservative sociopolitical environment precipitated by poor governance and a lack of quality education" (Gul 2009). The context for international development programming presented an unprecedented challenge. It was beginning to feel like this was a war not only in Afghanistan, but in Afghanistan and Pakistan alike.

Not long after arriving in 2010, I went to see the CIDA Program Support Unit Office. Upstairs on the second floor was a large mezzanine office, empty and dusty, divided by five or six cubicle offices and full of boxes of files, books, and posters on gender equality. It was the empty PAGE office. It looked like the team had just vacated their desks, leaving everything behind. I went back some months later to look through some of the boxes and retrieve a few of the numerous books left behind, with subjects ranging from Islamic laws and women to records of CIDA's lead role in coordinating the International Gender Advisory and Development Group. It was a rich mine of documentation: knowledge, research, lessons learned from the years of gender-responsive funds, slowly fading into dust. Framed posters from the 1990s on the repeal of the Hudood Ordinances lay against the wall in the dingy corner. It was the ghost of past hopes, a sad and symbolic image of what had happened to this pioneering women's human rights and empowerment fund during the period from 9/11 to 2010, its end coinciding with the pull-out of Canada's army from Kandahar in 2010.

Sadly, most of the files were destroyed by 2012 as they were determined to duplicate those in HQ. In retrospect, the many books and reports should have been donated to a feminist research organization. Now I understood the dark cloud that hung over the CIDA team working on the gender equality portfolio after 2009, lingering into 2010–11. All the years of working together towards a common goal were over.

The aid policy shift in 2009 brought on by challenging geopolitics reduced Canada's focus on gender equality in Pakistan to a few (though sizeable) projects on women's economic empowerment under the theme of inclusive economic growth (aligned with Canada's policy on Gender Equality and Sustainable Economic Growth). Although they reached more direct beneficiaries in specific geographic areas, the program was lacking the strategic reach to Pakistani grassroots organizations, the gender equality movement, and the policy work that the women's funds had provided. The move took Canada out of its central and strategic role in supporting a wide range of women's rights and gender equality organizations through Pakistani organizations and the policy discourse with government (as well as the ongoing dialogue with the network of gender equality partners).

The war against the Taliban was raging in Afghanistan but not going well for the NATO alliance, including for Canada in Kandahar, given it was the most difficult province in the country. By this time, there was likely concern at certain decision-making levels in ISAF and in Ottawa about the ability to completely defeat the Taliban in Afghanistan and in Kandahar in particular. Canada had taken three steps back on its gender equality and civil society programs in Pakistan at the height of its engagement in the war in Afghanistan. Aid program funding to Afghanistan and for women's rights and girls' education in Afghanistan increased even as Canada decreased its aid projects in Pakistan. Afghanistan, not Pakistan, was the top political, defense and security, and subsequently aid priority for Canada. Pakistan had taken a back seat. Many felt that the policy shift in Pakistan affected Canada's reputation and credibility with the rejection of PAGE II (2009), the final "nail in the coffin" for CIDA's gender equality programming, in the words of some CIDA staff at the embassy. It was a blow not only to the Pakistan women's organizations but also to the committed CIDA staff, both Canadian and Pakistani. CIDA cancelled one of its most successful mechanisms for supporting women's rights and feminist movements, and civil society activists and organizations throughout the country. Many of those organizations were linked to forging a democratic agenda and fighting more broadly for human rights and justice – efforts to address grievances in society. CIDA's support to SPO, the human rights NGO, also ended in September 2008, just as the environment in Pakistan was becoming more difficult for human rights organizations and activists, as the extremists were becoming bolder following the formation of the Pakistan Taliban in 2007.

— * —

The following years saw considerable turmoil in CIDA's program strategies for Pakistan, reflecting the broader shifting geopolitics of the region. In 2007 a new Country Program Development Framework (CPDF) had been put forward, retaining gender equality as one of three pillars along with basic education and democratic accountability. It also added a special program on Balochistan and FATA, which was never implemented. A year later, in 2008–09, there was another rethink, and the 2007 CPDF, which was supposed to be a ten-year strategy, was reduced to a focus on only two areas: economic growth (with women's economic empowerment placed under it) and education with a focus on children and youth. The gender equality and governance pillars were taken out, reversing the plans and high aim of 2006 to increase the budget and programs for gender equality. The laudable program objective of "Improvement in women's human rights, economic empowerment and access to social services" no longer appeared in the strategy. The reduced program also acknowledged that Canada had fallen to a middle-level donor in Pakistan against the rapid growth of other countries' aid programs to Pakistan, most notably those of the United Kingdom, the United States, Germany, Japan, and Australia. The Canadian strategy acknowledged the growing international focus on Pakistan because of its critical role in the global war against violent extremism as a way of linking it to the top foreign policy priority.

By 2011 there was another strategic-level review of the aid program with no conclusive outcome. New programming was put on hold; only the existing well-developed pipeline of planned projects remained on the books, but even these proceeded at a sluggish pace. The aid program had almost come to a halt. Canada, not surprisingly, was experiencing uncertainty on what to do with the aid program in Pakistan. During a visit by the HQ director general to Islamabad, we were informed that "Afghanistan-Pakistan relations were a sore point right now" in Ottawa, as the transition of NATO forces in Afghanistan was being discussed and decision-makers pondered what to do after the anticipated 2014 exit of international troops (announced in advance by the US). Canada's middle-level donor status soon fell to that of one of the smallest donors, the first time in over sixty years.

The same month CIDA cancelled the PAGE II women's fund in Pakistan, in Afghanistan the ISAF military command issued counter-insurgency guidance to all units to adopt village-level stabilization as a new approach in Afghanistan. It was meant to secure the population by working mostly at the grassroots and get services up and running, to have a more direct and lasting impact on the society beyond military campaigns to chase out insurgents. It was a model from Iraq, and the Canadian generals were compelled to make it work in Kandahar. It was a reflection of the influence of General Petraeus over the ISAF mission in Afghanistan and how his counter-insurgency or "COIN" doctrine was forming the pillar of modern military thought and also having some influence on development assistance in Afghanistan. The Canadian generals were taken with this innovation in their operations and pressured CIDA to undertake short-term stabilization programs. In Ottawa, the military's new stabilization approach met some resistance from the Afghanistan Task Force, led from the Privy Council Office by Deputy Minister David Mulroney. The ATF held firm to the position that the six priorities and three large signature projects for Afghanistan, and the benchmarks under them approved by Cabinet, were not to be changed. My report to Ottawa in 2009 on CIDA's plans on stabilization said that "over the next 18 months we will continue to support as the primary goal, the achievement of Canada's six priorities for Afghanistan and the success of CIDA's three signature projects. CIDA will continue to contribute to stabilization in a focused way. CIDA's contribution of development advice and planning expertise in the field as part of the civilian effort will continue. Our officers are already supporting the US surge and helping the US coordinate with the provincial government. CIDA will use every opportunity to help shape the direction of US program funds for development and stabilization," the latter a recognition that Canada was handing over its work to the Americans, and this would include stabilization programs. We reached a compromise with the military on support for their new stabilization approach, but it was a stretch for CIDA (and the Canadian military) at the time. With no experience in such programming in the agency, or in the Canadian military, we scrambled to devise a meaningful intervention alongside the military and help think out what was realistic and possible to do with aid funds while minimizing risk to CIDA (and the government of Canada). It added a new challenge for the aid agency on how to work closely alongside military security forces (not normally partners!) to implement development programs.

The CIDA offices were located at the Provincial Reconstruction Team headquarters – a fortified military base on the edge of Kandahar city that had once been a fruit canning factory built by the Russians. I was based there working as part of Canada's whole-of-government civilian surge to bolster the provincial government capacity to deliver basic services to its citizens, restore some essential infrastructure, and provide humanitarian aid. CIDA's mandate, "as part of Canada's whole of government mission, is helping the Government of Afghanistan to rebuild Kandahar province after years of war and conflict," read the public documents on the aid program. But the war was far from over and rebuilding in such a context proved impossible. A Kandahar Action Plan was developed, led by the civilian side as a "civ-mil" strategy, in 2008 under the leadership of Elissa Golberg, who had been appointed as the first Representative of Canada in Kandahar to oversee implementation of the Manley Panel recommendations. It employed a whole-of-government approach to contribute to the goals of stability, reconstruction, and governance. It was a solid strategy but was never fully implemented, as Kandahar was one of the most dangerous war zones in the world and the context was not yet conducive to post-conflict reconstruction and rebuilding.

The senior military officer responsible for the Dand district spoke to us one blistering hot day at a meeting on the district stabilization plan about their plans. "We've had a consultation with the district commissioner and have developed a plan. He has identified the development projects needed and we want CIDA to implement them," he said. "Can we see the plan?" the CIDA officer asked. The district officer pulled up a PowerPoint presentation that showed support to the school, the clinic, and the local government offices and a map of the area. "Was the community consulted?" asked the CIDA officer. "No, the district commissioner told us what was needed." It turned out the provincial civilian government departments responsible for services had not been consulted either, as they were not the usual counterparts for the military. We took the military district stabilization plan and retreated to our offices to discuss what to do. The next day we called our UN colleagues in Kabul, who emailed us a comprehensive community development plan for the Dand district that had been carefully developed by UN Habitat in consultation with the community and the local government the year before. It was a complete local development plan, outlining needs and priorities to restore basic services. We handed it over to our military counterparts, who accepted it in silence, not knowing what to say or even what to do with it. We reported to HQ that "the Village Stabilization pilot project has shown a somewhat rocky start both in terms of relations and working with the military and PRT civilians on the ground. Close management and monitoring to gauge the effectiveness of this approach along with trying other pilot approaches, will enhance the field and HQ's understanding as what works best under current circumstances in Kandahar."

A week later, after checking in and gearing up with protective equipment and helmets, we travelled to the Dand district office under a heavily armed contingent of soldiers for a launch of the Dand stabilization plan. We arrived after less than fifteen minutes on the road. It was then I realized just how precarious the situation was in Kandahar; this was an area we were working hard to stabilize so close to the PRT headquarters and just on the edge of Kandahar city proper – a sort of suburb just four kilometres south of the city. The room was packed with Canadian military and civilians and officials from the provincial government, including Kandahar Governor Wesa. He spoke first, followed by the head of the PRT and the district commissioner. There were no women present except for the few of us from CIDA and Canadian political staff. It was indicative of my experience in Kandahar; no women were ever present at any government meetings, much less had any central role in the provincial government (Tiessen 2017). It was a type of consultation to pave the way and garner full support from local authorities for implementation of the stabilization approach. CIDA allocated funds towards small projects such as water supply and school rehabilitation for re-opening and the district was stabilized for a short time by regular community security patrols by Canadian soldiers. We never really found out how stabilized it became, but it didn't last. The environment was not conducive to any kind of development programming, except emergency humanitarian aid. Counter-terrorism strategies and plans were nascent at the time (unlike today) and conflict prevention plans for development agencies were not yet a reality, at least for CIDA. On 30 December 2009, about two and a half months later, a deadly attack happened about 1,500 metres from the District Centre (which Canadian soldiers had rebuilt after a suicide bombing earlier in the year), killing four young soldiers and a young Canadian female journalist from Calgary on her first trip to Afghanistan. Their armoured vehicle struck a massive roadside bomb. It seriously injured four others including a young CIDA officer from Ottawa who lost her leg. It was her first field trip. She had been assigned to shadow the civil military cooperation (CIMIC) specialist. It shook CIDA and DFAIT staff both in the field and HQ to the core and brought into question the stabilization approach.

Reading the accounts of the Afghanistan papers years later, the findings of the US Office of the Special Inspector General for Afghanistan Reconstruction (SIGAR) was quoted: "We found the stabilization strategy and the programs used to achieve it were not properly tailored to the Afghan context, and successes in stabilizing Afghan districts rarely lasted longer than the physical presence of coalition troops and civilians," said the introduction to the report of May 2018. In Canada, former Cabinet minister Chris Alexander spoke on CBC Radio about Canada's stabilization efforts in Afghanistan: "Canada put an enormous amount of energy into stabilizing the country and it should not be forgotten" (CBC 2020). Others have assessed that this type of work – aid linked directly to military campaigns – has "been conducted at the expense of other development objectives" (Tiessen 2017, 135). The stabilization policy was pushing CIDA to match what the military was doing. There are many lessons learned from the early stabilization and COIN approaches showing why they were not more effective, especially in active war zones. The concept of stabilization and strategies for addressing violent extremism by aid agencies have changed dramatically from those early attempts.[1] The UN views stabilization programming within the context of a peace process, or to increase the legitimate government authority to help stabilize communities to move forward with recovery and development, usually immediately post-conflict or where conflict is sporadic and where the legitimate government is seeking to regain control and presence. The primary purpose is to build trust between communities and legitimate authorities and to lay the foundations for longer-term recovery, peace-building, and development programmes. Some form of restoration of local government presence is needed for it to be successful. Kandahar, as the heart of the Taliban, was not yet ready for this type of stabilization programming, much less traditional development projects. The local capacity to sustain stabilization programs was not there, either at the local government level, the provincial government level, or within the communities themselves. As an example, we found out at a meeting with the governor that the head teacher from the district had quit his job in education to work for the military on a cash-for-work initiative. I immediately informed the military, who corrected the issue, encouraging him to return to the school by hiring a member of his family instead. We also scoured resources to increase civil servants in the provincial government, but could hardly find anyone with a completed high school education.

One fundamental principle of development learned over the decades that applies even more critically to stabilization and PVE efforts, is that any assistance must be rooted in local contexts. Programs supported by aid actors should not be perceived as an outside imposition. Working with local organizations that are trusted by communities to shape and deliver programming is essential to prevent perpetuating cycles of radicalization and violence. Emerging research and global best practices on countering extremism are confirming that a whole range of structural and pull factors need to be addressed to combat extremism alongside a security response. Building community resilience through stronger engagement with community, particularly women, is one among many others (UNOCT 2023). As early as 2004, the lessons learned from the CIDA Women's Development Project Fund concluded that remaining strategic in an approach was enabled by addressing practical entry points on women's basic needs; that small injections of funds had led to policy initiatives and shifts; and that participatory approaches were essential, "partners who identify ground realities and design activities accordingly will achieve greater results. Community participation and involvement of local government structures can ensure a higher probability of achieving results." It also identified community ownership as key – a common and well-understood development principle by then: "when the communities['] basic needs are addressed, then the level of ownership, involvement, and willingness to carry the initiative forward and expand on is much greater. Long term sustainability can be achieved gradually through community participation and government's contribution however dependency on donors will continue in future due to lack of resources for projects" (CIDA 2004b). Recent approaches to women, peace, and security highlight collaboration and consultation with civil society to ensure inclusion. New guidance by the United States Institute of Peace (Schirch, Bosley, and Niconchuk 2023) to support the disengagement of people from extremist violence and their integration into local communities emphasizes pro-social engagement and building community resilience premised on involvement of local protagonists. The military often cited the urgency of time as well as security constraints, which meant short consultations with a few political authorities and security actors to move plans forward. The vision of the well-intentioned policies in Afghanistan was too far ahead of the ground reality.

In Pakistan, Canada's aid approach did not alter despite the growth of militancy and violent extremism, although its rationale did. It proposed concentrating on the education of youth and children, and on economic growth with a focus on women's economic empowerment to "enable Canada to combat extremism" (CIDA 2007). The program risk profile identified "militant driven insecurity" as the highest risk but was not accompanied by further analysis or guidance on what to do about it or where to target programs. While the theory behind education of youth and women's economic empowerment to combat extremism was plausible (since quality education, employment opportunities, and empowerment of women are important factors to address), it needed to be backed up by a closer examination of the problem and actions and implementation strategies, preferably in coordination with other donors and the government, to have a significant impact on this goal. Canada, along with most other aid donors, has supported education for decades in Pakistan. Early days of CIDA funding education in the 1980s even included support to madrassas (briefly), which at the time were expanding rapidly under Zia-ul-Haq's 1979 education policy. Education became one of two themes for Canadian assistance in 2009, although it was only a tiny fraction of the education aid to Pakistan when viewed against that of the UK, the US, the World Bank, and others. Education was the only sector where we eventually tried to be in sync on programming with the UK and the US (the biggest bilateral donors on education) on how to reach those most obscured and excluded in the population who could be at risk of radicalization. But the UK had little time to talk with Canada once the size and breadth of their program in education (and their overall aid program) were so large it was in no way even comparable to Canada's. They were preoccupied, with former UK Prime Minister Gordon Brown as the UN Special Envoy for Global Education, in leading a high-level political dialogue on education with the Pakistan government.

STEPPING DOWN AND HANDING OVER ON GENDER EQUALITY

After PAGE II faltered, the resilience of the Pakistan gender equality movement allowed them to quickly move their programs to more receptive donor partners. CIDA had played a key role for years, helping the gender equality movement to break ground and keep momentum when others were only marginally involved. Now, at a crucial time in Pakistan's history, the work Canada had supported made it possible for others to build on it. CIDA had been the innovator, an incubator of new groups and approaches, and had helped sustain the leadership needed at a critical time. Given the context in Pakistan and the urgency to place Pakistan as part of the solution to the Afghanistan war, it was time to pass the baton to bigger players to scale up programs to accelerate progress on women's equality and continue the policy advocacy.

By September 2009, the US Congress approved the Kerry-Lugar-Berman Bill allocating $7.5 billion in aid over five years to Pakistan. It included fighting poverty in the tribal regions and funding development projects in energy, health, and education. It also included massive funding for gender equality. The increase in US aid was linked to Pakistan's new efforts to counter militancy and stop militant attacks in Afghanistan. There was intense opposition to the bill in Pakistan, as its conditions were seen to violate Pakistan's sovereignty by micromanaging Pakistan's internal affairs. Hilary Clinton, then US Secretary of State, travelled to Pakistan that year and held town halls chaired by TV news host Nasim Zehra, attempting public dialogue on the relationship between the two countries. Despite the continuing controversy over the Kerry-Lugar-Berman aid to Pakistan, including the inability to spend even one-third of it in ten years, the bright spot was the funding for gender equality programs led by the capable organizations that Canada had initially nurtured and then supported for more than two decades.

CIDA watched as USAID launched its Gender Equity Program Fund of $40 million with the Aurat Foundation, one of CIDA's earliest and strongest partners on gender and women's rights through the 1990s. The Americans scaled up direct support to Pakistani women's organizations and women's human rights through gender funds based on the model and foundation Canada had laid over more than two decades. We felt envy and a sense of loss of relationship with and working in solidarity through support to the groups we had collaborated with for so many years. Some of them also felt the vacuum left by the end of the CIDA partnership. The coalitions of women's groups migrated with proposals and projects to USAID and UK DFID, both of which had increased aid to help counter radicalization in parts of the country.

END OF AN ERA IN CANADIAN AID TO PAKISTAN

Canadian disenchantment with Pakistan policies towards Afghanistan and the Taliban elements located in its border regions continued to play out in the context of the aid program. No new projects were approved for two years while Canadian aid to Afghanistan reached an all-time high. As the maple leaf flag was lowered for the last time at the Provincial Reconstruction Team base in Kandahar in 2011, the bureaucratic hand-wringing on "where the Pakistan aid program was going and how we could adjust to new realities" continued throughout the year. In April 2012, the final decision came from Cabinet to cut aid to Pakistan. We were told during a visit from senior management to Islamabad that the capacity to achieve results in Pakistan and the high operational costs of some programs were contributing factors. "There are concerns about how to achieve aid effectiveness in Pakistan and it has always been a difficult country for aid programs," we were told. The decision was taken within the context of the future of the war in Afghanistan and Canadian efforts as part of ISAF, as well as the government's major deficit reduction action plan severely affecting CIDA budgets that year. Pakistan was the worst-affected country among CIDA country programs, and it dropped from the list of priority countries for aid. For aid agencies, geopolitics and high-level foreign policy imperatives could swing and skew years of good development work and trusted relationships and collaboration, to meet the exigencies of the political moment.

— * —

Spring is a short but beautiful season in Islamabad, with flowering jacaranda trees and blossoms everywhere. We had just celebrated the Persian new year, *Naw Ruz*, with friends in Islamabad, a time for hope and renewal. It was an unfortunate time to deliver the message of cutting Canadian aid to the Secretary of the Planning Division in the Finance Ministry. We met in his office and, as expected, he took it graciously without much surprise. By then, Canada was a minor aid player from the Pakistan government's perspective, and it hardly made any difference to them as CIDA funds were not directed to government programs. They had bigger, more complex relationships to manage. Their main interest in Canada was accessing visas for Pakistanis to travel there. Those people-to-people ties remain a vibrant part of Canada's relationship with Pakistan.

CIDA retained a minor program in teacher training, continued the women's economic empowerment projects, and maintained the controversial and corruption-ridden debt for education conversion program. The Secretary told me that responsibility for both these thematic areas had been devolved to the provinces in 2010 under the eighteenth amendment to the constitution. CIDA had lost its last direct link to engage in meaningful dialogue with the federal government at the national level. It was indeed the end of an era for Canada's sixty-plus years of aid to Pakistan and for Canada's groundbreaking support for gender equality. Some in the Canadian government blamed the lack of success in Afghanistan entirely on Pakistan and its perceived double game with America – aiding ISAF and allowing logistics support, while turning a blind eye to Afghan Taliban leadership taking refuge in districts of the federally administered tribal areas such as Waziristan. There were even corridor rumours about stopping aid to Pakistan, and dramatically reducing the embassy staff in Islamabad.

"Unfortunately, the state has failed to effectively counter the extremist narrative, the rising religious intolerance and establish rule of law. The success of the latest [counter terrorism] operation depends on whether we have learnt any lessons from our past policy failures," wrote Zahid Hussain in his column in *Dawn News* on 1 March 2017. Now the Islamic State terror group[2] is active in Pakistan's border areas. The bombing of a mosque in Quetta during Friday prayers on 10 January 2020 that killed more than thirteen people, including a senior police officer, and injured twenty was undertaken by ISIL reportedly tracking an Afghan Taliban leader. In April 2021, the Quetta Serena hotel was bombed. Sectarian violence has not decreased. There has been a rise in Pakistan militant activity since the Taliban took power in Afghanistan. In July 2023 there was a suicide bombing at an ultra-conservative religious political party rally in Bajur district, 10 km from the Afghan border, killing more than 60 people. Islamic State – Khorasan Province claimed responsibility. There is still no end in sight to a situation that began as a small jihadist movement in the border areas of Afghanistan and Pakistan and is now a global threat. No one had predicted its reach.

PART THREE

Entry Points and Shrinking Spaces

13

Being a Feminist in Difficult Places

Just after Christmas on 28 December 2011, I picked up the *Pakistan Express Tribune* newspaper to see a report about Zarteef Afridi,[1] a social activist and human rights campaigner whom militants had gunned down in Khyber Tribal Agency (now a district of KP Province). He had been speaking at a gathering in Jamrud, his hometown, defending women's rights, saying that women and men were equal. The already-provoked crowd could not digest it. Some people chanted slogans, calling him a heathen who had come to throw away their centuries-old traditions (*Express Tribune* 2011). He then started receiving threats from the group that later claimed responsibility for his death, the Abdullah Azam Brigade; "what Zarteel was doing was in exact opposition of what is considered right here," said the news article. Reporting to Ottawa at the time, I wrote that "his death shows how vulnerable the situation is here yet ironically this is just two weeks after the landmark women's protection bills passed in the Senate. While one world of activists and organizations are working to protect women's equality and rights in Islamabad, another reality is operating elsewhere in the Country." The media reported that family sources said the deceased had been receiving threats because he was opposed to Taliban activities in tribal areas and supported women's rights. His brother was quoted at the time in the *Express Tribune*: "We cannot do anything against those who killed him. Impunity rei[g]ns for those who kill and abduct human rights activists in Pakistan." The shrinking freedom of activists promoting human rights and women's rights was manifesting everywhere. It was the culmination of decades of failure to recognize and understand the severity of the militant threat to society (Gul 2010).

After 2011 things regressed again, with more human rights activists assassinated, abducted, or disappeared. On 5 July 2012, Farida Afridi, co-founder of an NGO promoting women's rights in FATA, was shot dead (International Crisis Group 2015, n135). Two months later, protests erupted across Pakistan and other Muslim countries, instigated by a film released in the US denigrating the Prophet Mohammed by mocking him. Facebook and YouTube were blocked in Pakistan and a national holiday declared by the government as a "Day of the love of the Prophet," to release some of the anger from hardline clerics and their followers about the film trailer on YouTube. Mobile phone systems were also down. It was 2012, and anger grew to the point where police had to block off the diplomatic enclave with shipping containers on 22 September. We were not allowed out of our homes for close to a week. The protests turned into deadly anti-American action, with people clambering to reach the US embassy just beside our house. All embassy staff were in lockdown and were asked to prepare a safe haven inside our homes. We eventually spent that day at the Canadian Club with watery eyes from the tear gas targeting the nearby protesters, trying to interpret the local Urdu-language TV coverage of the event. In 2012, the KP office of the Canada-Pakistan debt for education project received a threat letter from the Taliban: "we know well your project financed by the infidels and Zionists fighting against our brothers in Afghanistan, this we will leave for now but you [the Pakistani staff] should leave. We see your dancing parties at night." It was a long letter, mostly disapproving of what was seen as unacceptable behaviour, but still a reality check for the aid program to see how Canada was portrayed as the enemy by extremists in Pakistan.

Barely two weeks after the protests settled down, on 9 October 2012, another brutal incident in Pakistan took place in the Swat Valley of Khyber Pakhtunkhwa province. A Taliban gunman from Mullah Fazlullah's Tehrik-e-Taliban Pakistan (TTP) attempted to assassinate fifteen-year-old Malala Yousafzai for her outspoken support for girls' education and her perceived promotion of Western culture and anti-Taliban views. This extremist group had occupied the Swat Valley and banned girls' education since Malala was eleven, four years earlier. The spokesman for the Pakistani Taliban, Ehsanullah Ehsan, accused Malala in his call to the media after the attempt on her life, claiming that she was propagandizing against the Mujaheddin, and that she was a Western spy and symbol of resistance to their ideology (and to their threats). "We did what we had to."[2] This should have been an ominous warning sign at the time of more social and political insecurity to come.³ The warning signs had continued in that area as the Taliban attempted to close girls' schools and ban education. The same month there were reports in the paper of a girls' schools in Mardan district being burned, along with several bombings of CD shops in the same district. I wrote at the time, "Violence in KP so close to Islamabad continues this month with seven charity workers murdered on New Year's Day in Swabi district, five of them female teachers. Life in Islamabad goes on, with parties, good restaurants, trendy coffee shops and concerts, but the brutal militancy is not far away – a mere two-hour drive and one is in the heart of it at the moment." My notes also recalled the police chief of Peshawar stating on 3 January 2013 that "we are in a state of war. The whole country is facing an insurgency, so we are revising the present security steps and working on a new strategy." The situation in KP became much worse that year.

Five months later, on 13 March 2013, Perween Rahman, a prominent social activist and development worker since the 1980s and the director of the Orangi Project in Karachi, was shot dead on her way back from work. "Perween believed that everyone, regardless of income, had a right to basic services," reported the *Dawn* newspaper in the month of her death. Parween was a defender of marginalized people living in slums in Karachi and had exposed illegal water supply rackets depriving the poor of access to water. As an architect and urban planner, she also documented encroachments on government land, championed land rights, and secured housing and livelihoods for the poor. She had received warnings to stop documenting land. Another employee was killed not long after. Her story has been made into a film, *Into Dust*, described by the filmmaker as a "universal story of bravery against powerful forces." CIDA had funded Orangi as early as 2003 ($88,000 under the PAGE women's fund) for improving livelihoods for women through a women's centre for training and trading.

Canadian foreign policy has consistently promoted human rights over the decades. The "promotion of human rights, diversity and inclusion" was considered at the core of Canada's foreign policy. By 2012, more than ever, civil society in Pakistan needed the international community's support as the tide of anti-democratic forces continued to swell, divisions deepened, and the forces of intolerance grew stronger in society. In 2012 Canada's official strategic messages stated that "the promotion and protection of human rights, in Pakistan and around the world, is an integral part of Canadian foreign policy.

Canada is particularly concerned about extremists, who are sowing hate and fostering religious intolerance, which is repugnant to Pakistan's values." That was the year that Canada made the policy decision to reduce its sizeable and long-standing development program in Pakistan, which had been a valuable tool to continue participating in this discourse, to a small and narrowly focused program.

— * —

The situation surrounding our daily life in Pakistan presented a confusing picture of a mix of freedom and suppression. It was not quite the rights-based and open democratic society many had hoped to see after decades of support to civil society and the rights movement, yet the media was surprisingly outspoken. Reading the English newspaper one morning, the barrage of headlines was once again an eye-opener. The front-page heralded: The government now ready to take on the irreconcilable militants; the government renewed its offer of talks with militant groups saying this is the spirit of Islam. "Our aim is to bring peace in Pakistan, particularly in FATA." Another article said the army were drawing up plans for a military operation against the Pakistan Taliban and would act if the TTP spurned the talks. Moving on, the same paper also reported that a jirga in Saragohda district of Punjab ruled on giving away two underaged girls to compensate the plaintiffs; a young child's tortured body was found; a woman was attacked with acid; a man claimed to have been sold into slavery; and an editorial lamented the bloodbath in Karachi, saying battlefield Karachi would bleed into its own gutters. The paper said Karachi was not under any government control. Media articles that year reported that Karachi was the most dangerous place in Pakistan, witnessing the most killings. News reports by the *Express Tribune* said that by the end of the year, there were about 2,700 dead and over 40,000 reported incidents of criminality. At the same time, another editorial lamented the weak development project agenda, saying money spent on most government development projects was a complete waste. That dose of daily news was a lot to take in.

Karachi's strategic role in the Afghan war included the logistics support for ISAF in Afghanistan; goods arriving at the port were taken onward by trucks in a continuous flow of hundreds per day, winding their way up through the Khyber Pass. It had also become a "main hub of radicalism" (Hussain 2010). Extremist groups established themselves there, while gradually, criminal gangs took control of parts of the city. Some have referred to it as a lawless megacity, where no one knows whether it is a stray bullet, car bomb, or suicide bomb that might take one's life on any given day. On a visit to Karachi that year, I took the opportunity to stop at the Tomb of Muhammed Ali Jinnah, the *Mazar-e-Quaid*, a beautiful white marble mausoleum built to house the remains of the founder of Pakistan. It was 45 degrees outside, the heat blurring the image. Jinnah's original house, now a museum, is another historic site in the city. One of his many messages resonated: "My message to you all is of hope, courage, and confidence. Let us mobilize all our resources in a systematic and organized way and tackle the grave issues that confront us with grim determination and discipline worthy of a great nation."

Thinking about Jinnah's revered role in Pakistan as the father of the nation made me reflect on the tensions evident in Pakistan, and the transition the country is undergoing between a centuries-old civilization, outdated social laws, and a different governance system and future. "Pakistan has been precariously balanced between past and present, between tradition and modernity, between Islamism and secularism throughout its brief history" (Ziring 2004). Everyone is impacted in some way by this transition, but women's rights are not only taking a step back in some parts of the country but are a matter of life and death. The WAF first articulated this in 1983:

> The position of women in Pakistani society has been disputed since the country was established in 1947. Muhammad Ali Jinnah's vision for the republic involved a separation of religion and politics, the equality of all Pakistanis, and the nurturing of an intelligentsia. He spoke out against "the curse of provincialism" and said in a speech, "It is a crime against humanity that our women are shut up within the four walls of the houses as prisoners." (Mumtaz and Shaheed 1987)

In the decades since Jinnah's death in 1948, those in power, most notably General Zia-ul-Haq, have eroded women's rights, often in "efforts to enforce a conservative, Islamic ideology" (Okeowo 2018).

— * —

By mid-March 2014, security in the capital had become worse again. The Americans had announced the troop withdrawal from Afghanistan. We were faced with soldiers with machine guns on most street corners, and getting into the diplomatic enclave to the office was an ordeal each morning. The security situation had not improved but life went on. After leaving my position at the embassy to work with the World Bank, Shahbaz and I had moved outside the diplomatic enclave to a house in the F7 area beside Jinnah Market. It was a new phase in our lives, and we began to experience Pakistan differently. Although we missed the comfortable support of the embassy, the freedom to live independently allowed us to see Pakistan through a new lens. We frequented the Afghan restaurant close by, where we shared tables with Afghans living in Islamabad and Pakistanis of all backgrounds. Everyone loved the charcoal-grilled kebabs served with the long flat Afghan bread and Kabuli pilau, jewelled saffron rice. The Saeed Book Bank down the street was chock-full of books on Pakistan and Afghanistan, from geopolitical history, the roots and rise of extremism, to poetry, art, and food adventures – we filled our bookshelves at home. The Canadian Second Cup coffee shop chain had opened an outlet at the end of our street, an air-conditioned haven to enjoy newly purchased books, weekend coffee, and newspapers. It was an unfamiliar freedom to walk the streets and frequent these places, even though the guards at the house gate wore flak jackets and helmets and carried machine guns.

On the morning of Muharram (the day observing the martyrdom of the Imam Hussain, a religious observance for Shia Muslims), we awoke as usual to the *azan*, the call to prayer that started at one distant mosque and cascaded to several others, each closer to the house. Heightened security was activated across the country in case of violence against religious processions for Muharram. Most offices were closed, cell phone service was suspended in sensitive areas, and thousands of police were deployed with the army on standby. It was a regular occurrence and one we were used to by then. It was just after a suicide attack in Punjab, at the Wagah border with India, that claimed sixty lives. The year ended with the deadliest terrorist attack in Pakistan's history – the bombing of an army public school in Peshawar on 16 December 2014. It killed 141 people, 132 of them schoolchildren between the ages of thirteen and sixteen. The Pakistan Taliban claimed responsibility. Every year Pakistanis hold a vigil to remember the Peshawar army public school attack, calling it a "massacre of the innocents." Both Ehsanullah Ehsan, one of the founding members of and spokesperson for the Pakistani Taliban (after the attempted killing of Malala), and TTP's Maulana Fazlullah claimed responsibility for the attack, justifying the killing of children and teachers at the school. Only months before, I had travelled to Peshawar to monitor a polio campaign. We were locked into the secure UN WFP guesthouse, unable to venture out after dark even in armoured vehicles – a veritable war zone, it reminded me of Kabul in 2009. It was also around the time when the visibility of the terrorist group Daesh first appeared in Pakistan. Pakistan's first National Action Plan against terrorism was drafted in 2014 in the aftermath of the gruesome army school attack. It marked a critical juncture in a new counter-terrorism and prevention of violent extremism strategy. Attacks on schools in the area continue; in October 2020, a blast at a madrassa in Peshawar killed seven children and injured 125.

SHRINKING DEMOCRATIC SPACE

Less than a year later, in April 2015, another well-known social activist, Sabeen Mahmud, was murdered in Karachi. She was shot in her car, her mother critically injured, while returning home from a talk on the silencing of activists in Balochistan. She was, in return, silenced herself. Mahmud was the director and creator of The Second Floor in Karachi, a community space for open dialogue and poetry, and where the talk had just taken place. Two years earlier she had gone into hiding as a result of threats for speaking out in defiance of the banning of Valentine's Day by the religious right. The 14 February celebrations were subsequently banned by the government in 2016 and 2017. "The Infidel West is conspiring against us to take away the *sharam* [modesty, humility, good manners] and *haya* [decency] of our women through Valentine's Day." Her killer said she was shot for holding an un-Islamic Valentine's Day rally (Inayat 2020). In the wake of her death, local media and fellow activists voiced their support of the outspoken organizer, who was just forty years old. "She was a pillar of support to all the voiceless people and her death is a huge loss for Pakistan," said one local media report. Reactions to her assassination on social media were unequivocal, saying, "a liberal and moderate voice silenced ... Another sign that freedom of speech in Pakistan is now gone ... An extraordinary Pakistani fighting for open dialogue shot dead in Karachi ... The end of civilization ... Even as we grieve our friend, we refuse to be silenced." Women human rights activists remember her as one of those who has fallen in the work against fundamentalism and defying extremism. I wrote an article in the Open

Canada media platform at the time, saying, "At a moment when civil society activists and intellectuals are being threatened and silenced in Pakistan, one can't help but think of the support Canada provided for voices of civil society over decades." The vision and hope of the 1990s of a vibrant, pluralistic, and rights-focused civil society in Pakistan seemed more challenged than ever. The investments of the international community to support a dynamic civil society and promote human rights in Pakistan, in which Canada led the way in the 1990s, had not kept pace with the swelling wave of its opposing forces.

Pakistan was a dangerous place for journalists too. It ranked eighth on the Committee to Protect Journalists' 2019 Global Impunity Index, with sixteen unsolved killings of journalists in the past ten years. Of the thirty-four journalists who were murdered there for their work since 1992, when CPJ began keeping detailed records, partial justice has been achieved in only three cases. On 28 March 2014, journalist, scholar, and development advisor Raza Rumi was attacked in central Lahore in his car, and his driver was killed. He said in the news, "I was dreading this day ... We [journalists] will continue to speak the truth and not back down" (*Express Tribune* 2014). He left the country for the US. Most journalists were calling these kinds of attacks a suppression of thought and of anything that goes against the "Muslim brotherhood views," as Imtiaz Gul told me over a dinner one night at the Chinese restaurant in our neighbourhood. But the Minister of Planning downplayed the incident, indicating that such incidents could happen even in Europe and the US.

In February 2021, four women working as crafts trainers in Ippi village in Mirali, North Waziristan, delivering vocational training for women for a local NGO, Sabawoon, were killed by terrorists. A fifth, Mariam Bibi, survived. It exposes the risks of engaging local women's groups in aid projects and begs the question of women's empowerment–type projects in Taliban strongholds and their life-and-death consequences. If this can happen to craft trainers, what can happen to women's rights activists? These women had put their lives at risk for a daily wage of only 1,000 PKR (about $10). In Pakistan, the International Crisis Group Asia reported in 2015, "militants target women's rights activists, political leaders and development workers without consequences" (International Crisis Group 2015). It was becoming an increasingly challenging environment for progressive liberal thinkers and human rights activists. Was all the hard work of civil society and women's rights organizations of the 1990s being rolled back? It appeared that all the support provided to those working for a more tolerant and democratic society had met with less success than hoped. Where was the women's movement in the face of this and how were they managing, given the societal movement towards increased conservatism and intolerance and violence?

Many accusations under the blasphemy laws remain grave human rights concerns. The blasphemy laws continue to be a source of oppression not only of religious freedom and human rights but, more poignantly, of women and girls. The Aurat March, a coordinated feminist protest that began in 2018 on Pakistan Women's Day, faced blasphemy allegations in 2021 – a potential violent threat, since "merely an allegation of blasphemy can cause vigilante killings or mob-driven violence" (Azmat 2022). Opposition to the laws exists but is limited. Support for the religious blasphemy laws, which are ingrained in Pakistan's legal framework, has been a position among the country's mainstream religious political parties – which represent both Deobandi and Barelvi Islam and include parties such as Jamat-e-Islami (JI), Jamiat Ulema-e-Islam-Fazlur Rehman (JUI-F), and Jamiat Ulema-e-Pakistan (JUP). They are united in their support for the blasphemy laws even as they criticize religious extremism.[4] The growth of the Islamic extremist political party Tehreek-e-Labbaik Pakistan (TLP) is attributed to its use of the blasphemy law as a main platform since the prosecution of the security guard Mumtaz Qadri (Kugelman and Weinstein 2021), who murdered the governor of Punjab in 2011 (see chapter 5) for his public stance against the blasphemy law and the Asia Bibi case.

The Islamist political parties have since then been stirring up wrath in youth on the blasphemy issue. Some now say the wrath of teenagers who become aligned to terrorists may have roots in Pakistan's "draconian blasphemy laws which call for the death penalty for any act or statement that maligns Islam or the Prophet Muhammad" (Gannon 2020). The blasphemy law has been used to discredit a range of critics. In early 2017, five human rights and social media activists disappeared in Pakistan, with some accused of promoting blasphemous content on social media. They were returned, but bloggers continued afterwards to be accused by the clerics of blasphemy. At that time, the government attempted to track Pakistanis posting material on social media that was considered offensive to Islam, which could be regarded as blasphemy, and therefore subject to a death sentence. Just a few weeks later, a university student in Mardan of KP province was lynched in April 2017 for allegedly uploading what was considered suspicious blasphemy content on Facebook. A former employee in the Canadian embassy was cautioned by his parents that year to reduce his opinions and views on Facebook and social media about the need for an open and free society in Pakistan. "Pakistan's deradicalization project must start in public schools and universities. We are already a few decades late in resetting our direction," said Raza Rumi (Rumi 2017).

— * —

Extremist groups frame women's human rights as "Western," colonialist, and/or immoral, and blame them for the alleged moral decline these groups fight against (Khan 2022). This has not changed from the early 1980s, when conservative religious groups accused WAF of being Westernized and un-Islamic and out to destroy the moral fabric of society (Mumtaz and Shaheed 1987). Asma Jahangir was branded early on as a traitor and an American agent trying to malign Pakistan and destroy the country's social and political fabric in the name of human rights when she tested the idea in late 1986 of a human rights organization for Pakistan. Others accuse Western aid and security programs of portraying women in Pakistan and Afghanistan as the poor and oppressed, who need to be "liberated" by Western intervention. This was the topic of discussion at a seminar at the Sustainable Development Policy Institute (SDPI) in December 2012 on "Conflicting Female and Feminist Identifies after 9/11." The concept of liberating women in Afghanistan was called an incomplete and hasty examination of the problem, ignoring historical redress. I listened to the panellists that day (a mix of Western and Pakistani women) speak about transnational feminist frameworks being used by the Pakistan women's movement since the 1990s, committing them to take a secular human rights-based approach. "There was a lack of Islamic authority in the women's movement – including in looking at honour killings without any nuanced understanding of the issues," said one speaker. In more recent discussions and dialogue, we have heard from Muslim women feminists expressing their concerns about the misinterpretations of Sharia by the Taliban.[5] The panel went on to conclude that many see the "Western orientalist feminist analysis" as dominating the discourse on women's issues. The book on *Women of Pakistan* written about the 1980s women's movement (Mumtaz and Shaheed 1987) specifically addresses this question. It is a discussion shaped by not only the questions and concerns raised by WAF but also those relating to Islam as a culture, a religion, and as a political force. It tackled the actors involved on either side and "traced the steps of Muslim women's struggle in the sub-continent and the role of Islam in contemporary history." The authors recount that "in the fifty years preceding Independence [of Pakistan], progressive Muslim groups justified women's education, emancipation, and rights from within an Islamic framework. As of 1947, having been monopolized by reactionary elements, Islam has been the medium used by those wanting to curb or deny women their rights" (ibid., 1). WAF's perception at that time was that extremist religious discourse was dominating the discussion on women's issues, not Western feminist analysis. For decades this has been a never-ending debate and perhaps a false dichotomy on who is dominating the discussion on women's issues and how. Is a future vision of equality between women and men limited to only two perspectives in the discourse? The panel lost the attention of its audience that day, who before the end had all left the session, as it did not appear to resonate with the majority of those attending.

WOMEN'S RIGHTS IN ISLAM

Islam provides some specific rights to women and mechanisms to protect them. These are defined through Islamic laws. The Quran builds safeguards into the social system to ensure women may not suffer injustices. Some of these are the right to have a dowry, to receive care and support, to own and inherit property. The role of mother is a highly valued and respected one. Although the male has the power of divorce, a woman can divorce herself from her husband, if she so stipulates in the marriage contract (Shakeel in GIANT Global Issues Awareness for National Trust Forum 1996, 104). Children after divorce are automatically in the custody of the father (intended to ensure a woman is not left to fend for her children alone), although this can leave a divorced woman vulnerable to losing her children. "It is well known that the advent of Islam was a herald of freedom for the exploited women of that era" (Iqbal 2006). The Sharia (or "path" in Arabic) that the Holy Book or Quran supplies remains the basis of all true Muslim life.

Although Islam in one sense defines the role of women, its various interpretations make any one authoritative prescription almost impossible. Islamic prescription, drawn from the Quran (Holy Book) and the Hadith (sayings and traditions of the Prophet Muhammed), has been subject to much interpretation. Islamic prescription is fairly explicit on marriage, divorce, custody of children, inheritance and property, and education. Areas that differ for women and men are marriage (the number of spouses) and divorce, purdah, inheritance and property, and witness. Islam gives a definite right of inheritance to women. In practice, this law has often gone unheeded in Pakistan and daughters often do not inherit the father's property. In the mid-1980s, the three controversial Islamic laws affecting women that were drafted by the Council of Islamic Ideology (CII) are the law of evidence, the law on adultery, and those on divorce. The one enacted was that on adultery. They were drafted and re-drafted and have been subject to constant debate and reform since 1980. The issue of women's rights and gender relations is one of the controversies between interpretations (and centuries-old misinterpretations) and has become one of the most challenging issues in Islam today. The various interpretations make one authoritative prescription impossible; therefore there are conflicts within the Islamic prescriptions with regard to female status. Interpretation has been influenced by many factors, including what has been deemed "culture." In some places where extremist groups are present at the local level, the mixing of customary law and Sharia law may be contributing to the conflicts within differing interpretations by those following extremist ideologies.

"QUESTIONS ABOUT CULTURE"

The human rights versus culture debate, the definition of gender as identity, the politicization of the definition of culture, and the accusations that criticism of harmful cultural practices is racial paternalism, neocolonialism, and cultural imperialism are all minefield debates holding policy-makers hostage to the culture question (Claros-Lopez and Nakhjavani 2018). The UN has many special rapporteurs working on such issues. The one on cultural rights said in August 2021 in the context of the takeover of Afghanistan by the Taliban, "Any efforts to justify such abuses [attacks on minorities and women human rights defenders, killing of artists and exclusion of women from employment and education] in the name of Afghan culture should be strongly opposed and denounced ... fundamentalism and extremism, and their harmful effects on cultures, everywhere in the world, threaten the rights and security of all" (UN News 2021).

In 2001, CIDA produced a corporate document entitled *Questions about Culture*, revised again in 2010. It attempts to give guidance on the issue of culture and gender equality and again raises the question, "Are we imposing 'Western' values?" It framed this in the context of the Convention on the Elimination of Discrimination against Women (CEDAW) and recommended using gender analysis and establishing a constructive dialogue with partners. It outlined ways to talk about gender equality with partners. The criticism against Western and human rights–based feminism has not disappeared and is rooted in many different arguments and perspectives. Sally Armstrong, the acclaimed Canadian journalist and human rights activist and author of two books on women in Afghanistan, asserts that improving the status of women is crucial to our collective surviving and thriving. "On a scale of 1–10, I think it is fair to say that religion and customs concerning women and girls score a solid 11 for a toxic mix," she said during a webinar on women's rights in Afghanistan during the early days of the peace talks with the Taliban. "We need to call out the Islamic extremists for this new form of patriarchy, this is not cultural, it's criminal."[6] The worry that day among the panellists was how the return of the Taliban to power in Afghanistan would affect women living under Muslim law around the world. "If women's rights are undermined in Afghanistan, it will undermine women's rights everywhere including Iran, Turkey, Mali, Somalia, Iraq and Syria," said the participant from the organization Women Living under Muslim Laws (WLUML). The Turkish writer Elif Shafak adds to this view, "For us, the rise of fundamentalism and the deepening of misogyny, the loss of basic human rights is not some abstract debate. We have seen enough to understand that when countries go backwards and tumble into authoritarianism and religious fundamentalism, it is women and minorities who have the most to lose" (Shafak 2021). "For feminists from Turkey, the rise of fundamentalism is an existential threat that is never far away." Transformation in culture should not mean upsetting the positive aspects of culture or disrupting cultural diversity. Instead it could mean changing the patriarchal traditions and gender roles that have been passed down through generations that can be obstacles to achieving equality or pose real threats to women's well-being. "Muslim women, in particular, have been placed at the heart of growing human rights versus Islam dynamic, a dynamic that has the potential to constrain the pursuit of inclusive and egalitarian peacebuilding processes" (Khan 2022).

— * —

By 2019, incidents of terror attacks in Pakistan had dropped significantly from 2009 levels. Following the series of National Internal Security Policies (NISP) from 2014 after the Pakistan Taliban attack on the military school in Peshawar, the government also issued national action plans combined with military operations. It is notable that the 2018 NISP was the first document to address gender dimensions of national security and took a multi-pronged expanded notion of security (Khan 2022). The UK removed travel restrictions and British Airways resumed flights to Pakistan. The US also acknowledged publicly that Pakistan's security environment had improved.

Pakistan is still a dangerous place for activists; despite improvements compared to a decade earlier, it still has unstable borders and is in a volatile sub-region. For anyone living in Pakistan, the continuing violence and extremism, threatening progressive voices in civil society and the women's rights movement, lends itself easily to a sense of uncertainty despite the combined efforts of activists and those working against it. Civil society activists and intellectuals are the silenced majority; as Kim Ghattas, a journalist, said at the Lahore Literary Festival in 2021, "the forces of pluralism are larger than we think, but they are sent to exile, pushed back, killed, jailed" – but they are not defeated.

14

Understanding Obscurities

Violent extremism is challenging aid actors and governments to rethink development approaches that can address not only some of the grievances but also the reasons for radicalization that can lead to violent extremism. "People need hope. They need choices and they need opportunities ... Lack of opportunity is a reflection of a failure of development," said UNDP Administrator Steiner at the UNDP and MISK Youth Forum in New York (Leiberman 2017). Steiner spoke about development as a "foundation for young people," arguing that development approaches need to take into consideration factors that make youth vulnerable to extremism. Since then, the UNDP has continued to research and understand this connection. In Pakistan around 63 per cent of the population is between the ages of fifteen and thirty-three – both a demographic dividend and a risk for Pakistani society. A UNDP report on Africa that same year found that people are being convinced the state cannot protect them. In the Sahel region, young people join jihadists not out of religious conviction but out of desperation in the face of bad governance, lack of employment, corruption, and state and militia abuses. Extremism thrives on anger, alienation, and a lack of inclusion, the report states (UNDP 2017). The vacuum left by the absence of state services has been filled by other groups.

The many books written before 2010 on the rise of terrorism in Pakistan point consistently to the lack of rule of law, the writ of the state failing to extend fully throughout the country, poor governance and injustice (particularly in remote areas such as the border districts near Afghanistan), the exclusion of parts of the population or a sense of alienation and feeling they do not have a place in society, lack of employment, and unending poverty as some of the underlying drivers. "A multilayered, multipronged strategy is needed that includes efforts to engage in the battle of ideas and address the structural factors – including issues of governance and injustice – that create the breeding ground for militancy," wrote Pakistan's ambassador to the UN, Maleeha Lodhi, in 2011 (Lodhi 2011, 351). The state's failure to address deep-rooted marginalization, socio-economic inequality, and insecurity in parts of the country fuel extremists' presence in areas of weak governance, where opportunities, employment, and equitable access to services of the state – including education, health, and justice – are limited. Equally, weak rule of law, impunity, inequality, and injustice are at the root of most protracted conflicts (UNDP 2022b). In Pakistan, violent extremists appeal to the concrete social circumstances of potential recruits – social displacement, precarious work, and systemic marginalization – and this material attraction appears to be the case for women as well as men (Khan 2022, n35). UNDP research has identified the link between the growth of violent extremism among vulnerable populations, notably youth, and limited socio-economic opportunities and weak civic engagement. A report by UNESCO found that 69 per cent of terrorist attacks happen in countries with low intercultural dialogue – in other words, supporting an environment where dialogue can thrive, bringing different groups together to talk, can help address the root causes and structural drivers of violence and can potentially lead to transformational impact (UNESCO 2022). Addressing deep-rooted socio-economic inequality and multi-dimensional poverty is a much greater challenge than merely increasing basic public services, although this in itself is not simple. The consecutive crises over the years in Pakistan have impeded the state's ability to focus on multi-pronged poverty reduction in the face of competing emergencies and security. Despite this, the Pakistan government has made strides in the past decade in extending state services in remote areas previously underserved such as the former FATA.

Other scholarly research has found inconclusive results on economic determinants such as poverty and income inequality, or education (including madrassas as a source of radicalization) and lack of governance, as factors conducive to radicalization. Research on Pakistan by Professor Christine Fair contributes to the evolving body of literature that suggests poverty, limited education, and time spent at a madrassa are poor predictors for determining either support for terrorism or participation in terrorism in Pakistan (Fair 2013). Research over the past decade has identified other factors that extend beyond the role of improved socio-economic development (better access to employment, services, justice), mainly an acute sense of grievance towards government (belief that government looks after only the interests of a few) and no confidence in police, military, or politicians, with security as an immediate (unfulfilled) need (UNDP 2017).

Knowledge and understanding of reasons for and sources of radicalization and determinants of violent extremism are evolving, particularly as the approaches and recruitment tactics of violent extremist groups evolve. Studies on what drives recruitment to the Lashkar-e-Taiba (LET) in Punjab found that fighters saw association with the group as a way to a more meaningful or purposeful life. They were motivated by a view that the perceived corruption and moral depravity in society are inappropriate for Muslims. The group was seen as an instrument for positive change (Fair 2013).

Findings from the behavioural sciences[1] to address the prevention of violent extremism have identified possible risk factors at the individual, social, and structural/institutional levels that are helpful in understanding what drives people to engage in violent extremism (UNDP 2021a). These findings show the complexity around the issue:[2]

RISK FACTORS FOR VIOLENT EXTREMISM

Individual

- Temporary emotional states.
- Individual psychological traits.
- Dissatisfaction with current social or political activities.
- The desire to take action to enact change.
- Empathy with victims and a desire to help.
- Openness to the use of violence: those who engage in and support VE must believe that there are conditions under which violence (including violence against innocents) is acceptable and effective.
- Expectations about the benefits of personal involvement in VE: the belief that participation in a VE group will bring individual benefits often accompanies initial and increased engagement. Such potential benefits might include feelings of "heightened status, respect, [and] authority."

Social

- Social network ties to VE members (in many instances, recruitment into VE occurs through existing social networks).
- Tensions and conflicts between groups.
- Groups experiencing a sense of injustice and/or stigma.
- Lack of social acceptance of diversity: when diversity is not valued, those who do not conform to social norms may see violent extremism as an alternate way of asserting dignity.
- Gendered lenses: socializations of gender often play a role. As one example, if a culture highly associates masculinity with employment, marriage, and/or protecting the women in their lives, and men are not able to achieve these, they may see VE as an alternate path to dignity or honour.

Structural/institutional

- State is unable or unwilling to engage marginalized groups in decision-making, and thus members of these groups may see VE as the only way to assert their collective voice.
- Root/historical/structural injustice: when marginalization and injustice are built into the structures of society (through laws/policies/economic exclusion, etc.), violent extremism may appear to be a way to radically alter power dynamics.

Violent extremism is a complex and multi-faceted phenomenon. "It is commonly understood that a confluence of multiple factors including structural, personal, and social drivers need to come together to lead to engagement in violent extremism" (UNDP 2021, n6).[3] This shows the complexity behind devising strategies and programs that can address root causes and structural drivers of increasing radicalization in society – again pointing to the need, as Lodhi states (above), for a multilayered, multipronged strategy that includes efforts to engage in discussion on ideas and address the structural factors.

How extremism gained such momentum from its roots in the early 1980s, during Pakistan's support for the US in its war against the Soviets in Afghanistan, was the subject of many conversations during our time in Pakistan and after. The failure of governments to appreciate the severity of the threat posed by militant groups during the 1990s and the 2000s led to their gaining ground, with drastic consequences not only for society as a whole but more intensely for women and girls, concludes Imtiaz Gul in his analytical work on extremism. The "Jihadi forces operating not only in Afghanistan but also in Kashmir in the 1990s over decades contributed to promoting a militant culture at home" (Gul 2009). He and others referred to this development as the "Talibanization of society," which had become abundantly clear by the mid-2000s but had been somewhat more obscure during the previous decade. Everyone, including Western countries, had underestimated the severity of the violent extremist threat in Pakistan and how strong the Pakistani Taliban coalition had become – including the state itself. "Islamic radicalism and militancy," to quote Zahid Hussain, "present an existential threat to the State of Pakistan" (Hussain 2022b).

In looking into the drivers and motivations of violent extremists more closely, it is an ever-evolving story, as extremists change tactics and adapt to trends to increase recruitment and support. However, they all have some similar motivations and goals: to defend Islam through a militant violent jihad (mainly against Western democracy but also the Pakistani state and military); to enforce (an interpretation of) Sharia law by force; to defend against Western attacks on Islam (a perceived US hostility to Islam increasingly since 9/11 but which had begun earlier with the formation of al-Qaeda); and to fight against perceived oppression of Muslims anywhere in the world. They also decry the role of religion in society as sorely lacking. Mona Sheikh, in her interview with Umme Hassan, wife of the imam of the Red Mosque in Islamabad, uncovered the concern of Islamic extremists about "[t]he lack of recognition of religion as a forceful and competing provider of key functions that are typically related solely to the state (order, security and justice)" (Sheikh 2016). Like other militants and extremists, Hassan's concern was over the corruption of Pakistan's politicians and the economic and military elite, and the deep social divisions in society, as well as the lack of justice.

The motives of extremist groups are many in addition to the above, but strikingly are driven by socio-political inequality, concerns over deep social divisions in society, socio-economic repression and socio-economic justice and moral corruption, and a quest for justice, equality, and the betterment of society (Sheikh 2016). They frequently refer to injustices, oppression, and corruption of security actors (Holmes 2017), and the rule of law system, which is seen as inhumane and complicated (Sheikh 2016). In a systematic review of studies on inequality and radicalization, the authors identified,

> The empirical findings of the inequality-radicalization relationship are frequently inconsistent and inconclusive, however, experiencing inequality is probably neither necessary nor sufficient for radicalization (nor terrorism). However, *it seems that socio-political, moreover (perceived) socio-political inequality is probably positively related to (cognitive) radicalization.* In other words, perceived exclusion, marginalization, and unfair treatment and individual or group injustice and discrimination play a more important role in radicalization thinking – where one study found this to be the case in Pakistan. (Franc and Pavlović 2021, 8)

The systematic review differentiated between extremists who remained at the level of belief and those whose behaviour led to violence.

> Manifestations of radicalization can range from general ideological beliefs through specific attitudes and justifications of violence to one's violent actions. Such beliefs and attitudes can, but do not necessarily, lead to violence and terrorism, both of which can be driven by distinct and different motives. (Ibid., 1n4)

Ironically, extremist ideologies glorify the supremacy of a particular group and oppose a more tolerant and inclusive society (UNDP 2021). Their views and actions display intolerance, and violent extremists frequently target religious and ethnic minorities and create divisions and conflict in society. The lack of religious tolerance for beliefs outside the Taliban's view of Islam and Sharia, for example, is one of the notable concerns about them, despite the teachings of the Quran on unity, oneness, and respect for all human beings. The lack of respect for diversity is present in the Taliban ideology and the vision based on their interpretation of Islam – there is no room for anyone who does not conform to their rigid definition of the correct behaviour, belief, and way of life. It is a divisive identity that may have roots in an oppressive past.

A "Case Study on the Role of Gender and Identity in Shaping Positive Alternatives to Extremisms in Pakistan," published by ICAN and funded by Global Affairs Canada, found that the curricula of the madrassas in Pakistan that teach an "ultraconservative version of Islam position Islamic religious identity as superior to other aspects of human identity, generating exclusion and rejection of other religious, national, and ethnic groups as threatening and inferior" (Schamber and Fransen 2022, 4). Extremist ideology inherently drives divisions and intolerance in society, fostering a sense of "us vs. them" to legitimize acts of violence against their targets. The prescription put forward by such extremists as a solution to their socio-political grievances is exacerbating the very same issues in society, rather than helping to address them. As noted in the risk factors above, engaging in violent extremism "as an alternate way of asserting dignity" can manifest when diversity is not valued.

WAF weighed in on the debate in 2020 on the national curriculum. WAF's analysis stated: "The overriding theme is the construction of a majoritarian religious nationalism, underlined by the national security narrative ... the proposed single national curriculum has been designed to further religious nationalism, homogenisation and centralism" (Hussain and Saigol 2020). A study on "The Role of Education and Gender in Shaping the Cultural Mindset in Pakistan" (Schamber and Fransen 2022) found that

> Pakistani schools – particularly madrassas and public schools – teach a rigid religious and nationalist ideology. By promoting the primacy of conservative religious identity, they undermine other aspects of human identity and foster exclusion and rejection of the "other" as threatening and inferior. This ideology is reinforced by strict gender norms that assert women's subservience to men.

Recent studies have found that, beyond madrassas, extremist and divisive rhetoric is embedded in Pakistan's mainstream public education system.

> The Pakistani education system, through both its structure and its content, drives divisions, inequality, and intolerance between identity groups, creating conditions that leave students vulnerable to radicalization and recruitment by violent extremist actors. Radicalization in the Pakistani school system is less a function of direct connections between specific schools and Islamic militants, and more related to the way in which the system at large produces divisions, inequality, and intolerance in Pakistani society.

Education systems that encourage divisions and hierarchies between students of socio-economic, religious, and gender identities create a society vulnerable to capture by violent extremist actors. Curricula that promote patriarchal gender stereotypes, assert a singular religion as central to national identity, and erase the experiences of minorities; and teaching methods that eliminate complexity and critical thinking all foster division, inequality, and intolerance. (Ibid.)

A series of ICAN studies on gender and identify extremisms found that "[s]implicity has been found to be appealing ... amid a changing and increasingly complex world that can exacerbate feelings of disempowerment, a lack of agency in men, and uncertainty of societal roles" (Fransen 2021). The role of critical thinking in education has been undermined in Pakistan "more systematically from the times of Gen Zia ul Haq's martial rule 45 years ago – religion has been used by the powers-that-be to undermine critical thinking and philosophical inquiry" (Khalique 2022). Critical thinking can foster a pluralistic educational environment that promotes questioning and open discussion of ideas. The potential of religious intolerance to lead to radicalization is exacerbated by students' limited knowledge about religion, lack of critical thinking skills, and personal grievances or experiences of injustice – often as a result of their lower-class status (Schamber and Fransen 2022).

In 2011, Karen Armstrong, a religious scholar and author, wrote "A Letter to Pakistan" putting forth some views based on Islamic teachings showing that the Islamic faith demands love and tolerance for their fellow human beings. In her words,

Today terrorists have used religion to authorize their atrocities, quoting scriptural verses out of context and violating some of the most sacred values of the tradition they claim to defend. Too many religious leaders behave like secular politicians, singing the virtues of their own faith and decrying that of others, with little charity or respect. (Armstrong 2011, 4)

The intersection of religion and politics has been a concern in Pakistan for decades. The Taliban want to implement a Sharia-compliant political order by force (Mir 2022). It is also an ideology that entrenches religion-based grievances against the Western world

(Khan 2022), in that Western democracy is seen as the enemy of Sharia. Islamic clerics who clash with the ideology of violent Islamic extremists have identified a number of areas that conflict with Islamic religious scholars' views, such as violating and using the religion for political purposes. Inventing stories and statistics that change the religion and putting in place charters of laws to protect Islam – such as forcing women to stay at home, not work, and remain out of the public sphere, or depriving women of their right to inherit property – are others. Many have commented on their misguided interpretations of Sharia. Although militant jihad is deemed urgent because religion, specifically Sharia, is under dire threat in their view, "the logical paradox in this discourse is that an omnipotent God requires protection of the Taliban" (Sheikh 2016).

More is now understood about the role that women play in supporting extremism. Social factors, including family networks, are key "pull factors" for female radicalization in Pakistan, where women have been motivated by both material and ideological factors, refracted as feelings of injustice and the prospect of living in a more just regime, run as an Islamic state (Johnston, Iqbal, and True 2020, n39). The Al Huda approach to fundamentalism, through its teachings of a very conservative interpretation of Islam, is one that targets women, although it does not advocate violent jihad. In November 2014, women students of Jamia Hafsa, the women's madrassa affiliated with Islamabad's Lal Masjid (Red Mosque), publicly declared their support for Daesh while backed by the mosque's chief cleric, Abdul Aziz, and his wife Umme Hassan. This incident marked the rising popularity of Daesh among women religious extremists, and in 2015–16 there were a number of reported incidents of women migrating to join ISIS in Syria and of women cells in various Pakistani cities involved in fundraising for ISIS/Daesh, such as the much-publicized case of the women-led "Al Zikra Academy" in Karachi (Phelan 2022). The female perpetrator of one of the deadliest terrorist attacks in the US, in San Bernardino, California (targeting a public health training event that killed sixteen people in 2015), was Tashfeen Malik, who studied in Multan between 2007 and 2014, and attended the local centre of the Al Huda from 2013 until she left the country in 2014. FBI investigators reported that Malik had become radicalized over several years prior to the attack. The Islamic State of Iraq and the Levant released an online article in 2016 praising the shooting and the two perpetrators.

A key recommendation of the UN Women–published report on the gender aspects of Pakistan's national security policies concludes that "laws and policies should not just focus on protecting women from violent extremism, but they should also encourage and facilitate women to proactively counter violent extremism (Khan 2022).

Addressing violent extremism (with its negative impacts on women and girls in society through the promotion of gender-discriminatory practices), versus a traditional role for development in poverty alleviation and gender equality, is not something aid agencies wanted to tackle in the past. The term "violent extremism" is also one that can be uncomfortable for development and humanitarian actors, given its association with security agencies and responses. It is not an area where development actors have taken a lead, although considerable research on development and extremism has taken place in recent years. Some say that sustainable development itself is preventative, especially by strengthening inclusive governance, human rights, justice, and the rule of law, given that socio-political grievances appear to be some of the bigger drivers of extremism. Supporting the work of NGOs and civil society to strengthen community-building processes is a critical contribution of development actors. Promoting gender equality itself is also seen as a powerful counter-narrative to extremist and violent extremist ideology, according to numerous studies on terrorism and extremism. If it weren't, why would extremists be so vehemently against it?

The gender equality approach CIDA put in place just before 9/11 and implemented between 2000 and 2005, before the cascading effects of the War on Terror reverberated down through aid policy decisions, could be viewed as a strategy for countering extremism and negative social forces, although no one knew it then. Preventing violent extremism was still a nascent field of research and policy and not considered an arena for development actors. As responsive funding mechanisms, the women's funds directed resources to organizations working for women's rights, those tackling gender-based violence and women's economic empowerment, and those working on the provision of basic health and education, as entry points at the grassroots. It consolidated networks from the grassroots to policy, an approach now at the forefront of gender equality policies and action. The PAGE Women's Fund between 2001 and 2010 – unique in this approach – provided sustained support to civil society organizations that were contributing to reducing the spread of extremism through addressing advocacy, awareness, alternative narratives, informal education, and approaches, and were expanding services for women (and families) at the grassroots. It supported organizations working with government at the policy level, including to further women's rights legislation. The organizations supported through the women's funds were networked with the democracy and human rights movement, amplifying principles of universal human rights, justice, and pluralism; they were connected as well with those working for poverty alleviation and the fight against inequality. Combined with the development cooperation support to the broader civil society fighting inequality and promoting rights, justice, and poverty reduction, this was potentially a successful combination contributing to social well-being and as such helping to counter extremism and divisive identities. The large bilateral gender projects that worked alongside PAGE, such as the AKRSP and the Aurat Foundation projects empowering women political representatives working at district level, helped scale the impact. Such programming efforts, including the increased participation of women in political processes, are recognized as positive elements in preventing extremism. Would the landscape of violent extremism today be the same had more sizeable funding had been directed to these efforts at the time by all donors together with the government? From the mid-1980s when WAF rang the alarm bells through the 1990s and the 2000s, supporting the women's rights movement and the growth of civil society and nurturing the development of a gender equality community (often on the front lines of injustice and human rights abuse), combined with practical entry points for needed services and support to marginalized areas, was a strategic response to a growing militancy. In addition, the early PAGE strategy specific to the border areas might have evolved to provide stronger support for that region (including the merged areas), for a targeted and contextualized area-based approach through continued partnerships with civil society, grassroots organizations, and local authorities. UNDP research on the prevention of violent extremism has noted that the majority of recruits in Africa who join a violent extremist group come from borderlands or peripheral areas that have suffered generations of marginalization (UNDP 2017).

Despite the global geopolitics impacting policy on Pakistan, CIDA could have stayed the course on defending and promoting women's rights and strengthening civil society and grassroots women's organizations by continuing the PAGE women's fund and allocating more resources to it (as was recommended, although tripling the budget would have been commensurate with the approach taken by USAID in 2010–11). The amount of money was less important than where it was directed and to whom, and there was much work to continue and build on. Even with the reduced aid budget, the PAGE fund alone would have been a solid and effective development investment. Canada would have maintained engagement in an important area of policy discourse and helped to support the bridging of women's organizations and activists with government at all levels.

Promoting tolerance, diversity, and inclusion is a challenge to governments, to development actors, to civil society, to communities. Anita Weiss in her 2021 book on countering violent extremism shows how people in Pakistan are pushing back on extremism through community initiatives, culture, poetry, writing, the arts, and education. The "sparks of hope," as she calls them, are everywhere (Weiss 2021). Development solutions are building on "people's agency to create avenues for enhanced community resilience, ultimately building and sustaining peace" (UNDP 2021b). Women's roles in promoting tolerance as well as perpetuating intolerance and extremism is important. Women's organizations and other civil society organizations have been working to change attitudes towards gender equality, tolerance, and attitudes towards violence. While this important work has been undergoing for decades, much more is needed to make the transformational and structural changes that will address the myriad of drivers of violent extremism and deep-rooted prejudice and gender inequality.

The re-emphasis on local organizations and channelling direct support to them is an essential part of current development approaches on gender equality. There has been little reference publicly to past decades of efforts by women's groups and the support provided by CIDA that had laid the groundwork and provided the knowledge and evidence for a feminist foreign aid policy such as the work in Pakistan. CIDA had put in place a mechanism to support women rights and civil society organizations and activists three decades earlier and had demonstrated commitment to emerging organizations in its willingness to pilot new approaches.

On the other hand, what is often referred to as "peace education" provides a counterweight to identity-based divisions by teaching universal messages about humanity, exposing students to the religious and cultural teachings of other communities, encouraging critical thinking and discussion, and incorporating elements of the arts and literature. The informal education initiatives aimed at women's empowerment that were supported by aid programs over decades through both women's funds and core support to human rights NGOs were all undertaking some form of this work. It is traditionally considered an area of development linked to building the capacity of NGOs and supporting the work of civil society.

The women's funds galvanized awareness of and support for women's rights at the community level and undertook different approaches on educating for gender equality and human rights, from working with parents, teachers, school committees, and district government officials, to dialogues and workshops with a wide range of community members, to specific training on gender equality and rights-based approaches to development for local CBOs and NGOs. Sub-projects funded gender-sensitive curriculum development in Quetta in Balochistan and adult education in Lahore, which integrated the knowledge and experience of local women (between 2006 and 2008). In Hunza, a sub-project addressed gender and rights in the education system through training teachers and creating a local CBO resource centre on gender and rights education in the Northern Areas (between 2002 and 2007). More research is needed to examine whether these more informal awareness-raising and education initiatives of the CBOs and NGOs have been or could be effective approaches in tackling drivers of extremism.

The limitations of state education have meant that more and more children attend religious madrassa schools. Pakistan has historically spent less than two per cent of its GDP on education.

> The distance between the educated and the undereducated
> many could not be ignored. Nor was it possible to prevent
> the poor and illiterate masses from seeking the services of the
> Islamic fundamentalists ... the representatives of the Islamic
> tradition more than secular politicians articulated the concerns
> and needs of the great, unspoken for majority. The secular
> symbols of independence and self government could not be
> expected to compete with the expositions of religious ritual.
> (Ziring 2004, 252)

Only a minority of madrassas, however, teach extreme forms of Islam: of the 45,000 madrassas in Pakistan today, an estimated 10–15 per cent are associated with the Wahhabi and Deobandi schools of Islam

(Schamber and Fransen 2022, n11). The number of female-only madrassas is growing: in 2009, there were already 1,900 registered all-female madrassas, making up 15 per cent of the total madrassas in the country, a marked increase from the 1970s (ibid., n32). They use rigid and selective interpretations of religious texts to inculcate an ultra-conservative version of Muslim womanhood that enforces traditional gender norms, teaching women that their power lies in their submission to men (ibid., n34). I thought back to Pakistan's sixth five-year plan of 1983 and its focus on mass education in rural areas and on education for rural women, pondering how and why it was never implemented.

15

Security, Gender Equality, and Development

The downward trajectory of gender equality indicators has mirrored the growth and spread of violent extremism in Pakistan. No one anticipated such a marked reversal of gender equality indicators during the rising internal militancy and the long war against the Taliban in Afghanistan. And there were other hard-won development gains lost due to violent extremism. The UN human development index shows a marked drop in countries affected by violence, militancy, and conflict. In the case of Pakistan,

> The State's security response to the threat of organized terrorism and violent extremism has had a deleterious impact on women and girls. The counter terror policies and security strategies of the government and security establishment, however, has so far not fathomed the multi-dimensional impact that conflict has on lives of women and girls. (Khan 2022)

Purely securitized responses have also exacerbated risks and vulnerabilities in communities through displacement and the disruption of livelihoods and informal trade, causing discontent with security forces in some instances. In 2015, the ICG wrote:

> Although women are among the main targets of militants' efforts to impose ultraorthodox Islam in Pakistan by force, they have been consistently excluded from military-led negotiations. The gender perspective has been largely absent from state strategies to counter violent extremism more generally. (International Crisis Group 2015)

Our historical look at Canada's support for gender equality in development in Pakistan has revealed the lack of substantive analysis of security or extremism and its impact on women and girls over the years. There was little or no mention of the impact of the rise in violent extremism on women and gender equality programs. There was thin analysis on the worsening security situation and its implications for development programs, despite women being killed and assassinated for simply attending schools or helping with training for small businesses in parts of the country. The increase in deadly attacks on schools, mosques, and markets, the silencing of women and human rights activists, and the rise in gender-based violence were not part of the gender analysis. And gender analysis was not something integral to political or security analysis in the past – it was considered initially a marginal issue, then a thematic one for the aid program to address through women's projects (this is not the case any longer with new approaches that take into account gender analysis). The relations between development programs and the policy/political and security world were also not strong enough to link gender equality issues with efforts to counter terrorism.

The study by Valerie Hudson and Kaylee Hodgson in 2020 concludes, like the many reports on women and extremism in recent years, that a gender lens is critical to counter extremism and the ongoing threat of terrorism, and provides valuable lessons for those looking at gender equality, international relations, and security policy (Hudson and Hodgson 2020). Hudson's study with Bowen and Nielsen demonstrates that

> nearly every dimension of national security is intertwined with whether women are subordinated or empowered within their society ... This means we need to examine the things that constrain women in their homes, in their personal lives – high levels of violence against women and impunity for their assailants, lack of property and inheritance rights, laws that favour men in divorce and child custody cases, polygyny, bride prices, dowries. These practices constitute the first political order of any society. The structure of the relationship between the two halves of humanity is the basis for the political order of every nation, and if that order allows autocracy, violence and extortion, a nation will arc in those directions as well ... It is time to say again what was said in Beijing a quarter-century ago: The fate of nations is tied to the status of women. (Hudson, Bowen, and Nielsen 2021)

Women's rights and equality are an essential part of all forms of the fight against fundamentalism, including preventive strategies, and should be an integral part of the strategy to counter violent Islamic (and other forms of) extremism. Breaking siloes will strengthen political, security, and development programming to develop a common understanding of the preventive policies and approaches. In an important step forward, Pakistan's National Internal Security Policies (since 2018) have recognized the signs of domestic violence against women as a major impediment to preventing violent extremism and include a broader definition of security that integrates a gender perspective. The NISP advocates for women's empowerment and the provision of equal opportunities in education and employment, partially as a strategy to counter extremism (Khan 2022, 55).

OBSCURED FROM HISTORY

Many insightful books on Pakistan's political and security analysis and history contain little reference to the women's rights movements, nor to the impacts of political and security policies and events on women or gender equality. Authors have left out the historic WAF protests against the Hudood Ordinances and Law of Evidence, which do not even appear in the chronologies of their books. They have been obscured from much of Pakistan's political history. Yet the WAF protests in the 1980s were an early indicator of the direction things were headed. The attack on the laws protecting women was the first sign of a rollback on women's rights, leading to a decline in most gender equality indicators and a much more dangerous period to follow. As the research since has confirmed, "[t]he restriction of women's rights is now recognized as a sign of radicalization – and therefore an early warning sign of violent extremism" (UNDP and UN Women 2020). These trends were evident at the time of the first CIDA mission on women in development in 1984.

Two risks were identified for CIDA programs for women's development at that time. First was a perception of exporting Western feminism to Pakistani women. This debate has not ended and has evolved into an intractable one rooted in differing perspectives. CIDA and its Pakistani partners were often criticized over the years for forcing a donor-driven gender equality agenda.

Second was the risk that the Islamization policies would further impact women's development. The assessment at the time was that

"Islamization is equated with politics, and within the political climate today, any solid predictions about how Islamization will affect women are at best open to challenge" (Gossen 1983). It concluded that there was "no evidence at the time that Islamization would hinder female education" (ibid., 29). Not long after the Mujaheddin took a stand against girls' education and the Taliban in Afghanistan banned it, the world has witnessed the ongoing impact on female education in Taliban strongholds in both countries.

The laws had a severe and detrimental impact on gender equality, constraining women's contribution to the economy and much more. In the 1986 Nation Builders strategy on women in development, CIDA stated that "laws and their interpretation fall in the sole jurisdiction of the Government of Pakistan," resulting in Canada focussing solely on social equity and extending benefits and services to uplift rural women. Ironically, the early CIDA WID approach (articulated in the 1984 paper on "Managing the Process of Change") identified the risks of not taking a systemic accountability approach to changing the policies, regulations, and practices that could adversely impact women. The latter, it proposed, would require special measures to remedy the effects of discrimination against women. Over a decade later, Pakistan's laws aimed at women's protection began to change policies and regulations by repealing elements of the discriminatory Islamic laws.

As this book was being written, more research was being published on the gender dimension of counter-terrorism policy and how gender analysis and mainstreaming must be an essential part of security policy. The new insights and understanding are providing evidence and policy advice on the link between misogyny and violent extremism to remedy the missing elements in responses. In major steps forward, the gender and extremism link is now fully on the radar of political, security, and development actors. The understanding of the threat and challenge of violent extremism to development at all levels is being researched by development and security actors searching for urgent policy and programmatic responses.

A key recommendation from a report in 2022 on gender analysis in violent extremism in ASEAN (Phelan 2022) is that policy-makers must engage women's CSOs and other women's groups in devising counter-narratives, as they often have extensive knowledge and understanding of local grievances that can serve as drivers towards violent extremism and they can offer alternative pathways at the local level. The women's funds were an entry point for policy-makers into this world. The blueprint was in place but not strategically viewed at the time as to their full value and the impact of the thousands of grassroots initiatives that continue year after year making progress. It points to the importance of forging closer policy linkages in the work of development, security, and political actors, and to the recognition of the essential role of development, despite the need for reform and discarding outdated approaches and models, to offer longer-term solutions.

The inability of feminist efforts, and the accompanying international aid and government efforts, to reach the majority of poor women in the country may still be the biggest challenge. CIDA's first research report on WID in Pakistan in 1983 asked whether bilateral aid could reach women at the village and grassroots levels. Thirty-four years later, in 2017, Canada's Feminist International Assistance Policy put this aim as one of its major objectives: "reaching women in communities as 'powerful agents of change' with an ability to transform their households and communities" (FIAP 2017). The prescription is clear; the question resides in the method, and in the changing operational and implementation approaches. The series of annual reports on rural women by the NCSW, UN Women, and Canada since 2017 reinforce the recommendations made by the 1980s reports and strategies, as well as WAF's recommendations. The needs remain very similar and even more urgent for the most vulnerable. WAF in its early days recommended a blueprint that formulates an effective strategy for incorporating the majority of Pakistani women. "Oppressed and victimized, the rural women and those of the urban poor have remained untouched by the current [1980s women's and democratic] movement which primarily expresses the concerns and fears of the urban bourgeois women. If the women's movement is to take root in Pakistan," Khawar Mumtaz and Farida Shahid said in 1987, "it will have to overcome ... the gap separating its activists from the majority of women – a gap that in itself is culturally articulated" (Mumtaz and Shaheed 1987, 157, 160). WAF may have been too hard on itself at the time. History has shown that WAF's efforts have touched oppressed rural women – the advocacy, the legal battles all led to gains in making what were previously considered cultural practices into illegal crimes, such as the use of girls to settle crimes and disputes between family groups – all this while battling the pressures of rising extremism in the country and raising awareness of the implications for women in Pakistan of the war on terrorism in Afghanistan.

Some in the women's movement in Pakistan are "challenging and deconstructing the hallowed private sphere of the family, community and society ... that what happens in the private realm is no longer simply personal but a collective experience," according to the Aurat March Network, established in 2018. Harassment and violence against women, whether in the home, in the workplace, or in public spaces, need to be addressed beyond the passage of laws so that women and their families do not forgo opportunities for social, economic, and political participation and growth (Center of Gender and Policy Studies 2018).

Development programs have made a difference in many women's lives, but there is more work to be done to address structural issues affecting the millions of unpaid women workers on family farms and enterprises. The gendered division of labour (women's inclusion in transplanting, weeding, cotton picking, vegetable and wheat harvesting, and the care and management of livestock) is a barrier to women's access to technologies, training, or microfinance. Adoption of more efficient, labour-saving methods by agri-business and dairy development organizations is ignoring women's work and role and marginalizing them as producers and managers. The development approaches in women's economic empowerment have included a focus on women in agriculture evident since around 2010, particularly in programs supported by the former DFID (UK Aid), USAID, and Global Affairs Canada.

In trying to figure out Pakistan, as so many authors have done in countless books, most conclude with an acknowledgment of the strength, resilience, and toughness in the face of colossal challenges beginning in 1979–80, when the "black wave"[1] of religious extremism swept the sub-region and the Middle East. Those years' events in Iran and Afghanistan influenced those in Pakistan, and the extreme schools of thought emanating from them spread globally. If Pakistan is an example of the march towards gender equality, it won't be defeated by violent extremists and their interpretation of women's rights and protection, despite the two steps forward and one step back, as WAF put it so many years ago. Certain strengths of the society have preserved Pakistan where any other country would have collapsed, said the chair of the Securities and Exchange Commission in 2012, speaking on a panel at a conference on development economics in Islamabad. Intellectuals, analysts, and authors have found a consensus on this point: those sustaining strengths include the binding support of the extended family social protection system, a diverse civil society, an energetic and active media, a growing urban educated middle class, and, not least, the greater visibility and role of women. The flourishing of art, music, literature, and creative voices continues to enrich society and culture. But the rural areas and the marginalized regions at the border with Afghanistan remain at high risk and are places where many women remain vulnerable.

After watching the Taliban takeover in Afghanistan in August 2021, questions and concerns swirled on what this meant for the situation of women, and not only in Afghanistan. The Taliban said at their first press conference after the fall of Kabul, "We will honor women's rights but within the norms of Islamic law." Given the differing interpretations of Islamic law and Sharia as a system of governance, especially between the Taliban, other Islamic extremist groups, and Islamic scholars and more moderate clerics and councils on Islamic law, the implications of this were murky at best. The Taliban interpretation of Islamic law when it converged with customary practices within informal justice systems in Afghanistan has been demonstrated as misogynist. As the UN Special Rapporteur on the human rights situation in Afghanistan, Richard Bennett, reported to the UN Human Rights Council on 19 June 2023, "The systematic violence against women and the shrinking civic space in Afghanistan present a dire situation. Women and girls in Afghanistan are facing severe discrimination that may amount to gender persecution, a crime against humanity ... Since assuming power on 15 August 2021, the Taliban has implemented 86 edicts, decrees, instructions, and new rules, without consultation, that profoundly affect all aspects of Afghan women's lives in society. These restrictions cover education, healthcare, employment, economic opportunities, media presence, and access to justice. The enforcement mechanisms, such as the Ministry of Virtue and Vice, and the systematic nature of these policies and practices aim to eradicate women from society entirely and diminish their role in the public life of the country."

If Pakistan is any example or holds any lessons on women's rights under Islamic or Sharia law, it is that strengthening state institutions and the justice system to legislate and enforce women's rights and associated services, supported by a robust women's rights movement working together with an active civil society (promoting socioeconomic equality, diversity, human rights, and inclusion), and buoyed by an outspoken and dynamic media reporting on women's rights violations, has worked as a countering influence against extremists in society. International donor programs have provided sustained commitment over more than four decades to this type of work at all levels in Pakistan. The diversity (vibrant civil society, energetic media) and strength (stronger judiciary, resilient society) of Pakistan have curbed what might have been a stronger suppression of women's rights under extremist interpretations (and misinterpretations) of Sharia. The state has strengthened women's protection legislation, strengthened women's divisions across federal and provincial levels of government, and improved legal systems, including police and courts and women's shelters, all with the push and help of civil society and Parliament (including women parliamentarians). But for poorer segments of the population, especially rural women in remote areas, the implementation of laws, access to justice, and freedoms and rights are not fully manifest, and progress has been slow, especially in the border regions near Afghanistan. The lives of women in the merged districts of KP near the border of Afghanistan remain under serious threat (UN Women 2022). Many remain outside of government services and institutions. Informal justice systems based on compensation and pardon rather than punishment continue to harm rural women in their unjust decisions that are not aligned to an interpretation of Sharia law used by scholars that is based on centuries of Islamic jurisprudence.

For women in Afghanistan living under the shadow of Taliban control of the country, the Taliban justice systems and informal councils hold inherent risk to their safety and security. After only one year in power, the Taliban banned women from work and girls from school, and "falsely claim that erasing women from public life is Islamic" (Anderlini 2020). Women are required to wear the hijab; they are banned from working for the UN or NGOs, from going to parks, gyms, or beauty salons, and from travelling more than 78 km without a male chaperone. The suspension of the Afghan constitution and of laws protecting women from violence, as well as the dissolution of the country's independent human rights commission (UN News 2023) and a severe curtailing of the media,[2] have taken away other protections. Since systematic and institutionalized discrimination against women and girls was at the heart of Taliban ideology and rule, the UN Special Rapporteur on Afghanistan said at the UN Human Rights Council, Afghanistan's de facto authorities "may be responsible for gender apartheid" (UN News 2023).

The political transition has left the state of gender equality in Afghanistan dire and may have potential reverberations in parts of Pakistan, with an uncertain and high-risk trajectory. The Pakistan representative at the UN Human Rights Council in September 2023 warned of the serious security, economic, and humanitarian impacts of the situation in Afghanistan on neighbouring countries (ibid.). The Taliban's return to governance in Afghanistan energized the TTP's violent insurgency and expanded the potential of the group, deepening its links with other militant groups in the region such as al-Qaeda and the Islamic State (Schamber and Fransen 2022). The concern in Pakistan was that the Afghan Taliban would continue to embolden the TTP. Pakistan has since experienced an escalation in cross-border terrorism from Afghanistan and the situation there remains a problem, with the TTP finding safe haven in Afghanistan. Violent extremism still poses the biggest threat to Pakistan's internal security. All forecasts point to trends of Islamic extremist ideologies in the region continuing to threaten gains on gender equality and women's security. As Afghan women activists have warned repeatedly, there are no moderate or like-minded Taliban.

As this book was being completed, the women's protests in Iran erupted against forced restrictions by the regime. "*Zan, Zendegi, Azadi*" ("Women, Life, Freedom") became the slogan to demand more freedom, the equality of women and men, and a fuller measure of equality, justice, and human dignity. The protests showed thousands of women refusing to be forced to dress and act as the regime required. They resulted in 22,000 arrests and more than 500 killed and thousands of schoolgirls poisoned in attacks that the government was criticized for not investigating properly (Lamb 2023). They demonstrated a significant challenge by young people to the Islamic Republic, who are building on nearly two centuries of feminist activism in Iran marked by the first woman, Tahirih, a renowned poet and scholar of Islamic jurisprudence, to publicly remove her face veil at a male-only conference in 1852.[3] She was condemned to death by the authorities, strangled with her own scarf, tossed into a well, and covered with stones. Before she was killed, she said, "you can kill me as soon as you like but you cannot stop the emancipation of women" (Nafisi 2023).[4] Young women today are saying the same thing, Azar Nafisi told the panel audience that day. Large portions of the population see very different visions of the future. One in five women in the Iranian capital are not wearing hijab – a quiet revolution (ibid.). Social dissatisfaction is cutting across all strata of Iranian society, and all of these have gender dimensions. Yet more than six months after the protests, the Iranian regime introduced a new and more stringent Hijab and Chastity Bill that includes a central role of "gender segregation" (Human Rights Activists News Agency 2023). It enforces stricter adherence to (and severe penalties for noncompliance with) the hijab regulations under the bill, which is entitled Support the Family by Promoting Culture of Chastity and Hijab. The state-sanctioned institutional oppression of women and girls in Iran, and the even more extreme version in Afghanistan, should be a concern for countries at risk for increasing extremism.

The region is witnessing pushback from elements of the population on rigid definitions of gender roles. Perhaps the Taliban edicts and regressive women's rights policies in Afghanistan is a partial factor in this along with the hardening position of the Iranian regime. The ideological and political spill-over effect of Taliban's takeover of Afghanistan upon anti-democratic, radical religious extremists in Pakistan will likely continue to impact gender equality. As one women's rights activist put it, what happened in Afghanistan has already impacted the world. Perhaps the cry "women, life, freedom" will reverberate across the three countries sharing borders in a volatile region and be once again a harbinger, this time of a trend towards a more equal and just global society.

Epilogue

Canada broadened and increased its gender equality programming under the development cooperation program in Pakistan starting in 2017 under the new Feminist International Assistance Policy. In 2018 Canada put in place a Women's Voice and Leadership Program in Pakistan to bring back the focus on funding women's rights organizations and revive the work that had halted with the closure of the PAGE fund. It was the first step back to supporting women's rights and gender equality after the dismantling of the legacy following the removal of the gender equality pillar of CIDA's Country Strategy in 2009 and was directed at grassroots women's organizations. It was time for Canada to come back, but could Canada regain the unique role it had carried from more than a decade earlier? This was especially questionable given the sizeable programs and funding of other donors on gender equality being implemented by then. Global Affairs Canada added new projects on women's political participation with Shirkat Gah (FemPower 2019), a new project with SAP-PK on democracy and empowerment of women, extended women's economic empowerment with AKRSP in Chitral and Gilgit-Baltistan, reproductive health and education programs, and an enhanced project with Kashf for Promoting Gender Inclusive and Equitable Growth, among others. Women's economic empowerment continues to be a central pillar of Canada's international development programming in Pakistan, with a strong focus in GB and Chitral with the Aga Khan Foundation.

Appendix

Chronology

1961	The Muslim Family Laws Ordinance is passed in Pakistan, marking early protective legislation for women.
1977–79	Administration of Zia-ul-Haq (following a coup in July 1977). His government extends President Bhutto's previous moves to make Pakistan an Islamic state. President Zia orders the creation of the Shariat courts. The role of Sharia law in the legal system is strengthened.
1979	The Hudood Ordinances become law in Pakistan, placing emphasis on Islamic codes of behaviour and criminalizing all consensual sexual intercourse between adults outside marriage. In rape (*zina bil jabr*) and adultery (*zina*) cases, the *Hadd* (Quranic) punishment was stoning to death if the offender was married and mandatory public flogging if unmarried.
	February: Iranian Revolution results in an extremist Islamic regime headed by Ayatollah Khomeni, which restricts women's employment and dress, including mandatory hijab.
	December: Soviet invasion of Afghanistan. The US extends massive aid to Pakistan, and together with Saudi Arabia and other states, the US and Pakistan build up the Afghan Mujaheddin forces to fight the Soviet troops and Afghan communist government. First beginnings of the Taliban in southern Afghanistan. Some 3 million Afghan refugees flee to Pakistan (Lieven 2011, 518).
1981	The Women's Action Forum (WAF) is formed in direct response to the Hudood Ordinances of 1979, to fight policy and legal discrimination against women.

1983	Protest by the Women's Action Forum in Lahore on 12 February against the Law of Evidence in Lahore turns violent, with police intervention and arrests. 12 February now celebrated annually as Pakistani Women's Day. Pakistan Expert Working Group on Women's Development Programs issues a report for the sixth five-year development plan of the government of Pakistan that results in the Plan espousing the integration of women in development, revitalization of the rural economy, and increased education for women. December: CIDA commissions a report on integrating Pakistani women into development. CIDA and AKRSP form partnership launching a program for social mobilization and community development including formation of grassroots women's organizations.
1984	February: CIDA sends mission to Pakistan to develop a CIDA Country Strategy for Women in Development. Campaign by WAF against the Shariat Law of Qisas and Diyat for its discrimination against women. The Shariat Law of Evidence becomes law in August that year, and is passed by the Majlis-e-Shoora (appointed advisory body to the president) and by the National Assembly (elected senate and lower house) in 1985.
1985	CIDA launches in Pakistan a WID research fund and leads formation of a donor coordination group called the Information Network on Women in Development (later becomes INGAD – the Inter-agency Gender And Development advocacy group). July: UN World Conference for Women in Nairobi and parallel NGO Forum '85 amplifies the voices of women from the global south and reinforces global networks of women's rights activists.
1986	Clauses added to the original blasphemy laws recommending penalties of death or life imprisonment. Human Rights Commission of Pakistan established. Aurat Foundation established as a feminist women's rights and development organization that becomes a key CIDA partner. CIDA creates SPO, a human rights NGO that launches a fund to support grassroots women's organizations. CIDA launches a major development strategy for women in Pakistan.
1988	6,000 women in jail in Pakistan, with *zina* complaints comprising the majority of cases.

	General Zia killed in air crash. Military and civil service manage a transition to democracy. Benazir Bhutto wins national elections.
1989	February: Soviet withdrawal from Afghanistan ends ten years of occupation. By year's end, Berlin Wall falls, and US President Reagan declares communism defeated.
1990	US cuts military and economic aid to Pakistan and imposes economic sanctions on Pakistan through the Pressler Amendment, targeting Pakistan on grounds of a nuclear issue.
1991	CIDA renews the 1989 Pakistan Women in Development Support Fund for an additional $500,000.
1992	Communist regime in Afghanistan collapses and a Mujaheddin government takes over for next four years. Beginning of civil war in Afghanistan under PM Hekmatyar.
1992–93	Washington imposes more sanctions on Pakistan under Missile Technology Control Regime.
1993–96	Second government of Benazir Bhutto. Pakistan switches its support in the Afghan civil war to the newly formed Taliban of Kandahar (Lieven 2011, 519).
1994	Pakistan signs the UN Convention on the Elimination of Discrimination against Women (CEDAW). CIDA approves new Women's Development Fund for an initial $500,000. Al Huda religious schools for women open in Pakistan. Taliban become prominent in Afghanistan.
1995	Beijing UN Global Women's Conference introduces women's rights as a priority. CIDA's Women in Development Program in Pakistan develops a new strategy prioritizing women's rights aligned to the new CIDA Gender Equity policy.
1996	April–June: Osama bin Laden returns to Afghanistan. September–October: Taliban capture Kabul. CIDA approves landmark $4 million women's development fund in Pakistan with a focus on women's rights.
1997	Qisas and Diyat Laws become part of the Pakistan penal code in between democratically elected governments.
1998	The US passes the Glenn Amendment against Pakistan and India, suspending all US aid as a result of nuclear tests conducted by Pakistan (under Nawaz Sharif's second government) in retaliation for similar tests by India. Pakistan approves a National Action Plan for Women.

1999–2000	October: General Musharraff comes to power in a coup. Pakistan National Commission on the Status of Women established under the Women's Development Ministry during Musharraf government.
2001	CIDA Country Program strategy for Pakistan (three months before 9/11) designates gender equality as one of three pillars. Significantly increases funding for gender programs over 2000–05. CIDA approves $7 million for a new expanded women's fund in Pakistan. 11 September: Al-Qaeda launches terrorist attacks on New York and Washington, causing destruction of the World Trade Center and damage to the Pentagon. Attackers are trailed back to Afghanistan and hence to Pakistan as well. October: US declares war on the Taliban and launches the military Operation "Enduring Freedom" in Afghanistan. Taliban flees Kabul 13 November, with the leadership of the Taliban and al-Qaeda escaping to Pakistan. Pakistan under Musharraf promises unconditional support for US and its war on terrorism. US lifts sanctions imposed on Pakistan under Pressler and Glenn Amendments.
2002	Highly publicized "honour crime" case of Mukhtar Mai in Dera Ghazi Khan, Punjab. Canada sends troops to Kandahar and takes leadership of the provincial reconstruction team (until end of 2010 with final rotation of troops into Kandahar).
2003	ISAF in Afghanistan is formed. *Charlie Wilson's War* published which identifies how America turned its back on Afghanistan after Soviet withdrawal.
2004	US offers new aid package to Pakistan and pressures Pakistan to launch a major campaign on Waziristan on border with Afghanistan against local allies of Afghan Taliban. Pakistan blames US policies for rise of Islamic extremism in the country.
2006	Protection of Women Act, passed by Pakistan's Parliament, returns rape from the Hudood Ordinances to the Penal Code, preventing rape charges from being converted into charges of extramarital sexual intercourse. CIDA launches a women's economic empowerment mission and strategy in Pakistan.
2007	January–July: Islamic radicals operating out of the Red Mosque/ Lal Masjid in Islamabad begin enforcing Sharia law in parts of the capital.

July: Pakistan military attacks the Red Mosque. Operation Silence marks "a critical watershed in Pakistan's struggle with Islamic militancy" (Hussain 2010).

September: Formation of the Pakistani Taliban, a loose alliance of mainly Pathan militant groups. On 9 October, US calls Pakistan an al-Qaeda safe haven for the first time publicly and the US announces a national strategy for combatting terrorism (Hussain 2010).

2007   Canada's Manley Panel proposes a whole-of-government strategy for Afghanistan with commensurate budget and deployment of civilians to Kandahar on governance and development.

27 December: Benazir Bhutto assassinated.

2007–09   US carries out drone attacks in Waziristan. The drone campaign contributes to a swelling of anti-American sentiment in Pakistan.

2008   September: Marriott Hotel suicide bombing in Islamabad, one of the worst terrorist attacks in Pakistan's history, marking the start of a period of intense attacks. Canada moves all diplomatic personnel to enclave. Asif Zardari (Benazir Bhutto's husband) elected president.

2009   April: Pakistan Taliban take over Swat and district of Buner close to Islamabad. KP provincial government imposes Sharia in the region by promulgating the Nizam-e-Adl Regulations as part of a peace deal with the Taliban-allied Tehreek e-Nifaz-e-Shariat-e-Mohammadi.

September: US approves Kerry-Lugar-Berman Bill allocating $7.5 billion in development aid over five years to Pakistan to fight poverty in the tribal regions and fund projects in energy, health, and education. Canada ends the continuum of the Women's Funds in Pakistan with rejection of PAGE II, marking the decline in Canadian aid to Pakistan.

Formation of Pakistan's Women's Parliamentary Caucus with UN Development aid.

2010   US troop surge in Afghanistan. Canada hands over PRT in Kandahar to the US.

The federal Women's Affairs Ministry is dissolved, and its responsibilities devolved to the provinces under the eighteenth constitutional amendment. Provincial Commissions for the Status of Women are mandated to review provincial legislation and policies to promote empowerment, ensure gender equality, and counter discrimination.

2011	Prevention of Anti-Women Practices Act passes in National Assembly, barring forced marriages, marriages to the Quran, giving away women in *vani*, and depriving them of inheritance. The Acid Control and Acid Crime Prevention Act, the Criminal Law (second amendment) Act, makes attacks with a substance such as acid punishable by fourteen years to life imprisonment. January: Governor of Punjab Salman Taseer assassinated by his bodyguard for criticism of the blasphemy laws. May: Osama bin Laden killed by US Special forces in Abbotabad less than one hour from Islamabad. Canada halts all new aid to Pakistan.
2012	Pakistan ranked second worst country on Global Gender Gap Index of World Economic Forum where it remains for more than a decade. Canada cuts aid to Pakistan by two thirds, to lowest level since the 1950 initial economic assistance package under the Colombo plan. September: Canada closes its embassy in Iran and expels Iranian diplomats from Canada; lists Iran as a state sponsor of terrorism. National Commission on the Status of Women (NCSW) Act transforms the Commission into a powerful and autonomous body with head equivalent to a Minister of State. Pakistan Taliban attempt to assassinate Malala Yousafzai in Swat. Farida Afridi, co-founder of an NGO working to promote women's rights in FATA, is shot dead.
2013	Militants distribute pamphlets in North Waziristan agency of FATA warning tribesmen against allowing women relatives to vote in federal elections because it clashes with Sharia, and clerics make similar announcements on mosques' loudspeakers. Honour killing of five women in Kohistan district of KP province for dancing at a wedding. Najma Hanif Jadoon, a human rights activist and ANP candidate for a reserved provincial assembly seat, shot dead in Peshawar. Murder of Parween Rahman from Organi development project in Karachi. Peshawar High Court forms an exclusively female bench – the nation's first. Madadgaar, a helpline headquartered in Karachi for "children and women suffering from violence, abuse and exploitation," sets up provincial headquarters in Peshawar and other provincial capitals.

2014	898 victims of honour killings officially reported according to the Human Rights Commission of Pakistan.
	Taliban attack a Peshawar school, killing 170 children. Pakistan formulates the first National Action Plan to counter terrorism and combat extremism.
	Sindh Child Marriage Restraint Act (2014), and Domestic Violence Prevention and Protection Act, Sindh (2013) and Baluchistan (2014), passed in provinces.
2015	Assassination of Sabeen Mahmud, intellectual and social activist in Karachi. Honour killing of social media star Qandeel Baloch in Multan by her brother. Punjab provincial women's protection bill and Marriage Restraint Amendment Act passed.
2016	October: Honour Crimes Law passes unanimously in both houses of Parliament through the National Assembly.
2017	Canada launches the Feminist International Assistance Policy Framework requiring all foreign aid to demonstrate gender equality outcomes and linking funding to GE results. Canada approves a women's political participation project for Pakistan to increase women parliamentarians and creates a documentary on the Journey of Pakistan Women highlighting Canada's support over three decades.
2018	Global Affairs Canada launches new Women's Voice and Leadership program in Pakistan.
2019	Pakistan's first Violence Against Women Centre opens in Multan, under the Punjab Women Protection Authority Act (2017).
2021	Taliban take over Afghanistan by force and declare women's rights will be allowed in conformity with Sharia law.
	Canada closes embassy in Kabul.

Notes

EPIGRAPH

This poem comes from the book of Urdu poetry entitled *We Sinful Women/Beyond Belief* (R. Ahmad 1991), a collection of poems by women expressing resistance to the government of Pakistan's Islamization policy in the early 1980s. One crore equals ten million.

CHAPTER ONE

1 Laws drafted by the Council of Islamic Ideology. The Qisas and Diyat Law has since been linked to increased crimes and violence against women by a number of researchers and analysts.
   The government of Zia-ul-Haq introduced a series of laws that reduced women's status in society. The legislation included the Hudood Ordinance, the Law of Evidence, and the Law of Qisas and Diyat. "The Law of Evidence and the Law of Qisas and Diyat became the focus of a raging controversy that pitched women's rights groups (particularly WAF) and right-wing obscurantist scholars and *maulvis* against each other" (Mumtaz and Shaheed 1987, 105).
2 The Advisory Council of Islamic Ideology was reconstituted under Zia-ul-Haq to support the Islamization policy.
3 Documentary film, *The Journey of Pakistani Women*, produced by Global Affairs Canada in collaboration with Islamabad's White Rice Communications and launched on 22 March 2018 at the High Commission of Canada in Islamabad as part of Canada's celebrations around International Women's Day.

4 22 June 2020: The "No Peace without Women's Rights: Breaking the Cycle of Conflict in Afghanistan" panel was presented in collaboration with the Women Living Under Muslim Laws (WLUML) online global discussion panel with Dr Sima Samar and Dr Sally Armstrong, McGill Centre for Human Rights and Legal Pluralism.
5 From *The Journey of Pakistani Women*.

CHAPTER TWO

1 Unfortunately, Holbrooke passed away unexpectedly just days after speaking at the Pakistan Development Forum in Islamabad in December 2010.
2 The Thomson Reuters survey of 2011 ranked Pakistan the third most dangerous country in the world for women after Afghanistan and the DRC. In 2021, Pakistan was ranked as the fourth most dangerous country for women (Sarfraz et al. 2022, n3). See also N. Akhtar and D.A. Métraux, "Pakistan Is a Dangerous and Insecure Place for Women," *International Journal of World Peace* 30, no. 2 (2013): 35.

CHAPTER THREE

1 The United Nations Development Programme (UNDP) is the UN's lead agency on development.
2 The Demographic and Health Survey (DHS 2017/2018) confirms this data on domestic violence. The UN WHO (2018) report "Violence against Women Prevalence Estimates" shows Pakistan in the lowest category of 15–19 per cent prevalence physical and/or sexual intimate partner violence (IPV) in the past twelve months among ever-married/partnered women aged fifteen to forty-nine years. (Also published in P.A. Ali and M.I.B. Gavino, "Violence against Women in Pakistan: A Framework for Analysis," *Journal of the Pakistan Medical Association* 58, no. 4 [April 2008]: 198–203.)
3 Pakistan's first children's and women's helpline. Madadgaar is working for children, youth, and women's rights and protection.
4 In 2022 Shirkat Gah, the women's rights organization, with the Democratic Commission for Human Development and Technology for People initiative of LUMS University, supported the *Humqadam* app to provide GBV response services, including information on the national and provincial laws and a step-by-step guide on how to respond to special cases of violence.

5 Canada's record of GBV is also concerning, with higher incidence in certain parts of the country. But this book is about a program of funding by Canada of Pakistan's social and economic development.
6 See chaps. 6 and 7 for explanations of the informal systems of justice operating in rural communities.
7 UNDP: Multidimensional Poverty Index (MPI) in Pakistan (2016). Available at https://www.undp.org/pakistan/publications/multidimensional-poverty-pakistan. Note that MPI is a measure that captures the severe deprivations that each person experiences with respect to education, health, and standard of living. The index has been calculated using the PSLM survey and is a product of two components: 1) incidence of poverty, 2) intensity of poverty.
8 See studies quoted in Khan (2022, 46), by Guilbert (2016); Ajayi (2020); Badurdeen (2018); Ali (2018); and Zeuthen and Sahgal (2019).
9 See references in Khan (2022, 16, 34, and 46).
10 The report cites the evidence found through the UNDP project LLDR, p. 36.

CHAPTER FOUR

1 Translated from Dari in Shahbaz Ehsani, ed., *Mirrors and Songs: A Selection of Poetry of Afghan Women* (CreateSpace, 2012).
2 Behbud's webpage states that it "has been instrumental in the uplift of over a million disadvantaged women and their communities since 1967. Behbud bases itself on the sole principle of working at the grassroots; physically reaching out and providing free of cost training in hand embroidery and needlework to women restricted to their homes and villages. Apart from our skill development programs and fair wages, we also provide free healthcare to our workers and their families, and open schools for their children in their communities." See https://behbud.org/about-us.
3 The original WID framework called for the baseline, targets, and measurement indicators – a systemic response to monitor the impact on women and change (a kind of precursor to the results-based management approach that CIDA utilized some years later), focusing squarely on results rather than intention.
4 The shift to gender equity in 1995 did obscure, for a time, the priority of addressing the basic development needs of the poor and marginalized, who were mainly women. It was after 1995 that support to women in agriculture also waned and fell out of donor priorities for funding.

5 This shift was in part due to reduced funding on agriculture, reflecting the norm in international donor priorities at the time (Jones 2012).
6 Today, education levels in the Hunza valley (the northern part of Gilgit-Baltistan) are 95 per cent for both genders, the highest in Pakistan. The majority of people in the Hunza valley are Ismaili, the religion following the Aga Khan.
7 In the ten-year AKRSP annual report in 1992, we read of Noor Bibi of Ahmedabad, and Hunza and Shahida Numa of Princeabad, Gilgit. The eighty-member Women's Organization of Ahmedabad, formed in 1984, has engaged Noor Bibi as a vegetable, poultry, and livestock specialist, regularly attending WO meetings, saving part of her earnings every week, and providing specialist training. Noor Bibi says, "AKRSP has told us about vegetable marketing and with increased produce I have been selling vegetables for the past three years ... Whatever income I earn from vegetables or other crops I spend on my child's education and household needs. We have educated our four sons and now wish that I had also educated at least one of my daughters ... Unlike before, all members of the women's organization (WO) are now selling fruit and vegetables" (Jones 2012, 57).
8 The first major CIDA evaluation of the WID Policy was undertaken in 1993. It was evaluated again in 1995 as part of a new performance review of six CIDA aid priorities – WID being one. It found that WID was still not woven into the fabric of CIDA operations: i.e., not being consistently implemented. (From Wendy Lawrence, CIDA GE specialist, March 2004, "Reflections on CIDA's Experience, An Historical Overview," presented to the 'Whither GAD' symposium, Ottawa, 3 March 2004. By permission of the author.)

CHAPTER FIVE

1 Salmaan Taseer's son was kidnapped in August 2011 by Islamic militants and taken to Afghanistan. He was eventually released in March 2016 after his father's assassin was executed.
2 In April 2021, the TLP staged protests across the country against France, accusing the French president of blasphemy for speaking out on the incident of the French school teacher who had shown the cartoon portrayal of the Prophet Muhammad, and who was subsequently beheaded on the street near his school in Paris by an Islamic extremist. Despite its banning as a political party in April 2021 after violent protests that caused the deaths of two policemen and left 340 people

injured (a ban that has since been lifted), Tehreek-e-Labbaik still holds powerful influence in the country because of its widespread support.

3 It built mostly on the USAID-funded programs for rural women focussing on economic empowerment by bringing a private-sector angle to development work.

4 Global Affairs funded another WEE project on dairy production in Southern Punjab through Plan International in subsequent years. UK Aid was also funding similar projects in the province.

5 Although aid donors coordinate by "sector" or "program," data is not easily available. Collating all data on WEE projects, for example, into a coherent picture of support by sector is almost impossible. This has long been a troubling issue, with attempts to tackle it through central government databases, many supported by development donors – none of which really work. But development donors continue coordination by sectors and themes on a regular although informal basis to avoid duplication and ensure complementarity of funding.

6 Information obtained through the course of my work with the UNDP Crisis Bureau.

7 Posted on Facebook by Canadian High Commission Pakistan.

CHAPTER SIX

1 The Karachi-based human rights lawyer and founder of Madadgaar National Helpline for victims of gender-based violence; see chap. 3.

2 The authors go on to say that "[a] study by the World Health Organization finds that one woman in three in the world will experience violence sometime during their lifetime and one in four will experience domestic abuse ... Domestic violence does not respect economies or social status' it is not specific to any one religion or culture. It ignores all frontiers" (Lopez-Claros and Nakhjavani 2018, 64–5). Countries such as Canada and the United States also suffer from unacceptable levels of GBV.

3 Chap. 4 by Jacqui True, "Sexual and Gender Based Violence Reporting in Asia."

4 Chap. 3 by Farhana Rahman, "Trajectories of Gender Inequality, Identity and Violent Extremism in Rural Bangladesh."

5 See explanations in chaps. 1 and 7.

6 Although passed in 1985 by the National Assembly, the law became part of Pakistan's penal code in 1997 between two democratically elected governments, championed by Zia-ul-Haq's finance minister from the 1980s, who was acting as interim president at the time.

7 Punjab is also known to have the highest rate of honour-related crimes in the country.
8 For more on SPO and its groundbreaking work for grassroots women's organizations see chap. 8.

CHAPTER SEVEN

1 Giving away women, mainly minors, to settle disputes as compensation to an aggrieved party is called *wani* or *vani* in Punjabi, *swara* in Pashtu. Marrying to the Quran is usually to keep a woman's inheritance in the family (*Parliament's Role in Pakistan's Democratic Transition*, Crisis Group Asia Report no. 249 [18 September 2013], found in International Crisis Group 2015, 9).
2 Fouzia Saeed, a social scientist, gender expert, and author, was the driving force behind this law. Her most recent book, *Tapestry: Strands of Women's Struggles Woven into the History of Pakistan* (Karachi: Liberty Books, 2022), is about the struggle of women to gain their rights from pre-1947 to 2016 and recounts much of this collaboration.
3 Aurat Foundation's Legislative Watch Programme for Women's Empowerment has published numerous papers on these issues over the years.
4 Compilation of research on CIDA funding for gender equality (1984–2013), my notes.
5 H. Khan (2015). Definition of informal law by Dr Noah Coburn in the USIP report.
6 Dr Muhammad Tufail Hashmi published his book on the Hudood Ordinance in Lahore in 2004.
7 A consultation on "Hudood Ordinances: The Islamic Perspectives," organized by Aurat Publication and Information Service Foundation, 4 January 2005, in Islamabad.
8 Patel published a survey in 1979 that demonstrated that women's knowledge of their Islamic and legal rights was very low.
9 Punishment ordained by the Quran and Sunnah; mandatory provision.

CHAPTER EIGHT

1 GAD was the label used to describe this change in gender approach at the time in development circles. Although touted as a major policy shift, the difference between WID and GAD can be difficult to discern.
2 Now part of the Afghan Taliban regime since their takeover in 2021.

3 The Al Huda Institute in Canada has come under the spotlight since it became known that the female shooter at San Bernardino had attended Al Huda School in Multan, Pakistan. The founder of the Al Huda schools, Farhat Hashmi, came to Canada in 2005 to start the Al Huda schools in Canada and the US. The Al Huda schools in Pakistan have raised questions among many Pakistani feminists regarding their philosophy on women's rights and equality and religious and cultural tolerance. In Canada, too, similar concerns have been raised by the Canadian Muslim community about Al Huda in Mississauga as far back as 2006 and up to today.

4 Since then, Al Huda has mushroomed into a chain of schools throughout Pakistan with additional locations in Canada, the US, Dubai, and the UK. It is now also considered a social movement and carries out social welfare projects.

CHAPTER NINE

1 The head of SPO for many years from 2001–02, Harris Khalique, became the Secretary General of the Human Rights Commission of Pakistan in 2018 – a non-governmental human rights organization registered under the law, recognized as the apex independent rights body in Pakistan. It monitors human rights violations and seeks redress through public campaigns, awareness-raising, legislative lobbying, policy advocacy, legal recourse, and action research through fact-finding missions. Besides other periodic and special publications it issues an annual report on the state of human rights in the country.

2 The project supported under PAGE worked to build the capacity of local NGOs to address gender issues through the Balochistan NGO Network, which represented 1,200 NGOs and CBOs.

3 AKRSP (1983, 44). Also in Jones et al. (2012, n10).

4 Simorgh was formed in 1985 in direct response to General Zia-ul-Haq's retrogressive legislation. Five members of WAF aimed to consolidate and build on issues raised by WAF through Simorgh as an advocacy and research organization, primarily on women's rights and violence against women.

5 From personal notes during this time in office.

6 RSPN was set up in 2000 and traces its history to AKRSP in 1982, funded by CIDA as the first major donor to AKRSP in Pakistan.

7 Awaz, literal translation "voice," was also the name of a Pakistani pop band that formed in Islamabad, in 1992.

CHAPTER TEN

1. The extremist groups that eventually formed the Pakistani Taliban were restricting women's development in parts of the country through tactics inciting fear and violence.
2. These are key examples of the kind of work undertaken during the period.
3. The NGOs identified three priority concerns: violence against women, the uneven impact of globalization on women, and a lack of women's participation in politics, power, and decision-making (CIDA 2001).
4. "As grassroots women's orgs and networks continue to play pivotal roles in conflict prevention & resolution, supporting them with flexible and sustainable funding is critical" (UNSC Open Debate on WPS, October 2022).
5. Hina Jilani speaking on video clip on Hellofuture.undp.org, September 2023.

CHAPTER ELEVEN

1. Robin Raphel tried to argue for continued humanitarian assistance to Afghanistan, but to no avail. US ended all bilateral aid to Afghanistan less than two years after Clinton took office (Coll 2004).
2. The role women played in support of Mullah Fazalullah and Tehrik-e-Taliban in some Tehsils during the militancy in Swat Valley 2007–09 is also well-documented (Khan 2022, 127). Women supporting violent extremists is covered in other reports and books on preventing violent extremism.
3. Early in 2007 the Lal Masjid (Red Mosque) was taken over by the madrassa students and their leader, Khateeb Maulana Abdul Aziz, along with his brother, Maulana Ghazi Rashid. It became a platform for popular fury over the American invasion of Afghanistan (Walsh 2020). The madrassa armed its students, along with their female counterparts in the attached Jamia Hafsa (the largest religious seminary for girls in the country [Sheikh 2016]), formed an armed resistance, and announced the imposition of Sharia. The government conducted a campaign against the Islamist militants called Operation Silence where Abdul Aziz was arrested trying to escape disguised under a burqa (Walsh 2020). The operation received widespread condemnation because of the number of people killed, including those who were innocent.
4. Composed of Australia, Canada, New Zealand, the United Kingdom, and the United States, who share intelligence information with each other.

5 As recounted by Sola Mahfouz in *Defiant Dreams: The Journey of an Afghan Girl Who Risked Everything for Education* (New York: Ballantine Books, 2023).

CHAPTER TWELVE

1 UNDP in 2016 referred to "[a]nother complicating factor within the larger phenomenon ... what might be called the 'securitization of development,' whereby military and security needs and priorities become enmeshed with development issues. Compounding matters, none of these issues are amenable to 'quick fixes'; they demand a long-term response that ultimately tackles structural or root causes" (UNDP, "Navigating Turbulence and Uncertainty," 15 November 2016, 16; see also Brown 2016).
2 The Islamic State of Iraq and the Levant (ISIL) is also known as ISIS (Islamic State Iraq Syria), IS, and Daesh. It was originally created by the wing of al-Qaeda in Iraq. Daesh is the (derogatory) Arabic acronym for ISIS (Brookings Institute).

CHAPTER THIRTEEN

1 He was the coordinator of the Human Rights Commission of Pakistan for the tribal areas. A schoolteacher and social and rights activist, he frequently advocated for education for girls and for gender equality.
2 Ehsan is his assumed name, believed in Taliban circles to be the name of one of the first Mujaheddin who "conquered" Kabul in 1996, brutally murdering former Afghan president Dr Najib and hanging his body from a traffic post (Owais 2020). His real name is Liaqat Ali. He fled into Afghanistan in 2016–17 and then surrendered and was held in custody in Peshawar, but escaped again in January 2020.
3 In 2017, the Canadian Government announced it was conferring honorary citizenship on Malala. On 12 April, she addressed Canada's Parliament. Her presence in Canada was widely covered by the media. Canada's Minister for International Cooperation used the opportunity to confirm that women and girls would be at the heart of the government's development policy, which was then under review, leading to the new Feminist International Assistance Policy (FIAP). Canada continues to fund global efforts in collaboration with other countries to get more girls in school around the world.

4 The UN Human Rights Commission has indicated that blasphemy laws should be withdrawn as they distort protection of minorities among other issues, and there are other protections in place to ensure religious freedoms and protections.
5 A podcast by the Philippine Centre for Islam and Democracy (*She Talks Peace*, episode 78: Huma Chughtai Talks Sharia and Conflict in Pakistan) referred to this. Chughtai also said they are using scripture to show CEDAW is not just a Western notion, it is supported by Islam. Fifty Ulema in Pakistan have developed a message talking about terrorism and peace and how the former is against Islamic injunctions (https://shows.acast.com/61ee08a05320a20013e729c6/episodes/ep-78-huma-chughtai-talks-sharia-and-conflict-in-pakistan).
6 The "No Peace Without Women's Rights: Breaking the Cycle of Conflict in Afghanistan" panel was presented on 22 June 2020 in collaboration with Women Living Under Muslim Laws (WLUML) as an online global discussion panel with Dr Sima Samar and Dr Sally Armstrong, McGill Centre for Human Rights and Legal Pluralism, and was moderated by Professor Payam Akhavan and Professor Vrinda Narain, with comments from Dr Mona Tajali and Professor Homa Hoodfar.

CHAPTER FOURTEEN

1 Behavioural science is the systematic study through observation and experimentation of how and why we behave the way we do. It draws on insights from psychology, economics, sociology, cognitive science, and other social science disciplines (UNDP 2021, 11).
2 This list is taken from the table in UNDP (2021a), adapted from Horgan (2009) and UNDP (2018, 14).
3 It is worth reviewing note 6 of the 2021 UNDP report for an indication of the range of analysis behind trying to understand drivers of radicalization and of violent extremism: John Horgan, *The Psychology of Terrorism* (Oxfordshire: Routledge, 2004); John Horgan, *Walking Away from Terrorism: Accounts of Disengagement from Radical and Extremist Movements* (Oxfordshire: Routledge, 2009); Harriet Allan et al., "Drivers of Violent Extremism: Hypotheses and Literature Review" (London: Royal United Services Institute, 2015), https://gsdrc.org/document-library/drivers-of-violent-extremism-hypotheses-and-literature-review; James Khalil and Martine Zeuthen, "Countering Violent Extremism and Risk Reduction. A Guide to Programme Design and Evaluation," Whitehall report 2–16 (London: Royal United Services Institute, 2016), https://static.rusi.org/20160608_cve_and_rr.combined.online4.pdf.

CHAPTER FIFTEEN

1 Coined by author and journalist Kim Ghattas in her 2020 book *Black Wave*.
2 Media is forbidden to publish content that is not in line with Taliban religious interpretations.
3 This act took place at a public gathering in northern Persia in 1848 and was seen as proclaiming an end to Sharia law.
4 Azar Nafisi, author of *Reading Lolita in Tehran*, recounted this infamous example of the Persian poet and scholar Tahirih, when speaking as a panellist on a webinar on Mahsa Ammi's death, "A Year of Protest and Reflections on the Future," by the Georgetown Institute for Women, Peace, and Security, 13 September 2023.

References

Abbas, Hassan. 2005. *Pakistan's Drift into Extremism*. New Delhi: Pentagon Press.
Aga Khan Foundation Canada. 1983. *First Annual Review*. Gilgit, Pakistan: Aga Khan Rural Support Program.
– 2006. *Canada and the AKRSP in Northern Pakistan*. Ottawa: Author.
Akhavan, Payam. 2017. *In Search of a Better World, A Human Rights Odyssey*. Toronto: Anansi Press.
Ahmad, Rukhsana, ed. 1991. *We Sinful Women, Contemporary Urdu Feminist Poetry*. Lahore, Pakistan: The Women's Press and ASR Publications.
Ahmad, Sadaf. 2009. *Transforming Faith, The Story of Al-Huda and Islamic Revivalism among Urban Pakistani Women*. Syracuse, NY: Syracuse University Press. Reprinted Oxford University Press Pakistan, 2010.
AKRSP. 1983. *First Annual Review, 1983*. Gilgit, Pakistan: AKRSP.
– 2009. "An Assessment of Institutional Development of Village and Women's Organisations." IDS Report for CIDA. Gilgit, Pakistan: AKRSP.
Altaf, S. 2011. *So Much Aid, So Little Development. Stories from Pakistan*. Baltimore: Johns Hopkins University Press.
Anderlini, S.N. 2020. "What Happened in Afghanistan Isn't Staying in Afghanistan." *Common Dreams*, 7 September 2020. https://www.commondreams.org/views/2022/09/07/what-happened-afghanistan-isnt-staying-afghanistan.
Armstrong, K. 2011. *A Letter to Pakistan*. Karachi, Pakistan: Oxford University Press.

Aslam, Fazeelat. 2012. "Saving Face." Karachi *Herald Magazine* (March): 76–9.

Ayesha, Imam, Isabel Marler, and Laila Malik. 2016. *The Devil Is in the Details: Development, Women's Rights and Religious Fundamentalisms*. Washington, DC: Association of Women in Development.

Azmat, Hira. 2022. "5 Years of Pakistan's Aurat March: The Young Feminist Movement Shocked the Nation into Paying Attention. But Where Is It Headed?" *No Niin* online magazine, issue 14. https://no-niin.com/issue-14/5-years-of-pakistans-aurat-march-the-young-feminist-movement-shocked-the-nation-into-paying-attention-but-where-is-it-headed/index.html.

BBC. 2019. "Afzal Kohistani: 'Honour Killing' Whistleblower Shot Dead." BBC, 7 March. https://www.bbc.com/news/world-asia-47480597.

Bigio, Jamille, and Rachel Vogelstein. 2019. "Women and Terrorism: Hidden Threats, Forgotten Partners." Discussion paper. May 2019. New York: Council on Foreign Relations.

Brown, S. 2016. "From Ottawa to Kandahar and Back: The Securitization of Canadian Foreign Aid." In *The Securitization of Foreign Aid*, edited by S. Brown and J. Grävingholt, 113–37. London: Palgrave Macmillan.

Bryant, Nick. 2017. "The Time When America Stopped Being Great." *BBC News*, 3 November 2017. http://www.bbc.com/news/world-uscanada-41826022.

Business Recorder. 2005. "Many Clauses of Hudood Ordinances Termed against Quran and Sunnah." 4 January 2005. https://www.brecorder.com/news/3116697/many-clauses-of-hudood-ordinances-termed-against-quran-and-sunnah-20050104111752.

CAC, Bytown Consulting. 2008. *Evaluation of CIDA's Implementation of Its Policy on Gender Equality*. Executive report. Ottawa: Government of Canada, Evaluation Division, CIDA.

Canadian High Commission Pakistan. 2000. *Canada-Pakistan Highlights, Winter 1999–2000*. Islamabad.

CBC. 2020. "Ex-Diplomats, Aid Workers Plead with the World Community to Stand By Afghanistan." CBC, 23 November 2020. https://www.cbc.ca/news/politics/afghanistan-taliban-peace-process-canada-1.5810962.

Center of Gender and Policy Studies. 2018. *Rural Women in Pakistan Status Report*. Islamabad: UN Women.

CIDA. 1984a. *Managing the Process of Change, Women in Development*. Ottawa: Canadian International Development Agency.

- 1984b. *Women in Development Policy Framework.* Corporate Policy. 18 December. Gatineau, QC: Canadian International Development Agency.
- 1985. *Administrative Notices.* CIDA WID News. Gatineau, QC: Canadian International Development Agency, January 25.
- 1986a. *Coming of Age,* CIDA *and Women in Development.* Policy report. Gatineau, QC: Canadian International Development Agency.
- 1986b. "Integrating Women into Development." Notes for a speech by the Minister for External Relations. 11 June. Gatineau, QC: Canadian International Development Agency.
- 1986c. *Women in Development:* CIDA *Action Plan.* Gatineau, QC: Canadian International Development Agency.
- 1989. *Women in Development. A Sectoral Perspective.* Gatineau, QC: Canadian International Development Agency.
- 1995. *From Plan to Action –* CIDA*'s Women and Development Program in Pakistan.* Islamabad: Canadian International Development Agency Women's Development Fund.
- 2004a. *Canada's Official Development Assistance ... in Pakistan, List of Projects.* Gatineau, QC: Canadian International Development Agency.
- 2004b. "Lessons Learnt from Women's Development Project (WDPr) 1996–2004." WDPr Team report, CIDA Pakistan: Sterling Swift, CIDA PSU. (Also found in R. Rashid 2016 as annex V, and in Moffat and Ehsan 2006 as annex 2006.)
- 2005. *Canada's Official Development Assistance in Pakistan.* Summary of Activities. Gatineau, QC: Canadian International Development Agency.
- 2006. "CIDA Pakistan Program Evaluation." October. Gatineau, QC: CIDA.
- 2010a. CIDA *Pakistan Program, Women's Economic Empowerment Framework.* Gatineau, QC: Canadian International Development.
- 2010b. *Gender Equality Policy and Tools.* Gatineau, QC: Canadian International Development Agency.
- 2010c. *Turning a New* PAGE *for Women,* CIDA*'s Programme for the Advancement of Gender Equality (*PAGE*).* Islamabad: Canadian International Development Agency Program Support Unit.
- 2014. "Pakistan Country Program Evaluation 2007–2008 to 2011–2012." Ottawa: Global Affairs Canada. https://www.international.gc.ca/gac-amc/publications/evaluation/2015/evaluation-pakistan.aspx?lang=eng#ann7.

Claros-Lopez, A., and B. Nakhjavani. 2018. *Equality for Women, Prosperity for All.* New York: St Martin's Press.

Coll, Steve. 2004. *Ghost Wars.* New York: Penguin Press.
Crisis Group Asia. 2013. *Parliament's Role in Pakistan's Democratic Transition.* 18 September 2013. Islamabad/Brussels: International Crisis Group.
Critelli, F. 2012. "Voices of Resistance Seeking Shelter Services in Pakistan." *Violence against Women* 18 (4): 437–58.
Daur, Naya. 2020. "Stop Using the Term 'Ghairat' in 'Honour' Killing Cases, Says SC in Landmark Judgement." *Nayadaur.tv.* 5 September 2020. https://nayadaur.tv/2020/09/stop-using-the-term-ghairat-in-honour-killing-cases-says-sc-in-landmark-judgement.
Dawn News. 2021. "EU Parliament Adopts Resolution Calling for Review of Pakistan's GSP+ Status over Blasphemy Law Abuse." 30 April 2021. https://www.dawn.com/news/1621254.
Devers, L., and S. Bacon. 2010. "Interpreting Honour Crimes: The Institutional Disregard towards Female Victims of Family Violence in the Middle East." *International Journal of Criminology and Sociological Theory* 3: 359–71.
Economist. 2011. "Now, Kill His Dream; What His Death Means for al-Qaeda; They Got Him." 7 May 2011, 22–6.
– 2012. "Perilous Journey: Special Report Pakistan." https://www.economist.com/banyan/2012/02/09/perilous-journey.
El-Ali, Leena. 2022. *No Truth without Beauty: God, the Qur'an, and Women's Rights.* Arlington: Palgrave Macmillan.
EU, Policy Department. 2017. *Women's Economic Empowerment at the International Level.* In-depth analysis for the FEMM Committee. Brussels: EU Policy Department, Director General for Internal Policies.
Express Tribune [Islamabad]. 2011a. "Keeping Women Down." Editorial, 19 October 2011. https://tribune.com.pk/story/277415/keeping-women-down.
– 2011b. "Violent Frontier Mourns Death of a Pacifist." 28 December 2011.
– 2012. "Editorial." 29 May 2012.
– 2014. "Under Siege: Express Media Group Attacked Once Again." 29 March 2014.
Fair, Christine, et al. 2013. *The Fighters of Lashkar-e-Taiba: Recruitment, Training, Deployment and Death.* West Point, NY: West Point Combatting Terrorism Centre.
Franc, Renata, and Tomislav Pavlović. 2021. "Inequality and Radicalisation – Systematic Review of Quantitative Studies." *Terrorism and Political Violence* 35 (4): 785–810. https://www.tandfonline.com/doi/pdf/10.1080/09546553.2021.1974845.

Fransen, Rosalie. 2021. "Reconstructing Identity: The Role of Gender in Driving and Dismantling White Supremacy in Sweden (Case Summary)." October 2021. International Civil Society Action Network. https://icanpeacework.org/wp-content/uploads/2021/10/Gender-and-Identity-Extremisms-Case-Summaries.pdf.
– 2022. "Institutionalizing Equality: Shifting Gender Roles in Jordanian Counterterrorism Responses." September 2022. International Civil Society Action Network. https://icanpeacework.org/wp-content/uploads/2022/09/Jordan-Summary-Gender-and-Identity-Extremisms-.pdf.
Gannon, Kathy. 2005. *I is for Infidels, From Holy War to Holy Terror: 18 Years inside Afghanistan.* Cambridge: Perseus Books Group.
– 2020. "Before Attack, A Pakistani Teen Sought Better Life in France." APN*ews.com*, 8 October 2020. https://apnews.com/general-news-12e45fe6e5ecb0b8e53f9ae61374bab8.
– 2021. "Taliban Tweet Threatens Malala; Twitter Removes Account." 16 February 2021. https://apnews.com/article/pakistan-malala-yousafzai-taliban58e421718cec6206cfcdf7a98113d8c5.
Georgetown Institute for Women, Peace and Security and Peace Research Institute Oslo. 2021. "Women, Peace, and Security Index 2021/22: Tracking Sustainable Peace through Inclusion, Justice, and Security for Women." Washington, DC: GIWPS and PRIO. https://giwps.georgetown.edu/wp-content/uploads/2021/11/WPS-Index-2021.pdf.
Ghattas, Kim. 2020. *Black Wave: Saudi Arabia, Iran and the 40 Year Rivalry that Unraveled Culture, Religion, and Collective Memory in the Middle East.* New York: Henry Holt and Company.
Global Affairs Canada. 2017. "Feminist International Assistance Policy." June 2017. Ottawa. https://www.international.gc.ca/world-monde/issues_development-enjeux_developpement/priorities-priorites/fiap-paif.aspx?lang=eng.
Global Issues Awareness for National Trust Forum. 1996. *International Conference on Islamic Laws and Women.* 22–23 December 1996. Islamabad: Giant Forum, Maktaba Jadeed Press Lahore.
Global Village Space. 2020. *What Does Mera Jism Meri Marzi Mean?* 29 January 2020. Islamabad.
Gloekler, A., and J. Seeley. 2007. "Gender and AKRSP – Mainstreamed or Sidelined?" In *Valleys in Transition: Twenty Years of AKRSP's Experience in Northern Pakistan,* edited by G. Wood, S. Sagheer, and A. Malik, 120–95. Oxford, UK: Oxford University Press. (Also cited as: A. Gloekler and J. Seeley. 2003. "Gender and AKRSP: A Policy Analysis." AKRSP: Gilgit, Pakistan. In AKRSP "Lessons Learned" Exercise.)

Goss, Gilroy. 2006. CIDA *Pakistan Progamme Evaluation*. Ottawa: Goss Gilroy Management Consultants, commissioned by CIDA Performance and Knowledge Management Branch.

Gossen, Rhonda. 1983. *The Other Side of Purdah, Integrating Pakistani Women into Development*. Research study. Hull, QC: Canadian International Development Agency.

Guardian. 2021. "Virginity Tests for Female Rape Survivors Outlawed by Pakistani Court." 6 January 2021. https://www.theguardian.com/global-development/2021/jan/06/virginity-tests-for-female-survivors-outlawed-by-pakistani-court.

Gul, Imtiaz. 2009. *The Most Dangerous Place, Pakistan's Lawless Frontier*. New York: Penguin Group.

– 2012. *Pakistan Before and After Osama*. Mumbai, India: Roli Books Private Limited.

– 2017. "NOC for (I)NGOs or Tool for Corruption?" Islamabad *Daily Times Newspaper*, 8 November 2017.

Haq, F. 2016. "Bombs and Burqas: Muslim Women and Extremism." 24 March 2016. https://www.wilsoncenter.org/article/bombs-and-burqas-muslim-women-and-extremism.

Holmes, Melinda. 2017. *Preventing Violent Extremism, Protecting Rights and Community Policing: Why Civil Society and Security Partnerships Matter*. Washington, DC: International Civil Society Action Network (ICAN).

Hudson, Valerie. 2020. "What You Do to Your Women, You Do to Your Nation." *New York Times*, 6 March 2020. https://www.nytimes.com/2020/03/06/opinion/global-womens-rights.html.

Hudson, Valerie M., Donna Lee Bowen, and Perpetua Lynne Nielsen. 2020. *The First Political Order: How Sex Shapes Governance and National Security Worldwide*. New York: Columbia University Press.

Hudson, Valerie, and Kaylee Hodgson. 2020. *Sex and Terror: Is the Subordination of Women Associated with the Use of Terror? Terrorism and Political Violence* 34: 1–28. http://doi.org/10.1080/09546553.2020.1724968.

Human Rights Activists News Agency. 2023. "Iran's New Hijab Bill Stirs Controversy and Concern." 7 September 2023. https://www.en-hrana.org/statements/irans-new-hijab-bill-stirs-controversy-and-concern.

Human Rights Commission Pakistan. 2018. *Annual Report*. Islamabad: Author.

Human Rights Watch. 1999. "Crime of Custom? Violence against Women in Pakistan." https://www.hrw.org/legacy/reports/1999/pakistan.

Hussain, Neelam, and Rubina Saigol. 2020. "Policy, Education for One and All?" 6 September 2020. https://www.dawn.com/news/1577990.

Hussain, Zahid. 2010. *The Scorpion's Tail, The Relentless Rise of Islamic Militants in Pakistan – and How It Threatens the World*. New York: Free Press, Division of Simon and Schuster, Inc.

– 2017. "Silencing Dissent." *Dawn Newspaper*, 13 December 2017. https://www.dawn.com/news/1376190.

– 2020. "The Rise of the Opposition." *Dawn.com*, 4 October 2020. https://www.dawn.com/news/1583018.

– 2021. "Daniel Pearl's Murder Case Strains US-Pakistan Relations." *Arab News Pakistan*, 30 January 2021. https://www.arabnews.pk/node/1800966.

– 2022a. *No-Win War*. London: Oxford University Press.

– 2022b. "Trapped in a Jihadist Quicksand." 15 August 2022. https://www.dawn.com/news/1704690.

Inayat, Naila. 2020. "Damage Caused by Valentine's Day to Pakistani Ideology Is Bigger than Any Existential Threat." *The Print.in Opinion*, 13 February 2020. https://theprint.in/opinion/letter-from-pakistan/damage-caused-by-valentines-day-to-pakistani-ideology-is-bigger-than-any-existential-threat/364465.

International Crisis Group. 2015. *Women, Violence and Conflict in Pakistan*. Asia Report, no. 265, 8 April 2015. Brussels: International Crisis Group.

Islam, A., and A. Carlos Lopez. 2021. "Using Laws to Protect Women from Violence." 3 August 2021. https://blogs.worldbank.org/developmenttalk/using-law-protect-women-violence-does-it-work.

Jafri, Amir. 2008. *Honour Killing, Dilemma, Ritual, Understanding*. Karachi, Pakistan: Oxford University Press.

Johnston, Melissa, and Jacqui True. 2019. *Misogyny and Violent Extremism: Implications for Preventing Violent Extremism*. Melbourne, Australia: Monash University, UN Women.

Johnston, Melissa Frances, Muhammad Iqbal, and Jacqui True. 2020. "The Lure of (Violent) Extremism: Gender Constructs in Online Recruitment and Messaging in Indonesia." *Studies in Conflict & Terrorism* 46 (4): 470–88. https://www.tandfonline.com/doi/full/10.1080/1057610X.2020.1759267.

Jones, Linda, et al. 2012. *Review of Women's Economic Empowerment in Gilgit-Baltistan*. Aga Khan Foundation Canada.

Jones, Linda, (MEDA), and Perveen Shaikh (ECDI). 2005. *Middlemen as Agents of Change: MEDA and ECDI in Pakistan*. June. Washington,

DC: The Practitioner Learning Program in BDS Market Assessment Learning Paper and the SEEP Network.

— 2006. "MEDA, The Double-X Factor: Harnessing Female Human Capital for Economic Growth." *International Journal of Emerging Markets* (Emerald Insight Publishing) 1, no. 4. https://www.emerald.com/insight/publication/issn/1746-8809.

Khalique, Harris. 2011. *The Latent Transformation, Challenges, Resilience and Successes of Pakistani Women*. Islamabad: Aurat Foundation.

— 2022. "The Uncritical Era." *Dawn News*, 18 September 2022. https://www.dawn.com/news/1710724.

Khan, H. 2015. *Islamic Law, Customary Law and Informal Afghan Justice*. Washington, DC: United States Institute for Peace.

Khan, Rabia. 2009. *Situational Analysis and Mapping of Women's Human Rights in Pakistan*. Islamabad: Report Commissioned by Canadian International Agency.

Khan, Sheharyar, et al. 2022. *Resilience, Community Security and Social Cohesion through Effective Women's Leadership*. Islamabad: UN Women.

Khan, Shoaib Sultan. 2009. *The Aga Khan Rural Support Programme, A Journey through Grassroots Development*. Karachi, Pakistan: Oxford University Press.

Khan, Simbal. 2022. *Gap Analysis of Pakistan's Security Protocols through a Gender Lens*. Islamabad: UN Women Pakistan.

Khan, Sumera. 2012. "Fighting for Women's Rights; Supreme Court Urged to Declare Jirga System Illegal." Islamabad *Express Tribune*, 17 March 2012.

Kugelman, M., and A. Weinstein. 2021. "In Pakistan, a Tale of Two Very Different Political Movements." *Lawfare*, 4 January 2021. https://www.lawfaremedia.org/article/pakistan-tale-two-very-different-political-movements.

Lamb, Christina. 2023. "A Year since Mahsa Amimi's Death, What Changed for Women in Iran?" *The Sunday Times*, 17 September 2023.

Lari, Maliha Zia. 2011. *A Critical Appreciation of the Prevention of Anti-Women Practices (Criminal Law Amendment) Bill 2011*. Islamabad: Aurat Foundation Legislative Watch Publication and Information Service Foundation.

Lawrence, Wendy. 2004. "Gender Equality and Development: Reflections on CIDA's Experience." Presentation to the "Whither GAD" Symposium, 3 March 2004, Ottawa.

Lieberman, Amy. 2017. "Bloomberg Says Cities Will Lead in Youth Development, Fighting Extremism." *Devex*, 15 September 2017. https://www.devex.com/news/bloomberg-says-cities-will-lead-in-youth-development-fighting-extremism-91037.

Lieven, Anatol. 2011. *Pakistan, A Hard Country*. London: Penguin Group.

Lodhi, Maleeha. 2011. *Pakistan beyond the Crisis State*. Karachi, Pakistan: Oxford University Press.

Maher, S. 2018. *The Sensational Life and Death of Qandeel Baloch*. New Delhi: Aleph Book Company.

Mahmood, Arshad. 2017. "Ending Child Marriage in Pakistan." Islamabad *Express Tribune*, 21 November 2017.

Mai, Mukhtar. 2007. *In the Name of Honour*. London: Virago Press.

Mamdani, Mahmood. 2004. *Good Muslim, Bad Muslim: America, the Cold War, and the Roots of Terror*. New York: Doubleday.

Masood, Salman. 2011. "Pakistan Top Court Upholds Acquittals in Notorious Rape Case." *New York Times*, 12 April 2011.

McAllister, Elizabeth. 1984. *Managing the Process of Change, Women in Development*. Presentation to the President's Committee. January 1984. Hull, QC: Canadian International Development Agency Policy Branch.

— 1997. *Institutionalizing Gender Issues*. Washington, DC: World Bank.

Miller, John, Michael Stone, and Chris Mitchell. 2002. *The Cell: Inside the 9/11 Plot, and Why the FBI and CIA Failed to Stop It*. New York: Hyperion.

Mir, A. 2022. "Pakistan's Twin Taliban Problem." United States Institute of Peace, 4 May 2022. https://www.usip.org/publications/2022/05/pakistans-twin-taliban-problem.

Moffat, Linda, and Lubna Ehsan. 2006. *Evaluation of the Women's Development Project and the Program for the Advancement of Gender Equality*. Islamabad: CIDA Pakistan.

Moser, Caroline. 1993. *Gender Planning and Development: Theory, Practice, and Training*. London: Routledge.

Muhungi, W., and E. Edwards. 2017. "Supporting Women's Rights in Troubled Times." *Stanford Social Innovation Review* 16 (1): A9. https://doi.org/10.48558/0TJ0-BH77.

Mumtaz, Khawar, and Farida Shaheed. 1987. *Women of Pakistan, Two Steps Forward, One Step Back?* London: Zed Books.

Naheed, Kishwar. 2001. *The Distance of a Shout*. Karachi, Pakistan: Oxford University Press.

Naqeeb, Bilal. 2006. SPO: *A Brief History*. Islamabad: SPO, Khurhseed Printers.
Nasr, Vali. 2013. "The Inside Story of How the White House Let Diplomacy Fail in Afghanistan: The War Issue Special Report." *Foreign Policy Magazine*, 4 March 2013.
O'Donnell, M., and C. Kenny. 2020. *With Ten Years to the SDG Finish Line, Laws Need to Change for Gender Equality*. Washington, DC: Centre for Global Development.
Okeowo, Alexis. 2018. "Daughter of Pakistan." *New Yorker*, 9 April 2018.
Owais, Tohid. 2020. "Runaway Taliban Frontman: Ehsanullah Ehsan, the Man and Myth." *Arab News*, 10 February 2020. https://arab.news/cty2p.
Packer, George. 2019. *Our Man, Richard Holbrooke and the End of the American Century*. New York: Alfred Knopf.
Patel, Rashida. 1979. "Women's Awareness of Legal Rights: Results from a Survey." *Legal Status of Women in Pakistan* 97. Islamabad.
Paterson, Isla. 2004. *Operational Review, Program for the Advancement of Gender Equality. Final Report*. Gatineau, QC: Commissioned by CIDA Pakistan Program.
Paton, Julia. 1986. *Nation Builders: Women in Pakistan, A Development Strategy*. Gatineau, QC: Marsters Associates, BMC Consulting; commissioned and published by Canadian International Development Agency.
Phelan, Alexandra, Jacqui True, Irine Hiraswari Gayatri, Amporn Marddent, Yolanda Riveros Morales, and Sittie Janine Gamao. 2022. *Gender Analysis of Violent Extremism and the Impact of COVID-19 on Peace and Security in ASEAN*. Melbourne: Monash University. https://doi.org/10.26180/19731589.v1.
Phelan, Alexandra I.H. 2022. *Gender Analysis of Violent Extremism in ASEAN*. Melbourne: Monash University and UN Women.
Qazi, Sabina. 2012. "What's Culture Got to Do with It." Karachi *Herald Magazine* (March): 60–4.
Quetta Voice Web Desk. 2020a. "Honor Killings, Domestic Violence Claim 23 Lives of Women in Balochistan." *Quetta Voice*, 19 June 2020. https://www.quettavoice.com/2020/06/19/honor-killings-domestic-violence-claim-23-lives-of-women-in-balochistan-since-january-1st-2020.
– 2020b. "Women Empowerment in Balochistan." *Quetta Voice*, 9 October 2020. https://www.quettavoice.com/2020/10/09/women-empowerment-in-balochistan.

Quresh, Shaheen. 2011. *Major Laws Relating to Women in Pakistan.* Peshawar, Pakistan: Blue Veins.

Qureshi, Muzaffar. 1998. *Fifty Years of Pakistan-Canada Relations: Partnership for 21st Century.* Islamabad: Quaid-i-Azam University, Area Study Center for North America.

Rashid, Ahmed. 2001. *Taliban, The Story of Afghan Warlords.* New Haven, CT: Pan; Yale University Press.

– 2002. *Taliban: Islam, Oil and the New Great Game in Central Asia.* New York and London: IB Tauris.

– 2011. "The Afghan Conundrum." In *Pakistan Beyond the Crisis State*, edited by Maleeha Lodhi, 305–17. London: Hurst Publishers UK.

Rashid, Rukhsana. 2013. "CIDA Women's Economic Empowerment." Islamabad: Report commissioned by CIDA.

– 2016. *The Power of Pakistani Women: 30 Years of Canadian Programming in Gender Equality.* Islamabad: Sterling Swift, CIDA PSU.

Reed, Alastair, and Kateira Aryaeinejad. 2021. "2020 Trends in Terrorism: From ISIS Fragmentation to Lone-Actor Attacks." United States Institute of Peace, 8 January 2021. https://www.usip.org/publications/2021/01/2020-trends-terrorism-isis-fragmentation-lone-actor-attacks.

Renzetti, Elizabeth. 2019. "Violent Misogyny *Is* a Threat to Half Our Population. We Need to Call It What It Is: Terrorism." Toronto *Globe and Mail*, 30 November 2019.

Rubin, Barnett. 2022. "Afghanistan under the Taliban: Findings on the Current Situation." *Stimson*, 20 October 2022. https://www.stimson.org/2022/afghanistan-under-the-taliban-findings-on-the-current-situation.

Rumi, Raza. 2017. "Pakistan's Radicalisation Problem Begins at School." *Islamabad Daily Times*, 8 April 2017.

Sarfraz, Azza, Zouina Sarfraz, Muzna Sarfraz, and Zul Qarnain. 2022. "Gender-Based Violence in Pakistan and Public Health Measures: A Call to Action." *Bulletin of the World Health Organization* 100 (7): 462–4. http://dx.doi.org/10.2471/BLT.21.287188.

Sarwar, Beena. 2014. "The February 12 Pledge, Terrorism, and the Malala Connection." *Journeys to Democracy* (blog), 12 February 2014. https://beenasarwar.com/2014/02/12/the-february-12-pledge-terrorism-and-the-malala-connection.

Schamber, S., and R. Fransen. 2022. "Signs of the Times: The Role of Education and Gender in Shaping the Cultural Mindset in Pakistan."

Case study. International Civil Society Action Network. https://icanpeacework.org/2021/10/gender-and-identity-extremisms.

Schirch, Lisa, Chris Bosley, and Michael Niconchuk. 2023. RISE *Action Guide: Rehabilitation and Reintegration through Individual, Social, and Structural Engagement*. United States Institute of Peace, 14 November 2023.

Shafak, Elif. 2021. "Elif Shafak's Diary: Publishing Heroes, Afghanistan's Forsaken Women, and the Lessons of Turkey's Autocratic Turn." *The New Statesman*, August 2021. https://www.newstatesman.com/politics/2021/08/elif-shafak-s-diary-publishing-heroes-afghanistan-s-forsaken-women-and-lessons.

Shah-Davis, S. 2011. "A Woman's Honour and a Nation's Shame: Honour Killing in Pakistan." In *Gender, Sexualities and the Law*, edited by J. Jones, R. Fenton, and A. Grear, 188–200. London: Routledge.

Sheikh, M.K. 2016. *Guardians of God, Inside the Religious Mind of the Pakistani Taliban*. New Delhi: Oxford University Press India.

Shinwari, N. 2015. *Understanding the Informal Justice System, Opportunities and Possibilities for Legal Pluralism in Pakistan*. Islamabad: CAMP.

Shirkat Gah. 2007. *Talibanization & Poor Governance*. Lahore, Pakistan: Shirkat Gah Women's Resource Centre.

Siddiqui, Zuha. 2022. "Pakistan Floods Pose Urgent Questions over Preparedness and Climate Reparations." *The New Humanitarian*, 5 September 2022. https://www.thenewhumanitarian.org/news-feature/2022/09/05/Pakistan-floods-urgent-questions-climate-crisis.

Smith, Joan. 2019 (2016). *Home Grown: How Domestic Violence Turns Men into Terrorists*. London: Quercus.

Tiessen, R., and S. Baranyi, eds. 2017. *Obligations and Omissions: Canada's Ambiguous Actions on Gender Equality*. Montreal and Kingston: McGill-Queen's University Press.

Torwali, Z. 2012. "Letter to the Editor." *Swat Express Tribune*, 6 October 2012.

True, J., and S.W. Eddyono. 2021. "Preventing Violent Extremism – What Has Gender Got to Do with It? Gendered Perceptions and Roles in Indonesia." *European Psychologist* 26 (1): 55–67. https://doi.org/10.1027/1016-9040/a000434.

UK Home Office. 2020. *Women Fearing Gender-based Violence, Country Policy and Information Note Pakistan*. London: UK Government.

UN. 2022. *Women, Peace and Security Report*. New York: UN Security Council.

UNDP. 2017. *Journey to Extremism in Africa: Drivers, Incentives and the Tipping Point for* Recruitment. New York: Regional Bureau for Africa. https://journey-to-extremism.undp.org/v1/en/findings.
– 2021a. *Applying Behavioural Science to Support the Prevention of Violent Extremism: Experiences and Lessons Learned.* New York: UNDP Arab States with Nudge Lebanon and B4Development.
– 2021b. *Preventing Violent Extremism Annual Report.* New York: Author.
– 2022a. *Enhancing Efforts to Prevent Violent Extremism by Leveraging Behavioural Insights Lessons Learned from Practical Experiments.* New York: Author.
– 2022b. UNDP *Crisis Offer.* New York: Author.
UNDP and UN Women. 2020. *Conflicting Identities: The Nexus between Masculinities, Femininities and Violent Extremism in Asia.* Bangkok: UNDP Asia Pacific Bureau.
UNDP Pakistan. 2009. *Facets of Violence against Women.* Project report, Gender Justice and Protection Project. Islamabad: UNDP.
UNESCO. 2022. *Framework for Enabling Intercultural Dialogue.* 20 September 2022.
UN Office of Counter-Terrorism (UNOCT). 2023. *Visibility Report.* June 2023. New York: Author.
UN News. 2021. *Afghanistan Is Facing a 'Cultural Disaster', Says* UN *Rights Expert.* 17 August 2021.
UN Women Pakistan. 2020. *Khyber Pakhtunkhwa. Status of Women and Girls in Khyber, Kurram, Orakzai, North Waziristan & South Waziristan – Gender Profile of Merged Districts.* Islamabad: Author.
Walsh, Declan. 2020. *The Nine Lives of Pakistan.* London: Bloomsbury.
Walsh, Sinead, and Oliver Johnson. 2018. *Getting to Zero, A Doctor and a Diplomat on the Ebola Frontline.* London: ZED Books.
Warraich, S. 2005. *Honour Killings and the Law in Pakistan.* London: Zed Books.
Weiss, Anita. 2021. *Countering Violent Extremism in Pakistan: Local Actions, Local Voices.* Boston: Oxford University Press.
Weldon, S. Laurel, and Mala Htun. 2013. "Feminist Mobilization and Progressive Policy Change: Why Governments Take Action to Combat Violence against Women, Gender & Development." *Gender and Development* 21 (2): 231–47. http://doi.org/10.1080/13552074.2013.802158.
White, Jessica. 2023. *Gender Mainstreaming in Counter Terrorism Policy, Building Transformative Strategies to Counter Violent Extremism.* United Kingdom: Routledge

Woodyatt, Amy, and Sophia Saifi. 2019. "Pakistan to Open More than 1,000 New Courts to Fight Violence against Women." CNN, 21 June 2019.

Yusuf, Huma. 2017. "Mind the Gap." *Dawn Newspaper* (Karachi), 6 November 2017.

Yusuf, Zohra. 2006. "My Years with WAF." *Journeys to Democracy* (blog), posted online 13 February 2013. https://beenasarwar.com/2013/02/13/my-years-with-waf-zohra-yusuf-on-the-pakistani-womens-movement.

Ziring, Lawrence. 2004. *Pakistan at the Crosscurrent of History*. Lahore, Pakistan: Vanguard Books.

Index

Afghanistan: Af-Pak Strategy, US's, 20, 122; border regions with Pakistan, 135, 206–8; decline of foreign aid to, 103, 105; deployment of American troops in, 141; impact on Canadian aid to Pakistan, 156, 165; informal justice system, 94; ISAF war and Canada's role, including development assistance, 144–5; Pakistan's pivotal role in, 11; relationship with Pakistan, 18; stabilization approach in, *see* stabilization approach in Afghanistan; Taliban, *see* Taliban (Afghanistan); US war against Russian invasion, 6, 15, 79, 103
Aga Khan Rural Support Program (AKRSP), 45–6; women's programming and women's organizations, 39, 45–8, 117–18
agriculture, women's role in, 4–47, 204, 221
Al Huda Schools for women, 107, 193, 225n3 (ch. 8)
All Pakistan Women's Association, 4, 76; CIDA funding for, 81

al-Qaeda, 136, 140; 9/11, 140, 143; links to ISIL, 227n2 (ch. 12); murder of journalist Daniel Pearl, 142
Aurat Foundation, 91; local governance projects, 92, 147

Balochistan, 117, 225n2; domestic violence in, 27, 117; gender-disaggregated data, 17; gendered development divides, 30; provincial *Child Marriage Restraint Act* and *Domestic Violence Prevention and Protection Act*, 217; special aid program, CIDA's, 157
Bhutto, Benazir, 106, 150, 213, 215
bin Laden, Osama, 59, 140, 148
blasphemy laws, 50–2; human rights concerns with, 179
border region, Pakistan-Afghanistan, 117–19, 184, 208, 214; al-Qaeda insurgents in, 135–6; anti-Americanism in, 140–5; cross-border terrorism, 214, *see also* Afghanistan; ISIS active in, 166–7; PAGE strategy

for, 195; regional disparities, 31, 185, 205–6, see also Khyber-Pakhtunkhwa Province; US drone strikes on, 150

Canadian aid, 89, 92, 114; cuts to levels of, 157–8, 165–6, 103, 104, 216
CARE (NGO), CIDA-funded project, 60–3
CEDAW, 183
CIDA, 10, 16, 38, 39, 148; gender policies, 41, 48–9, 110. See also Women in Development Policy; Feminist International Assistance Policy
CIDA Pakistan, 148; civil society, funding for, 114–15, see also Aga Khan Rural Support Program, Strengthening Participatory Organizations, South Asia Partnership in Pakistan; country strategy, 63, 143, 157; country strategy, gender equality pillar in, 209; cuts to, see Canadian aid: cuts to levels of; donor coordination on gender equality, funding for, 122–3; education programs, 163; gender equality approach, 2006–09, 132, 194; gender program size, 147; gender strategies, 14, 20, 42, 98, 110, 202, 203; impact of Afghan war against Taliban on aid to Pakistan, 156; women's development fund, 99, 108, see also CIDA Pakistan women's funds; women's economic empowerment policy, 23, 55; women's rights, funding for, 104, 108, 111, 195. See also Afghanistan
CIDA Pakistan women's funds: closure of, 156–7; lessons learned, 162; review and evaluation of, 112, 127, 128, 129; role of, 138, see also Program for Advancement of Gender Equality; support for legal rights, 89, 90, see also gender justice, Simorgh women's resource centre
Commission of Inquiry on the Status of Women, Pakistan, 130
Council of Islamic Ideology, 182, 219n1
countering violent extremism, programs for, 36, 122; counter-terrorism strategies, gender dimensions of, 177, 202; lessons learned and principles, 162–3; links with women, peace, and security policy, 26; women's roles in, 35, 196. See also prevention of violent extremism
customary laws, 74, 93–4; links with Islamic laws, 95

Diyat Ordinance, 3, 12, 53; links to honour killing, 76–7; significance of and campaign against, 13; use of by American government, 53

education of girls, 119, 156, 202; attacks on, and closing of girls' schools, 109, 173; banning of, 106, 109, 112, 146, 202; Malala Yousafzai, 172

early warning signals of violence
against women, 76, 138; as
indicators of extremism and
violent extremism, 32, 112,
138, 201

Feminist International Assistance
Policy of Canada (FIAP), 40–4,
132, 203, 217
feminist movement in Pakistan,
107; Canadian support for, 108,
137; early Muslim women's
movement, 181

gender-based violence (GBV), 27,
32, 62; links with violent
extremism, 75, 76, 83, 202
gendered division of labour, 204.
See also agriculture
gender equality indicators, 33, 144;
and violent extremism, 76
gender justice, 91, 122–3; gender
apartheid, 206; gender-based
courts, 90–1; gender
persecution, 205
Gilgit-Baltistan northern regions
of Pakistan: education levels in
Hunza valley, 222; sectarian
violence in, 121. See also Aga
Khan Rural Support Program
grassroots women's organizations,
129; AKRSP support for, 118;
CIDA support for (under
WDPR), 125, 133, see also CIDA
Pakistan women's funds; SPO
support for, 116–17, 147

honour killings and crimes, 27–8,
74, 217; increased media
reporting on, 132; Kohistan case,
29–30, 95; law against, 77,
83–5; Mukhtar Mai case, 79.
See also Diyat Ordinance
Hudood Ordinances, 4, 131;
debate on, 98; history and repeal
of, 8, 97, 124; retaining roots
of religious extremism, 100
Human Rights Commission of
Pakistan, 89, 217, 225n1.

inheritance laws, 45; as barrier
to women's economic
empowerment, 58. See also
Islamic laws pertaining
to women
Islamic laws pertaining to women,
99, 181–2; misinterpretations
of, 99, 180, 193, 205; protests
against, 5. See also Qisas and
Diyat Ordinances; Law of
Evidence for Women;
inheritance laws
Islamization policy of Zia-ul-Haq,
5, 43, 98; impact on women's
development, 201–2
Iran: Islamic revolution, 6, 14, 211;
women's protests, 207–8

Jahangir, Asma, 8, 79, 93, 180
jihad, 189; ideology of, 149, 185
jirga, 93–4; rulings violating
women's protection legislation,
29, 92. See also panchayat

Kandahar (Afghanistan), 159;
Provincial Reconstruction Team
(PRT), 144
Karachi, 142, 174–5; founders' day
of WAF in, 7; murder of social
activist Sabeen Mahmud, 177;

murder of social development activist Parween Rahman, 173
Karwan (NGO), 96–7, 134
Kashf (NGO), CIDA-funded project, 57, 62, 209
Khyber-Pakhtunkhwa (KP) Province, 27, 28, 32, 56; differences in levels of development and gender disparity in merged districts of former FATA, 30–1, 112, 206; honour killing of five women in Kohistan district, 216, see also honour killings and crimes: Kohistan case; Kalash Valley, 121; Khwendo Kor (NGO), 135; levels of and responses to GBV, 90; murder of seven charity workers in Swabi district, 173; murder of Zarteef Afridi, human rights activist, in Khyber district, 171; Sarhad Rural Support Program (NGO), 119; security threats to NGO operations, 117, 135, 139, 141, 153, 172; Swat district militancy of Pakistan Taliban, 96, 146, 172, see also Yousafzai, Malala

Lal Masjid (Red Mosque), 193, 226; affiliated women's madrassa, 193; eight-day siege of, 148; wife of imam, 90
Law of Evidence for Women, 4, 13; came into effect, 8. See also Islamic laws pertaining to women
Lawyers for Human Rights and Legal Aid, 27, 137

madrassas, 104, 186, 190–1, 197; female-only, 198

Mahbub ul Haq, 14, 45
MEDA (Canadian NGO project funded by CIDA), 54–5
mujaheddin, 103, 105; against girls' education, 202; fighting in Afghanistan, 11
Mukhtar Mai, 78–9, 214; girls' school and women's shelter, 80
Multan, 60, 78, 85, 116; first violence against women centre, 79; local Al Huda school, 193; murder of Qandeel Baloch, 217
Musharraf, General, 97

National Commission on the Status of Women Pakistan, 29, 45, 61, 130, 214; Act, 87, 88, 216

panchayat, 73–4; ruling in Mukhtar Mai case, 79; rulings' impact on women, 93–4, 96. See also jirga
Peshawar, 11, 15, 90, 137, 173; bombing of army school by TTP, 176; murder of Najma Jadoon, human rights activist, 216
poverty, 17, 30, 44, 56, 75, 186; community-based programs, 122; determinant for radicalization, 148, 186, 190; feminization of, 44; rural women in poverty reduction, 62, 203; socio-economic inequality and multi-dimensional poverty index, 186, 221
Prevention of Anti-Women Practices Act (also *Women's Protection Act*), 86–7, 93, 194–5, 216

prevention of violent extremism, 25; lessons on, 135; risk factors, 187; small projects for, 82, 138; strategies for, 61, 139, 177, 206; UNDP research on, 195. *See also* countering violent extremism, programs for

Program for Advancement of Gender Equality (CIDA PAGE fund), 80, 129, 132; closing of, 153; for human rights, 111. *See also* CIDA Pakistan women's funds

Punjab Province, 60, 62; CIDA-funded projects on women's economic empowerment, 53, 56, *see also* Karwan, Simorgh women's resource centre; governor's murder, 179, 216, *see also* Taseer, Salmaan; honour killing of Qandeel Baloch, 78; Mukhtar Mai, *see* Mukhtar Mai; provincial government's protection of women legislation, 84, 100, 126; Safia Bibi blasphemy case, 4; Southern Punjab militancy and LET, 79

Punjab Women Lawyers Association, 5, 12

purdah, 7, 55, 107, 151; CIDA study of (1983), 235

Qandeel Baloch, 78, 85, 217
Qisas and Diyat Ordinances, 13, 76–7

radicalization, 191–2; detecting early signs of, 138, 201; factors conducive to, 186–90, 228; female, 34, 193; programs that help prevent, 122, 162; role of women against, 112

Red Mosque. *See* Lal Masjid

sectarian violence, 121, 167
Sharia law, 4, 5, 14, 76, 110; creation of Shariat courts, 211; extremist interpretations of, 109, 141, 146, 180, 190; mixing with customary law, 95, 182

Sharif, Nawaz, 85, 104
Shirkat Gah women's organization, 61, 134; addressing GBV, 96; Fempower project, 92

Simorgh women's resource centre, 123, 225n4 (ch. 9)

Sindh Province, 28, 116, 122, 132, 217; *Child Marriage Restraint Act* and *Domestic Violence Prevention and Protection Act*, 217; Indus River floods, 15–17

South Asia Partnership in Pakistan (SAP-PK), 113, 125, 129, 209

stabilization approach, in Afghanistan, 145, 158–9, 161

Strengthening Participatory Organizations (SPO), NGO, 115; work with grassroots women's organizations, 116–17

Taliban (Afghanistan), 7; formation of, 106; gender apartheid, 206; ideology, 206; impact on women's rights in Muslim countries, 183; policies on women, 110, 206; takeover (2021), 205

Taliban (TTP), Pakistan, 146, 149; attack on Marriott Hotel, 151; bombing of Peshawar army public school, 176; links with

ISIL and al-Qaeda, 207; view of Islam and Sharia, 190, 192–3
Talibanization of society, 143, 189
Taseer, Salmaan, governor of Punjab, 50

UK Aid (formerly DFID), 91, 126, 204; Aawaz civil society program, 126
United States, relations with Pakistan, 53, 59; Af-Pak strategy, 152, *see also* Afghanistan: Af-Pak Strategy; aid cuts and nuclear sanctions, 103; anti-Americanism, 172; drone strikes on border with Afghanistan, 150; increased aid, 143, 164; post-9/11, 142
United States Institute for Peace, 134, 163

violence against women. *See* gender-based violence

women human rights defenders, 178
Women in Development Policy (WID) of CIDA, 3, 5, 40, 48, 212; change in CIDA strategy, 104, 110; early strategy in Pakistan, 201–2
Women, Peace and Security, 108, 125, 163, 229; Canada's ambassador for, 37; Georgetown University Index, 26
Women's Action Forum (WAF), 4, 204; formation and founding, 7
women's economic empowerment (WEE), 23, 58, 204; addressing GBV in, 37, 62; Aga Khan Foundation approach, 45; CIDA first mission, 147, 214; CIDA framework, 47, 124, 209; CIDA projects, 47, 55, 62; legal barriers to, 45; market system approach to, 45; WEE forum, 83
Women's Protection Act, 93. See also *Prevention of Anti-Women Practices Act*
World Economic Forum Gender Equality Index, 33, 216

Yousafzai, Malala: assassination attempt by Pakistan Taliban, 14, 172, 216; honorary Canadian citizenship, 227

Zardari, Asif, 215
Zia-ul-Haq, 4, 10, 13, 98, 175; blasphemy law, 52; creation of Shariat courts, 211; education policy, 163, 192; introduction of Islamic laws, 219, 223; Islamization policy, 5, 8, 43. *See also* Islamization policy of Zia-ul-Haq; blasphemy laws
Zina Ordinance, 4, 6, 100